The Book of Buckfastleigh

A Time for Remembering 1930–2002

Sandra Coleman

HALSGROVE

First published in Great Britain in 2003

Copyright © 2003 Sandra Coleman

All rights reserved. No part of this publication may be reproduced, stored in a retrieval system, or transmitted in any form or by any means without the prior permission of the copyright holder.

British Library Cataloguing-in-Publication Data
A CIP record for this title is available from the British Library

ISBN 184114 233 6

HALSGROVE

Halsgrove House
Lower Moor Way
Tiverton, Devon EX16 6SS
Tel: 01884 243242
Fax: 01884 243325
email: sales@halsgrove.com
website: www.halsgrove.com

Frontispiece photograph: *Fore Street, Buckfastleigh, c.1900.*

Printed and bound in Great Britain by Bookcraft Ltd, Midsomer Norton.

Whilst every care has been taken to ensure the accuracy of the information contained in this book, the publisher disclaims responsibility for any mistakes which may have been inadvertently included.

Foreword

Buckfastleigh has a long and diverse history and has experienced many changes, particularly over the past 70 years. Now that many of the older people I grew up with are no longer here I am conscious that much of the town's recent history could be forgotten or lost unless it is recorded.

The desire to have the history of the town documented is shared by several local people who recognise that a way of life which was enjoyed by so many has gone forever. However, because of the forward thinking of our forebears, we have been left a legacy of fine buildings, good facilities and a strong community spirit. This is our heritage which we seek to preserve for present-day inhabitants and future generations.

The writing of this book has been a fascinating and rewarding experience thanks to nearly 200 people who have shared their reminiscences, observations and local knowledge, and have contributed in so many different ways.

Sandra Coleman
Buckfastleigh
2003

A general view of Buckfastleigh, prior to 1976.

Market Street, Higher Town, 1920.

This photograph shows a pageant which was held in Buckfastleigh to celebrate the silver jubilee of King George and Queen Mary in 1935. At this point the procession of schoolchildren is marching through Plymouth Road.

CONTENTS

Foreword		*3*
Acknowledgements		*7*
Chapter One	A Shadowy Picture of Buckfastleigh	9
Chapter Two	The 1930s: And then the War Came	17
Chapter Three	The 1940s: Those Who Remained Behind	23
Chapter Four	The Evacuees: A Flux in the Population	31
Chapter Five	The Yanks	35
Chapter Six	Welcome Home!	41
Chapter Seven	The 1950s: An Industrial Town	49
Chapter Eight	Carnivals and Carnival Queens	57
Chapter Nine	The South Devon Railway	61
Chapter Ten	The Races: A Stirring Sight	65
Chapter Eleven	The 1960s: A Better Quality of Life	67
Chapter Twelve	The Primary School: A Precious Resource	75
Chapter Thirteen	The Woollen Mill: Part of Daily Life	85
Chapter Fourteen	The 1970s: Reorganisation and Deterioration	91
Chapter Fifteen	The Churches: Looking out to the Community	99
Chapter Sixteen	The John Loosemore Centre: A Rounded Experience	109
Chapter Seventeen	The Local Hospital: Small and Friendly	113
Chapter Eighteen	The 1980s: A Town in Decline	117
Chapter Nineteen	Sport: Playing for the Town	123
Chapter Twenty	The 1990s: Working for the Town	133
Chapter Twenty-One	Farmers and Farming: A Way of Life	139
Chapter Twenty-Two	The New Millennium: Looking to the Future	147
Business Subscribers		*157*
Subscribers		*158*

The Buckfastleigh contingent of the Devon Regiment, 1918. Left to right, back row: J. Ford, H. Joint, T. Peters, T. Voisey, C. Hurrell, E. Gill, W. Black, W. Boyer, J. Thorne; **middle:** *S. Myhill, W. Parsons, W. Saunders, J. Casely, R. Gillard;* **front:** *G. Bowden, R. Walters, C. Barnes.*

Station Road, Buckfastleigh.

Acknowledgements

I am indebted to the community for their help, support and goodwill in the writing and preparation of this book, especially for the contribution of written material and photographs by Gordon Adgey, Dom Gabriel Arnold OBM, Larry and Diana Areco, Martin Baker, Stuart Barker, Hilary Beard, Bob Beard, Margaret Berry, Joan and John Bickford, Gerald Billing, Joyce Blank, Violet Boon, Betty Bovey, Annette Bowen, Barbara Bray, Alan and Jacqui Butler, R. Campbell, Bill and Sybil Chaffe, Alan Chaffe, Elsie and Fred Churchward, Julia Cross, Edith Coleman, John Coleman, Peter Collings, Edward Coode, Margaret Coombes, Audrey Coulton, Fernley Cox, Margaret Dawe, Adrian Dawe, Rose and Neil Dalgleish, Dartmoor National Park Authority, Robert Dennis, Judith Dewdney, Cyril Doidge, Paul and Jennifer Dove, Noel Downie, William Drake, Trish Durman, Ann Eales, Nigel Edworthy, Jim Elliott, Jill and Richard Elliott, David Evans (Buckfastleigh), David Evans (Birmingham), Libby Faubert, Elsie Foot, Victor and Margaret Foot, Ken Fricker, Reg and Gwen Gill, John and Joan Gill, Debbie Griffiths, Garth Grose, Terry and Joy Hallett, Hilary Hammond, Revd David Hardy, Colin Harmes, David Harris, Helen Harris, Laura Harris, Marian Harvey, Cyril Heath, Dr James Hedger, Pat and Derek Hedges, John Henle, Mick and Peggy Henley, Lyn Heseltine, Val Hoare, John and Marian Hoff, Joe and Sheila Horak, Kathryn Hughes, Florence Humphries, Revd John Irwin, Nora Jackson, Donald Joint, Harry and Doris Kayley, Jacquie Kilty, Dr Ann Klemm, Philip Knowling, Maurice Lane, Michael and Cynthia Lane, Michelle Lee, Mary Lee, Bill and Doreen Legg, Rene Lewis, Jens-Peter Linde, Rhoda Look, Maureen and Andrew Maclean, Pauline Manfield, Eileen Manley, Suzanne Manley, Vera Marks, Barbara Martin, Betty and Bill Major, Bruce McLellan, Carole Millman, Dr Derek and Marjorie Moore, Brian Norman, Betty Northcote, Joan Norwell, Amy Peachey, Keith Pearson, Richard Pickles, Adelaide Pinney, Jeanne Pinney, Richard Rogers, Revd John Rowland, James Searle, Bill Selley, Margery and Jack Setters, John Shinner, Phyllis Short, Dianne and Roger Simmons, Sarah Small, Ken and Ruth Smart, Ann and Horace Smart, Dorothy Smith, Jack Smith, Ruth Smith, Vic Sparkes, Jean Starkey, Major Charles Stewart, Annette Stirling, Kaz and Marjorie Stryjski, Jaine Swift, Robert Tarasiuk, Esther Taylor, Jack Tillyer, Pamela Thompson, John Thorn, Michael Tolchard, Doreen Trude, Betty Tucker, the staff of the Valiant Soldier Heritage Centre, Doris Vine, Phyllis Voisey, Doreen and Michael Voisey, Jan Walker, Ronald Weeks, John Weir, John Wellingham, David and Ann Werry, Sheila Whipp, Nils White, Lucille Whitehead, Margaret Wigram, Jenny Wigram, Idwal Williams, Sarah Woodman, Jill Yolland.

I am especially indebted to Catharine Sparkes for her support and for typing the book to disk for the publishers, Elizabeth Knowling for her local knowledge and the use of material from her archives, Patricia Cairn-Duff for her up-to-date photographs of Buckfastleigh town centre and to Peter Thornhill for his assistance with the selection and scanning of photographs.

Thanks to the following sources: *The Ashburton and Buckfastleigh Cottage Hospital, A Short History*, Peter Webb; *Britain 1918–1951 – Institute of Contemporary British History*, Peter Catterall, reprinted by kind permission of Heinemann Educational Publishers; Buckfastleigh Primary School log-books, 1940–93; Cassette of Robert Dennis' war experiences, narrated by Robert Dennis; *Devon at War (1939–1945)*, Gerald Wasley, reprinted by permission of Halsgrove; *Devonshire Leaders*, Ernest Gaskell, 1907; Listing Records of English Heritage of Holy Trinity Church; 'The Post-War World – Dream and Reality: 1945–1949', *The Short Oxford History of the Modern World, Empire, Welfare State, Europe: History of the United Kingdom 1906–2001* (Fifth Edition), T.O. Lloyd (2002), reprinted by permission of Oxford University Press; *The Story of St Luke's Church – Buckfastleigh*, Helen Harris; *The Story of the Sepulchre – The Cabells of Buckfastleigh and the Conan Doyle Connection*, Susan Cabell Djabi; *Structural Investigation of Holy Trinity Church*, BMP Structural Investigations, Buckfastleigh, Devon, 1992; *This Sceptred Isle: Twentieth Century*, Christopher Lee, 1999; *The Wheatsheaf*, the in-house journals of the Co-operative Wholesale Society, 1927.

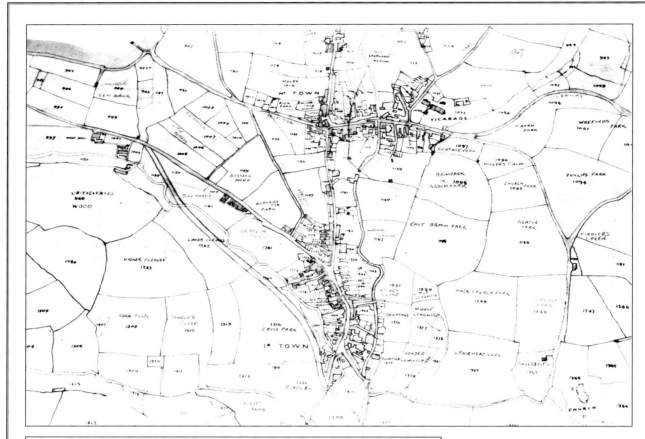

Above: *The 1840 Tithe Map of Buckfastleigh.*

Left: *The Avenue, Dean, 1910.*

Right: *Market Street, Higher Town, c.1900.*

One

A Shadowy Picture of Buckfastleigh

Buckfastleigh stands on the southern edge of eastern Dartmoor at the confluence of two rivers surrounded by lush and fertile land. Archaeologists believe that the town originated as two distinct and separate settlements, one being Higher Town (Market Street) and the other Lower Town (Fore Street). A road or lane (now Chapel Street) would have linked the two settlements and fields or orchards would have existed where churches and houses now stand.

'However, there is no evidence for a Domesday settlement here,' said Debbie Griffiths who is head of archaeology and historic buildings at the Dartmoor National Park Authority. 'Buckfast was here when the Domesday Book was compiled but not Buckfastleigh.'

The Domesday Book was compiled in 1086 and one of the first recorded entries for Buckfastleigh was, according to the Place-Name Society book, in 1350. Clearly the town, or settlements, were established by then, if not earlier.

Phil Knowling, a local writer, conjectured that most communities would have chosen to settle near their religious leaders, which would have made Buckfast the favoured spot. However, people may have been encouraged to settle a little further away in what was to become Buckfastleigh in order to allow the Benedictine Order the solitude required as part of its monastic life. The attributes of the area around Buckfastleigh would have encouraged the orginial settlers to remain and become an established community.

Debbie Griffiths, despite being uncertain about the relationship between Buckfast Abbey and the settlements of Buckfastleigh, speculated that the settlement was founded at the confluence of the Dean Burn and River Mardle in order to make use of the water in the processing of wool and manufacture of cloth. The Abbey remained lord of the manor until the Dissolution of the Monasteries in 1539. Debbie explained:

Historic research in Devon can be extremely frustrating and difficult because record survival can be patchy, partly due to land ownership in the past but also because some records were lost during the Second World War. If you look at the 1839 Tithe Map for Buckfastleigh the medieval town plan is very evident, suggesting that little change had occurred between the Middle Ages and the mid-nineteenth century. If you look at the changes between 1839 and 2002 you can see that in those 150 years or so, the town has extended well beyond its medieval limits. The Tithe Map is giving us a small, albeit shadowy, picture of an earlier Buckfastleigh.

One thing is certain, both Higher Town and Lower Town are indisputably medieval in origin. There is one main thoroughfare of tall, narrow buildings with long, thin strips of land – burgage plots – extending behind them. During medieval times, holding property in the town was one of the essential rights of merchants so it is not surprising that, like any business person today, merchants wanted their property to front the main shopping area where customers could easily be attracted. As many people would be vying for such a position the houses were designed so that as many as possible could be fitted into the street. The burgage plot comprised land on which outhouses, livestock and suchlike could be kept.

In view of the rapidly changing face of so many town centres it is rare to find medieval houses in the twenty-first century. The homes were constructed

Left: *The weir and River Dart, Dartbridge, c.1900.*

from wood and many would have been ravaged by fire, a regular occurrence in medieval times. By the seventeenth century most houses had been rebuilt using the original layout but, as time progressed, the medieval styles were phased out. Nils White, a former employee of the Dartmoor National Park Authority, stated that 'Buckfastleigh has one of the best examples of medieval town layout in England.'

'The burgage plots are visible on both sides of Fore Street and are bounded by the Mardle to the north and the Dean Burn to the south,' said Debbie Griffiths, 'and visible also, to a lesser extent, east and west of Market Street.'

Later developments in Buckfastleigh occurred behind the principal street frontages – a feature common to medieval towns. If one has occasion to wander through the 'ope' ways – the narrow alleyways that lead to courtyards – it may feel as though one has wandered back in time. Perhaps not as far back as medieval times but certainly into the 1800s.

Many of the courtyards were workplaces for local inhabitants with the rivers being used for the washing of wool by those engaged in the wool trade. John Warren, a saddler, used to ply his trade in Warren's Court, opposite the Valiant Soldier. In the 1800s there was a coaching inn on Fore Street (next to the newsagents) called the London Inn, which backed on to Fowler's Court. In 1883 a Yealmpton builder by the name of Henry Fowler came to live in Buckfastleigh with his wife, Sarah, and bought a long lease on the London Inn, which he converted into workshops and dwelling-houses. Whilst living in Buckfastleigh they had two sons, Richard and John. When Sarah died Henry moved to Plymouth.

Henry's link with Buckfastleigh is significant because two of his grandsons, Henry (junr) and his brother Frank, compiled the first edition of the *Concise Oxford Dictionary* and the *Pocket Oxford Dictionary*. Henry (junr) also compiled *Fowler's Modern English Usage*.

Geologically, Buckfastleigh is a fascinating area. The ruins of Holy Trinity Church stand on a great limestone hill at the eastern entrance to the town. The Devonian-period limestone is the oldest type of limestone found in the British Isles and occurs almost exclusively in Devon and Cornwall. Scientific investigation has proved that the limestone was formed from sponges, corals, sea urchins and shellfish in the warm shallow sea that covered the area 350 million years ago. Through this timeless hill run a series of caves and, at Higher Kiln Quarry with its main entrance near Dartbridge Road, sediments have been discovered which suggest that there was at one point a massive disturbance which could have been caused either by an earthquake or by freezing.

Edgar Reed, who once owned the grocery and provision store Reeds (now Costcutters) in Market Street, and Wilf Joint, local historian and a former Town Mayor, were keen cavers. They discovered two caves in June 1939 which were subsequently named Reed's and Joint Mitnor Caves. Joint Mitnor Cave (named after Wilf Joint and two other men who were with him, Mitchell and Northey) is, according to the Devon Spelæological Society, the richest interglacial bone cave in Britain. The remains of hippopotamus, straight-tusked elephant, slender-nosed rhinoceros, boar, fallow deer, red deer, giant deer, bison, hare, wolf, fox, wild cat, cave lion, cave hyena, badger and bear have been found there.

It is difficult to imagine that these animals roamed this part of the earth 100,000 years ago or that further back in time the area that is Buckfastleigh was covered by sea. What is more remarkable is the fact that the remains of these beasts and various sediments have survived undetected and unharmed until their discovery in the mid-twentieth century.

Baker's Pit, near the ruins of Holy Trinity Church, and Reed's Cave, at Higher Kiln Quarry, form the longest cave system in the county, the overall passage length being $3\frac{1}{2}$ km. The two caves, which are connected in numerous places, form one distinct cave system. It is quite likely that the River Dart flowed through Baker's Pit one-and-a-half million years ago, the river flushing away all the rubbish and silt to form the existing large chambers.

Well known to cavers and naturalists, Higher Kiln Caves became the headquarters for cave research following a meeting between the Society for Promotion of Natural Reserves, the Devon Naturalist Trust and the Devon Spelæological Society, at which the Pengelly Cave Research Centre was founded in March 1962. The centre was named after William Pengelly, the nineteenth-century excavator who discovered Kent's Cavern in Torquay.

Two other noteworthy caves in the vicinity of Buckfastleigh are the Pridhamsleigh Cavern, on the site of an old quarry with a lake in which eels can be found, and Bunkers Hole at Dean Prior.

The year 1947 saw the formation of the Devon Spelæological Society of which Wilf Joint was once president. The society still meet at their clubhouse in Crest Hill, Buckfastleigh, although at the time of writing the group has no members from the town.

In 2003 Baker's Pit came under the control of the Devon and Cornwall Underground Council which is

Fore Street, c.1900.

a regional body of the National Caving Association who administer the caves with permission from English Nature and the landlord. The Pengelly Trust, on behalf of the Devon Wildlife Trust who owns the freehold, administers Reed's Cave and only allows limited access (25 trips per year) to bona fide caving clubs. Communal access is not permitted and visits must take place outside the bat-roosting season which runs from October to April.

The caves, our geological heritage, need to be firmly guarded and administered because open access to Devon's caves over the past 50 or so years has led to such vandalism that remarkable examples of stalagmites have been destroyed. Most cavers are responsible people with respect for the environment they love but the sheer volume of visitors can have a detrimental effect.

A number of thriving industries have developed in and around Buckfastleigh over the years. In addition to the wool industry there has been quarrying at the limestone quarry of Bulley Cleaves, the Whitecleaves basalt quarry at West End, as well as copper and tin mining.

Brookwood and Wheal Emma Mine were two of a group of mines that existed about 2 miles northwest of Buckfastleigh, situated on both banks of the River Mardle. The other mines were Old Wheal Emma (also known as Brook), Wheal Treebly, New Brookwood and East Brookwood – at one time all of these worked under the name of the South Devon United Copper Mines.

Brook Mine was situated in a wooded valley near Brook Farm and started producing copper ore in 1845. In 1856 Wheal Emma had opened and Brookfield followed in the early 1860s. Between 1856 and 1877 34,000 tons of copper ore had been produced and thus confirmed the mines as the largest copper producers in the area. By 1885 work had ceased in all of the mines except for New Brookfield, which continued until 1891.

When it first started Brook Mine was known as Macclesfield Mine, the proprietor being the Earl of Macclesfield, a landowner who not only possessed the estate of Brook Manor but also a considerable amount of land in and around Buckfastleigh. For the past few centuries the lives of the owners of Brook Manor have been closely tied up with the affairs of Buckfastleigh. Much has been written about the Cabell family who held Brook Manor for at least 100 years. The manor was built, or extended, in 1656 by Richard and Elizabeth Cabell. Richard was the third Richard Cabell and the likeliest contender for the title of 'wicked Squire' which was bestowed by local inhabitants – he was also one of the contenders for the man upon whom Conan Doyle based his book *The Hound of the Baskervilles*. Susan Cabell Djabi has written a definitive booklet on the Cabell family called *The Story of the Sepulchre – The Cabells of Buckfastleigh and the Conan Doyle Connection*, which would be of great interest to anyone intrigued by the Cabell family.

'The Little Man' in Baker's Pit, 1960.

Suffice to say that in 1674 the Cabells were the wealthiest family in Buckfastleigh and Brook Manor was the largest house in the parish and the sixteenth-largest house in the whole of Devon. The Brook Manor estate included the manor-house and farm, gardens and orchards and several surrounding farms including Button, Wallaford and Bowden. It also included properties in the villages of Holne, Coombe and Scoriton, and the town mills of Buckfastleigh as well as properties elsewhere in Devon.

It was through the unfortunate first marriage of Richard and Elizabeth Cabell's daughter, also called Elizabeth, to a Cholmeley D'Oily, and her second happier marriage to Richard Fownes, that her great inheritance was squandered. Elizabeth died before her husband and their son, Thomas, on his father's death, was forced into selling the whole estate to Sir Thomas Clarke, Master of the Rolls, in 1758. He left it to his patron, the Earl of Macclesfield, in his will.

According to Ernest Gaskell's *Devonshire Leaders* (1907?), the Earls of Macclesfield derived their descent from Thomas Parker of Leke in Staffordshire who was knighted in 1705, becoming the First Earl of Macclesfield. The book then mentioned George, the Second Earl, Thomas the Fifth and Thomas the Sixth, but with no dates or further information. The author then referred to the 'present Peer' as being born on 24 May 1888, and commented that he is the fortunate possessor of an immense amount of property, 15,000 acres, much of it in Buckfastleigh.

The estate of Brook Manor remained in the hands of the Macclesfield family until 1914 when the family divided up the property and sold it off in lots. The manor-house passed into the hands of Albert Mitchelmore, Lord Macclesfield's agent, who came from Buckfastleigh, and from there into the hands of various owners, including those of Gilbert Pye, probably the owner best remembered in recent times.

The owners at the time of writing hailed from Buckinghamshire. During the 1980s they spent about four years looking for a property and in 1990 finally discovered Brook Manor. The house and gardens were in a state of disrepair but they saw great potential in the beautiful and historic property and so

Left: *Austins Bridge, c.1900.*

Below: *Jordan Street, c.1900.*

Below: *Church Steps, c.1900.*

Outside the Black Rock (now the Abbey Inn).

bought it and began the mammoth task of restoring it. The renovation took two years and the new owners encountered all kinds of problems. The property is listed Grade II so a great deal of care had to be taken during the building work. English Heritage and the Dartmoor National Park Authority both made a contribution. English Nature was also involved because Brook Manor is a roosting site for the Greater Horseshoe bat. The bats were removed from the attic during the renovation and were later returned. Special provision had been made to enable the bats access into the roof space.

In 2003 the family have been in residence for ten years and are enjoying the property. The house is supposed to be haunted but so far nothing has been experienced, however horses are perceptive to atmosphere and seem very wary of the area surrounding the quarry.

The drive to Brook Manor is three-quarters of a mile long and the copper mine, now boarded up, is situated in a quarry approximately halfway between the entrance to the estate and the house itself. It is a gloomy, forbidding area, especially in the evening. The owner of Brook Manor said:

What does frighten our guests is the fact that the Greater Horseshoe bats come into the house. We had to be very careful, when restoring the house, about using Death Watch beetle treatments and the woodworm treatment. We tried to restore the house sympathetically, and we found all sorts of treasures... such as original fireplaces, one beautifully decorated, and original doors. The two main front doors are originals and one has the initials RC (Richard Cabell) carved on the iron handle. The doors themselves are oak and are of double thickness, the planks go horizontally on the inside and vertically on the outside so they are extra strong. The bolts are great big ones which make us think that the house was once a fortified manor.

It is certainly a very historic building, and we have learned a lot about the history of the house. We have also learned that anyone who is interested in the Hound of the Baskervilles *wants to come and have a look at it.*

It is hoped that the family will stay for a good while yet. Living there with their extended family they have brought Brook Manor back to life and a gardener from Buckfastleigh has lovingly restored the grounds that were so unkempt when they first arrived. A small, shadowy glimpse, perhaps, of what Brook Manor might have been like in the 1600s.

Buckfastleigh should not be viewed in isolation. The whole town is softened by the green hills surrounding it and, from the top of these hills, views of Dartmoor can be seen framing the town. Buckfastleigh provides access to both the neighbouring countryside and to the West Country's seaside resorts, which allows local inhabitants to enjoy a quality of life often denied to those living in more industrial areas.

In earlier years Buckfastleigh was covered and surrounded by many fields and orchards ensuring that the town centre was smaller and more compact. The 1840 Tithe Map revealed a wide spread of orchards in and around the town, including Jordan Street, New Road, Orchard Terrace, Plymouth Road, Dartbridge Hill through to Buckfast and Old Totnes Road out as far as Colston. 'Nearly every farm had apple orchards,' said farmer John Thorn, 'and there was quite a good income from them at one time.'

Bob Beard, whose farm is in Buckfastleigh West, bordering Buckfast, said:

There was a Round down under the cottage at what is now the Abbey Inn, and the poor horse would walk round and round in circles driving the shaft of the machinery which ground the apples into pulp. When the pulp was pressed the casks of apple juice would be loaded onto a horse and cart and taken over to Simmons' Cider Store in the Old Totnes Road.

The bottom floor of the cider store was built into the side of the hill – that kept the temperature fairly stable. The casks of apple juice would be taken around to the back of the building which is level with the first floor, the casks would be rolled off the cart and taken inside.

Fortunately for inhabitants of the town in 2003 Buckfastleigh abounds with a unique and rich historical heritage that is ever present despite our often-unseeing eyes. In addition to Fore Street and Market Street's medieval layout the houses themselves reveal intricate details of design and usage. Debbie Griffiths noted:

The character of the town as a whole is essentially a late-eighteenth to early-twentieth century landscape, still with an industrial feel to it, unusual in a Devon town. As well as the mill buildings themselves there are many examples of industrial housing, most of which were built by the Hamlyn family or the Co-operative Society. Distinctive amongst these are the Jordan Street terrace, and the turn-of-the-century terraces at Pioneer Terrace, Bossell Terrace, Orchard Terrace and Sherwell Court.

In Lower Town the buildings along Fore Street are a mixture of private houses, commercial properties and public houses and are predominantly outwardly late-eighteenth to early-nineteenth century in character. They exhibit a variety of styles, shapes and sizes which lend character to the area. The building line is staggered, roof heights vary, some front elevations are decorated, others plain.

A walk through the town and its side streets and lanes, with time to stand and observe, can be historically enlightening and aesthetically satisfying. For example Park View, opposite The Christian

Above: *Churchward's Mill, which was destroyed by fire in 1906.*

Inset: *A view of the school from Glovers Park (Bossell Road), c.1900.*

Above: *A Mothers' Union outing, c.1920. Included in the picture are Ivy Jackson, Annie Lane and May Arscott.*

Right: *A Mothers' Union outing, 1928.*

Plymouth Road, c.1900.

Community (formerly the YMCA) in Chapel Street, was once a house built for the Hamlyn family, c.1860. The original cast-iron railings are still in place and to the left of the house are the gates to the former coach yard.

Further down Chapel Street are four seventeenth- or eighteenth-century cottages with a tentering loft used for drying cloth in earlier days. Just below Plymco, and on the same side, there is a former builder's yard which is a rare example of a group of late-Victorian industrial buildings and a surviving piece of medieval rear-plot development. Next to the yard there is a doorway with a plaque above it indicating that it was once the Golden Lion Inn, built c.1820.

Standing in Plymouth Road one can take a good look at Tollmarsh which was built for the Hamlyn family, or note that the White Hart Inn, near Weech Corner, was built on the site of a former mill and that the building that is now the fish-and-chip shop was built in 1733, as indicated on the date stone. The initials 'HC' on the stone are possibly those of Henry and Catherine Callard who owned the building.

The cartway leading into Fowler's Yard, where the London Inn once stood, has a small tap in a niche on the left-hand side that dates the 1892 piped-water system which followed an outbreak of typhoid.

Walking into Station Road from Fore Street one immediately comes to Bridge Cottage, a rather attractive house. Built some time around the 1820s, it was once the home of John Bovey, the registrar for births and deaths who was also an ale-and-stout agent, vaccination officer, sanitary inspector and insurance agent!

Further along Station Road is Church Bridge which crosses over the River Mardle. Elizabeth Knowling has noted from the date stone that it was built in 1749 with the name S. Meafield on it. She has discovered that the bridge was described as being in decay in 1670.

And have you noticed the Kissing Steps halfway up Church Steps? They are the ones that have pitched stone treads at right angles to the treads on the other steps. When you have found the steps and the repair mason's initials of 'TW', turn around and look out over Buckfastleigh. You will find that the shadowy picture of the past has become a little clearer.

The people of Buckfastleigh enjoying the Mission at Glovers Park, c.1900s.

Left: *Hoff & Son (butchers), Market Street, c.1930.*

Right: *The Hoff & Son butcher's van outside the shop, c.1930.*

The Town Hall, c.1940.

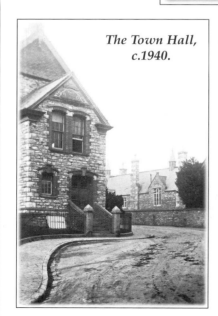

Above: *Jack Honeywell* (left) *and Ralph Abbott* (right) *taking it easy, c.1900.*

Two

THE 1930S: AND THEN THE WAR CAME

The authors of a booklet titled *Devon Historic Industries* who visited Buckfastleigh in 1934 formed a very favourable view of the town:

> ... the impression was received quickly of a unique rural settlement, yet largely occupied with its woollen, paper and foundry industries, immune from slum dwellings, well housed and blessed with modern water supply, sanitation, public lighting and welfare institutions...

Buckfastleigh was a busy and lively town during the 1930s. It had never been a prosperous community, but it was self-contained, there was employment, albeit low paid, and local people worked hard to make a decent life for themselves and their families.

Nationally the situation was grim. At the start of the decade the Labour party lost power and an all-party government, the national government, took over. It was the first time that this had happened during peacetime and the events took place against a backdrop of world recession following the 1929 Wall Street crash. New inventions, such as vacuum cleaners, electric ovens and other domestic appliances, were discovered alongside a growing economic depression. In spite of this situation Buckfastleigh Urban District Council continued with an ambitious building programme which had started during the 1920s and would continue through to the early 1950s. Council-houses were built on Glovers Park, Plymouth Road in 1926, at West End in 1928, and houses at Elm Bank, Fairy Lane and Gipsy Lane were completed between 1934–36. The town boasted more than 40 shops and businesses in the early days. One local man recalled:

> From the bottom of Fore Street up there was a shop behind every window. There was the paper-mill, the quarry, the gas works (Buckfast) and electricity works, leather works, Willcocks' iron foundry (in Dial Court), and the Co-operative Wholesale Society which was a big employer and owned the woollen mill and tan yard.

The Buckfastleigh Co-operative Society first started in 1869 when a small shop in Fore Street was opened opposite the Post Office. Nine years later a grocery store (est.1878) was opened, followed by the drapery department, the bakery (est.1884) and the butchery (est.1887), all in Chapel Street (where Plymco supermarket and Searle's premises stand).

Ken Smart worked for Willcocks, the engineers. The firm, which worked in marble and stone, was established in 1835 and contributed to most industries in the area, manufacturing water-wheels, corn pressers, manhole covers and even gravestones. Ken started there in the early 1930s until he was called up during the war and went into the Navy. He returned to work at the foundry to complete his apprenticeship before working for Richard Beare and Sons.

Bulley Cleaves Quarry had been bought from the famous historian and writer Revd Sabine Baring Gould in the 1840s by the great-great-grandfather of Charles Stewart, a member of the Coulton family. The Coultons then owned virtually the whole of the hill on which the church and the graveyard stand.

Reginald W. Coles started his career in quarrying in 1924 when his family's firm of civil engineering contractors secured a contract to widen Dartbridge. They leased Bulley Cleaves Quarry at Black Rock in order to obtain the necessary stone masonry and crushed stone for the task. It was on the completion of the widening of the bridge that Reg Coles decided to enter the quarrying industry and went into partnership with the Coulton Trust and Charles Stewart,

Buckfastleigh paper-mill, c.1900.

acquiring a long-term lease on Bulley Cleaves Quarry in 1934.

A man who became happily involved in the life of the town, Reg was elected as a member of the Institute of Quarrying in 1931 and later became both chairman and president of the institute. In 1946 he was elected to the Buckfastleigh Urban District Council and became president of the cricket club and vice-president of the amateur dramatic society.

Local man, Cyril Heath, joined R.W. Coles (Quarries) in 1936:

I was 16 when I joined the company and when I first started working there the men used to break the stones with a 14-pound sledgehammer. Of course the stone would be blasted first but sometimes after blasting you would be left with a very large stone – bigger than a dining-room table – and you couldn't put a stone that size in a crusher. You would have to break it down and sometimes it was easier to break the stone than blast it. They worked from 7.30a.m. to 5p.m. breaking stones.

There was a 32-hour guaranteed week at one time. If the weather was bad and you couldn't work the management would guarantee you 32 hours pay. But normally the men would work in bucketing rain in order to get their hours up to the normal hours of 46 hours a week.

One of the drillers was a man called Lester Davies who would be let down the cliff by rope onto a ledge with his pneumatic drill and would drill down to about 40 feet and then blast. He would be there from 7a.m. until lunchtime and then go back again. I have seen him working up on the ledge for about three hours in pouring rain and I would have an awful job to stop him working. Nowadays it would all be done by machine. [Cyril laughed.] He used to work Saturday mornings from 8 to 12 and then, after drilling all morning, he would go and play rugby in the afternoon! The men I worked with were all great chaps, and it was a way of life.

Much later, Cyril was encouraged by Reg Coles to take the examination which would qualify him to become an associate member of the Institute of Quarrying. When Cyril passed in 1952 Reg was delighted that a local man, and a member of his staff, had succeeded at a time when no other quarryman in the country had done so. Cyril continued:

We had a happy life when we were young. On Sundays we would go trouting in the streams, or climb trees in the woods. Sometimes we would play in the fields or play cricket in the Recreation Ground. It was a happy environment and a healthy one. What a different world it is now.

Born in Buckfastleigh, Maurice Lane said that he and his brothers, Les and Alan, and sister Lil had a very happy life growing up in the town, although times were tough and their parents had to work very hard. Maurice's father was Jack Lane and his mother a Willcocks before her marriage. Maurice said:

My maternal grandfather was a stonemason by trade and he had ten in the family. My great-grandfather once owned Abbotswell in Crest Hill.

We were Anglicans and as children we all had to go into the choir. We used to go to Sunday school in the morning then up to Holy Trinity Church for the morning service, go home, change and stay indoors. We lived in Silver Street and the vicarage was nearby and Mum would say, 'The vicar mustn't see you in the street on a Sunday'. Then in the evening we used to go to the service in St Luke's, in Plymouth Road.

John Gill, who was born and brought up in Jordan Street, said:

I joined the choir with Bill Selley and Roy Miller. I was the longest-serving choirboy of the three of us. We used to go to Sunday school in the National Schoolroom, then at ten to eleven we would go to Holy Trinity Church for the morning service. Home for lunch. Then back to Sunday school again in the afternoon, and then we went up to the Parish Church for the half-past six evening service – but only in the summertime. In the winter we went to St Luke's Church.'

Bill Selley remembered:

I joined the church choir at an early age and we used to be invited out to tea at the Nesbits who gave us wonderful cream teas and suppers. At Christmas we were invited up to Bigadon to sing carols in the lovely hall up there. The singing was followed by a sumptuous supper and Mrs Fleming used to take a present off the tree for you. The Flemings and the Churchwards were local benefactors. If the church needed anything the benefactors would see to it.

Ken Smart recalled:

In those days everyone went to church on Sundays. Coming down Church Steps from Holy Trinity Church was like coming away from a football match because there were so many people. 25 to 30 men sat regularly in the church choir, and in fact, there were more in the choir then than go to church now!

Everyone joined in or supported local events and clubs. Marian Harvey noted:

The rugby club was especially popular. The rugby team was stronger than the soccer team and it used to get a lot of support.

There used to be an annual show in the Town Hall when pigeons and chickens and garden produce were shown. I won the shoe-cleaning competition and the silver-cleaning competition when I was 12. You had to clean the shoes and silver and display your efforts.

Maurice Lane remembered:

The Co-op used to have a gala at Molefield, up Crest Hill. On the right-hand side going up the hill there were some old buildings and then a field which used to belong to the Co-op where their horses were kept. At the gala there was a marquee with fancy cakes and everything, sideshows and sports with prizes. There was also a competition to see who could clean the most boots with Co-op polish whilst sitting on an old wagon!

There was always something going on. There was a Boys' Club even then, which used to meet in the National Schoolroom. We used to play table tennis, football, box and have paper-chases in the winter. There was always something to do. But the youth club boxing club was the thing! Before the Second World War we used to have boxing contests in the King's Arms on a Friday night. It was a real do, that was. Percy Voisey, Nancy Voisey's father, used to be our trainer and we would train in the King's Arms.

The Lane men, 1920. Left to right: Jack Lane, Dick Lane, John Lane.

Marjorie Setters remembered how carnivals were a big event before the Second World War. 'The sports day at the Recreation Ground and the Sunday school trip to Teignmouth were annual events,' said Marjorie, 'and all the fathers used to come down and wave off the mums and toddlers.' Bill Selley recalled how popular the Anglican Sunday-school trip was:

It was always held on the last Wednesday in June. There were over 100 children in the Sunday school then and about 400 people in total went on the train. The trips were suspended when the war came.

Maurice Lane noted:

The Co-operative Society used to have trips too. We went to Guernsey once, in either 1937 or '38. We got down to Torquay at six in the morning and everything was lovely when we started out. Then, once on the ferry boat, everyone was sick and we didn't see each other until we got to Guernsey!

Another popular pastime was going to the pictures at the cinema in Station Road. Ernest and Vera Pickles had left Cornwall for Buckfastleigh in 1934, just after they were married. Ernest and his father had been running the local cinema in Liskeard in the days when several new ones were being built and then Ernest came to run The Picture House in Buckfastleigh. Previously it had only shown silent films and had closed down because the owner, from Torquay, had not put in the equipment necessary for 'talking' films.

One of the most important events in the town calendar was Buckfastleigh Races. The races were started by a group of Buckfastleigh sportsmen and were held at Dean Court, which was farmed by the Coulton family who were tenants of Lord Churston. Audrey Coulton, who married Guy Coulton in 1939, said:

The races were organised by a family committee and everyone in the town was involved one way or another. What they made financially they put back into the races.

In the 1930s many of the properties near Buckfastleigh had stables and there were also stables scattered around the town. Horses would be allocated to a particular stable including one at Rose Cottage in Silver Street, owned by Guy's uncle, and Dean Court, of course, which had a great many.

Rene Lewis remembered:

When there was racing on at the racecourse some of the girls, including me, used to stand at the top of Station Hill, by Station Tree (now sadly gone), and see all the jockeys come in by train. We would go dancing when the jockeys were here. There were always dances on Whit Saturday and Whit Monday.

Maurice Lane recalled:

We used to go to the races, and we would go down to the railway station and wait for hours for the horses to come in by train. All the pubs had stables and there were stables up at Silver Street where we lived.

Growing up in Buckfastleigh was great and I never really wanted to live anywhere else. My family lived in Silver Street and Joan, my wife, also lived in Silver Street when she was growing up. We boys used to play in the meadow and jump the leat. Joan, who was two years younger then me, used to come down too.

Joan and I did our courting in Buckfastleigh and used to go dancing at the Town Hall. She wasn't allowed out very much as she was brought up by strict grandparents.

Rene Lewis and her friends said how much they enjoyed going for walks when they were growing up:

We often went for walks, usually a whole group of us. We used to go to the woods and pick columbines and primroses. Then we would pack up the flowers in a box and send them to London hospitals.

Marian Harvey laughed:

Many people were keen gardeners and had allotments up at Wallaford Road and at Fairy Lane – before the housing estate was built. There was a barn at the back of Gipsy Lane, where the back of the gardens are, and the local boys used to box there on a Sunday afternoon. They made us pay a halfpenny to leave!

At harvest time people would turn out to help local farmers. There was much more of a community spirit as everyone knew, and was involved with, each other. Front doors were never locked – there was no need to lock up as we all went in and out of each other's home. A great sense of humour existed as we were all in the same boat. Even the employers mixed with the men and women they employed and did as much as they could for them.

There was easy access to larger towns such as Newton Abbot and cities like Exeter and Plymouth, and the regular bus service was more frequent than at the beginning of the twenty-first century. Both the Western National and Devon General ran double-decker buses into Buckfastleigh. The red Devon General used to stop outside the Town Hall, go along New Road and down Chapel Street. The green Western National used to turn around by butcher Hoffs, on the corner of Jordan and Market Street, and stop outside the YMCA on the corner of New Road, on its way down through the town.

Few people had their own transport beside the use of a horse or a bicycle. Postmen and doctors were among the group of people who had to walk their rounds. The postman's round involved carrying a bag of heavy mail on foot to Hayford Hall and Scoriton! Horses were an important part of town life; Ken Smart remembered Jack and Kenny Setters, with their father George, delivering coal to the tan yard, the paper-mill and Buckfast Mill on horseback. They owned six or seven horses and in those days it was the only way to deliver goods.

At the beginning of the 1900s Ken and Jack Setters' grandfather went into partnership with a man called Blackmore, using horses to draw big timber wagons full of huge logs from trees at Dean and Brook Mill. Following Blackmore's death, their grandfather, who owned the Bridge Inn at Barter's Bridge (also known as Damarell's Bridge) in Elliott's Plain, became the sole owner, and when he died in 1916 he had 16 horses stabled in Fore Street. The business went to Ken and Jack's father. In addition to the timber trade the horses and carts were used for carrying hay, coal and helping out farmers. By 1934 Jack, at 14, was working in the family business:

We would go out on a winter's morning to the station to meet the trains and if it was raining we would be soaked through by dinner time. We would go home and mother would have a hot meal and fresh clothes. Then we would go out again in the afternoon and get wet through again. This would go on week in and week out and in those days summers were summers and winters were winters! One day I said to my father, 'You think more of those horses than you do of us!' He loved his horses. He gave me a slap on the ear, kicked my bottom and said, 'Those horses cost me a hundred pounds – you cost me nothing!' I never forgot that!

Jack Coulton's men came down to our stables one day and asked how many horseboxes we had. We had four boxes then and we would go to the railway station on Friday evenings to meet the trains so we could pick up their gear for the races on Saturday and Monday and take it all to wherever the races were being held.

Local people were used to seeing animals around the town. The Wakehams, who were farmers, used to drive their cows through the town to be milked and there were also several slaughterhouses in Buckfastleigh. The slaughterhouse belonging to the Co-op was at Glebelands (before the housing estate was built) and pigs and cows were kept there. Butcher Hoffs had a slaughterhouse behind the premises in Market Street and Gerald Lang, also a butcher, had a slaughterhouse in the yard next to the Valiant Soldier.

Maurice Lane recalled working for the Co-op:

I worked for the Co-op before I got called up during the war. They had four or five milk rounds in those days and we used to deliver the milk by horse and trap. The horses were stabled at the back of the Co-op. The first round was at 6a.m. First the harness had to be checked to make sure that it was in good condition and then I had to load up with big churns of milk. Milk was ladled out of the churns in pints and half-pints in those days and I had to take cream, eggs and butter with me, of course. In the afternoon I did the bread round up at Cross Furzes and Pridhamsleigh up to Beara – all by horse and trap. You got promoted from one round to another. I eventually finished at 6p.m. It was a long day.

Gradually, however, mechanised transport took over and the use of horses became less common. Maurice illustrated that in some cases there was a reluctance to change:

You could do better with the horses than a van. The horse knew what to do! When I got off the trap with the churn and walked up to someone's front door the horse would walk slowly behind me. I ended up talking and having conversations with the horse!

Jack Setters talked of the transition:

THE 1930S: AND THEN THE WAR CAME

We did quite a bit of work for Reed and Smith Mill. One of the Reed brothers said to my father, 'Look, George, the horses are too old-fashioned you'll have to get yourself mobile.' So we bought a new Ford lorry which meant my brother and I had to pass a driving test. Ken first and then, when I was old enough, I took the test and passed first time. Father was thinking of getting another lorry as the business was expanding but then the war came and that was that. My brother Ken managed to postpone getting called up because of the business as we used to help with the paper-mill and it was considered essential work. I managed to get a postponement, too, but only for six months and then I got called up and volunteered for the Air Force.

Finally in 1939, when Germany and Russia invaded Poland, the British government became aware of the depth of fear of Adolf Hitler held by other European countries. The reality of the situation, which Prime Minister Chamberlain had striven to hide from the government and the British people for so long, became clear. For nine years Britain had watched the rise of the Nazi party in Germany and had seen Adolf Hitler's growing power as chancellor and then Führer of the country. Moreover, Britain had observed as the atrocities committed on the Jews by the Nazis unfolded. A growing European fear of Hitler had been read about in the newspapers but the country had not taken it seriously.

The economic crisis in Britain had been exacerbated by industrial strikes, discontentment, growing poverty and the country's preoccupation with the abdication of Edward VIII and King George VI's subsequent accession to the throne. These factors had disinclined the nation to consider war but Britain half-heartedly began to make preparations.

The people of Buckfastleigh were not wealthy and, during the war years, life became harder as a result. Villagers survived by eating chickens, pigeons, partridges and rabbits. It was the sense of responsibility held by local businessmen that kept the town going – their lives were bound up with those of other people in the community.

Stuart Barker, Buckfastleigh Mayor from 1997–2001 stated:

This was the time when your peers judged you by the amount you did for the community. In the social history of many towns there has always been a significant group of people who have had the money and who were prepared to reinvest in their town. The difference here was that those employers and benefactors were also leaders of the Urban District Council. So if the town needed anything they provided it. They recognised that Buckfastleigh was a working mill town and they acted accordingly. They didn't need ten million pieces of paper to get planning permission to do something like you do today. The Urban District Council built many houses meaning a high proportion of 'council-houses' to those privately owned.

West End snowed in, 1928.

The most prominent benefactors, of course, were the Hamlyns, who had owned the woollen mills until they were purchased by the Co-operative Wholesale Society in 1920. The Hamlyns had built new cottages and, together with other well-known benefactors such as the Coultons, the Churchwards, the Hoares, the Hunts and the Symons, were instrumental in the building of the Town Hall in 1887. Bill Selley reflected on the undertaking of this construction, which had an extension added in 1924:

It was built in two parts. After they built the first part they had to raise more subscriptions and then the Hamlyns and John Furneaux donated the funding required for an extension. We have a wonderful Town Hall for the size of the town.

The Hamlyns also provided land for public amenities including the playing-fields, the tennis courts, Victoria Park and the swimming-baths, which had been inaugurated as part of Queen Victoria's jubilee memorial.

Buckfastleigh was 'one of the first towns to have a swimming-pool,' said Maurice Lane, 'and we all used to swim there and in the river down by the Dart, and later we used to go to Spitchwick at Newbridge.'

Stuart Barker believed that the generosity of the town's employers and benefactors in looking after the community had ultimately proved to be a problem:

If there was a row of cottages needed for the mills' managers and supervisors then the employers built them. In reality the Hamlyns owned much of the town that they gave so much to. This kind of generosity from the Hamlyns and other employers went on from one generation to another which was very good for the town in one way. The problem was that the population came to rely on that generosity. Local people never had to do anything for themselves and they were never involved in decision-making and if they needed anything it was provided. The number of trusts that exist in Buckfastleigh bearing the name Hamlyn is significant. In the 1930s it was a town that was well advanced of its time.

Then the Second World War started and life was never quite the same again.

Above: *Waterman's Corner, Higher Town, c.1900.*

Above: *A French family wedding, c.1930.*

Above: *The Valiant Soldier pub was decorated in honour of King George V's silver jubilee in 1935.*

Right: *Celebrating the coronation of King George VI at Damarell's Bridge, 1937.*

Three

THE 1940s: THOSE WHO REMAINED BEHIND

During the 1940s life was very different for those who fought in the Second World War. For the people who remained behind in Buckfastleigh the change was just as dramatic, albeit far less dangerous and frightening. According to 'The Attlee Years Revisited' by Nick Tiratsoo in a book entitled *Britain 1918 to 1951 – Institute of Contemporary British History* by Peter Catterall: 'Everywhere the most common experience of war was disruption – of home, family, jobs and leisure time…'

Many of those who went to fight were from families whose roots were in Buckfastleigh – the well-known names of whom are easily traced through parish records. Until the war, incomers were mostly folk from other Devon towns and villages, from the West Country generally, or young men and women who married a local person and came to settle in the town. Wherever they came from the incomers arrived in small numbers and were easily absorbed into the local community.

During the 1940s, however, groups of Land Army girls lived at Fullaford House and both British and American servicemen were stationed in and around Buckfastleigh. Many families took in young evacuees from London who attended local schools. All of these people were only temporary residents but their presence had a great impact on the town, not least because they were present in such large numbers. Additionally, many families uprooted themselves from cities like Plymouth, where the bombing was relentless, and came to settle in the town as permanent residents.

It was at the height of the First World War in February 1916, and with a desperate shortage of land workers, that the government appealed for 400,000 women to continue agricultural labour in the name of patriotism. The Land Army was formed as a result and was such a success that the appeal was repeated during the Second World War. It was no easy task to care for such a large number of young women, many of whom had left home for the first time to work in isolation in the backwaters of rural Britain.

Sheila Whipp was such a Land Girl. Born and raised in Liverpool, and not wanting to be called up for the Forces when she reached 18, she promptly applied for the Land Army. After four weeks' training in Exeter Sheila was posted to a 150-acre farm just outside Staverton. It was a primitive existence, which included muck spreading, sawing logs and potato picking. There was no water or electricity and the food was primitive, too. 'Fortunately my good friends, the Harris family in Buckfastleigh, did my washing', said Sheila. 'I used to spend my day off, which started after I finished the milking, with the Harrises and have my bath in their house!' Their friendship and hospitality made up for the conditions experienced at the farmhouse.

Land Army girl, Ann Smart (née Hegarty), was based in Buckfastleigh:

We had to work hard, very hard, for very little money. We were all city girls – I came from Leeds, none of us were country-bred, and there was nothing to do in Buckfastleigh except to go to the pub. The only thing we could afford was the cider – and I didn't like that very much! The Picture House had just burnt down so we had to go to Newton Abbot if we wanted to see a film on our day off on Saturday afternoon; it used to cost us 11d.

The first farm I worked on was Mr Tooley's at Tordean. We used to go around in the lorry and we were dropped off at different farms. But I was so green, I didn't even know what a hoe was! But they were good years.

Margaret Wigram has lived in Buckfastleigh for 56 years, first coming to the town with her parents and young brothers before the war:

We were actually staying with the Rowlands at Bilberry Farm and we were in Holy Trinity Church when war was declared in 1939. Mr Mylchreest, the vicar, was preaching when the verger opened the door and walked up to the pulpit carrying a paper in his hand. He handed it over to Mr Mylchreest who said, 'I am very

Left: *Land Army girls in the garden of Fullaford House, Wallaford Road, where they were billeted during the Second World War, 1943.*

Right: *Land Army girls in uniform, c.1940. Left to right, back row: Jean Woods (née Croft), Florence Prowse (née Bedford), Kathrine Gallagher, Alice Baron, Louie Groom; middle: Irene Dawson (née Clements), Bette Marles, Irene Vokes, Mary Skirrow, Jean Young, Agnes Holt, Lilian Cairns, Connie Wilson, Betty Wilson; front: Pat O'Leary, Dorothy Blueman, Anne Smart (née Hegarty), Eileen Edwards, Hetty Allen.*

Left: *Tollmarsh viewed from Plymouth Road.*

A photograph of Chapel Street showing the mill buildings on the left-hand side and the Co-operative Society stores on the right-hand side, c.1940.

sorry to announce that we are at war with Germany.'

During the war I joined the Land Army and worked at Rill Farm for a while. I was still living at Bilberry Farm and used to cycle from there to Rill to do the early morning milking and do the same thing at the end of the day. It was exhausting.

Margaret eventually left Buckfastleigh in order to look after her mother but was employed on a farm by the Bedfordshire Land Army for the duration. When she married at the end of the war she returned to live in Buckfastleigh with her husband, Dr Michael Wigram, who joined the existing medical practice.

With increasing labour shortages women were enlisted to work in other industries in order to fill the gaps left by men. The Buckfastleigh Woollen Mill had employed women before the war and there were, in fact, as many female workers as male, both before and after the war. Usually the women did the spinning, weaving, warping, and sewing of rugs, while most of the men worked in the tan yard. Even in the tan yard some men were replaced by women, although this was before mechanisation and the heaviest jobs in the tan yard were those such as pulling. This involved putting the skins over a beam and pushing the wool down off them.

Doris Vine was born in Tavistock and moved to Buckfastleigh as a child; she started working in the mill as a weaver just before the Second World War:

I loved the work, all the workers were women except for the loom-tuners and we worked very hard. Our orders came from Russia and I remember working on a Russian order. Because I was quick I was given five learners to teach, for which I was paid an extra £2.

Violet Boon went to work in the mill when she left school at 15 and worked there during the war, after a short period of employment at Hawson's Court:

I was an invisible mender. In those days they used to weave the cloth and dye it navy-blue. There was no tweed or anything then. Another girl and I were the youngest of the menders and we were good. There were a lot of flaws in the material and we had to put them right. If there was a piece of big yarn we had to pull that through and leave little tails, and when the material went over to be dyed pickers would cut off all those little tails.

'I made sheepskin rugs for a few years, from the age of 14,' said Joy Hallett. 'After a time the skins were sent away to make airmen's jackets, etc. No more rugs were available.'

Marjorie Setters worked in the invisible-mending department too, then moved to Exeter to a factory making parachutes. 'The hours were long,' she said, 'and we had to work nights, so I moved to another factory where I worked day shifts only.'

Adelaide Pinney and her friend, Winnie Stuart, had the choice of going into the Forces or into other war work. They chose to work in munitions which meant leaving home and going up to the Midlands. Adelaide remembered:

It was our first time away from home and it took us all day to get there. We changed lodgings several times until we were satisfied. In the end we cooked our own meals, which was alright until we went on to night shifts. We had to do two weeks on night shift followed by two weeks on day shift.

Our job was to put explosives into shells. By the end of the shift we would be covered in yellow sulphur which wouldn't wash off. My friend became ill from doing another job using cordite, probably from inhaling the powder into her system, and she never really recovered from it.

The factory was right out in the wilds and fortunately we were surrounded by tall trees. Often whilst we were working we would hear enemy planes flying overhead. We would have to switch off the lights and be extremely quiet.

I enjoyed the experience of being away. We could go to the theatre and do different things. Then my fiancé said 'come home', so I came back to Buckfastleigh, we got married and I went back to working in the mill which I had been doing before I went away. I went into the weaving department. I enjoyed the company but we had to lip-read because it was so noisy and we couldn't hear each other speak.

Most of us were glad to be back to a normal life when the war ended. Glad to be housewives and to raise a family. However, quite a few of us continued to work part-time in the mill even then.

Nick Tiratsoo, in 'The Attlee Years Revisited', stated:

... a closer inspection of the evidence suggests that the war was generally less subversive than has been claimed. Women were not suddenly 'liberated' by working in factories, for example. In fact, most were given the worst jobs and could not wait to return home as a consequence.

Elsie Churchward decided she wanted a job in the mill and asked Ralph Dunning if he would employ her in the weaving shed. A neighbour said, 'Oh, Mrs C you'll never do that!' 'Well I'm going to try,' she replied, and she did; she worked there for two or three years.

The government decided to open workers' restaurants across the country which would provide cheap but nourishing meals during a period of rations and food shortages. The Buckfastleigh Urban District Council opened a British Restaurant in the town during the early years of the war. It was based in the Methodist Church for two or three years before

Members of the Hunt family in the doorway of Hunt's (now the Baker's Oven), Fore Street, c.1930.

being moved to the National Schoolroom. Just before it opened Mr Willcocks, manager at the mill, asked Elsie if she had applied for the supervisor's job at the restaurant:

I said, 'No, Mr Willcocks, I don't want to, really.' 'You must put in for it,' he said. So I did, because my father worked for him and Mr Willcocks had been good to him, which I appreciated. However, Mr Dunning was furious with Mr Willcocks for commandeering me because during the war you were not supposed to leave your job.

I got the supervisor's job. Of course, I had a lot of experience from working in the White Hart which was a hotel in those days. The food for the British Restaurant came from a canteen in Bovey Tracey which delivered meals to other canteens in the district. Well, we had the first lot of meals and I never met with so many grumbles in my life! It was stewed lamb and it was practically devoid of any meat – it was just bones. People were grumbling to me and I was having to apologise over and over again.

Eventually, I did the cooking myself and members of the local voluntary organisations used to come and help with the cash till. We were on rations of course and a Miss Pratt, who represented the Ministry of Food, used to visit to dish out the ration coupons. Fancy having to run a restaurant on coupons! Once I overspent and she wrote me an awful letter. She made me feel so bad I thought I was going to prison!

Margaret Foot came to Buckfastleigh in 1939 when she was 12 years old. Her father was a bookmaker in Torquay but many races had to be cancelled by the authorities who were afraid the crowds might be bombed. Margaret explained:

Dad took the opportunity of coming to Buckfastleigh and we ran the Waterman's Arms until 1959. Rationing was one of the worst things but I don't think that we suffered as much in the country as they did in the towns. Things like butter were hard to get. Mother used to mix margarine and butter together, to make it better, and add a drop of milk. But we had meat, rabbits and pigeons, and eggs. Local people kept fowls so you could get eggs and you could get things from local farmers. The farmers used to kill their pigs and come into the pub and say: 'I'm killing a pig at the weekend, Missus, would you like a joint?' We never went hungry and rabbits were a very good standby. We used to make rabbit pie – you could roast or stew a rabbit. The only thing I remember queuing for in the shops was oranges, if you had three people in your family you were allowed three oranges.

Organisations like the Women's Voluntary Service (WVS), now the Women's Royal Voluntary Service, and the Red Cross were involved in supporting men and women in the Forces. Sybil Chaffe, the clothing officer for Buckfastleigh, collected items for the WVS, which she and others packed up into small parcels made up of such articles as sheets and underwear. The Exeter WVS then collected the parcels and distributed them to those in need.

Sybil also collected weekly premiums from local people who belonged to the hospital treatment scheme; this included nursing care if it was needed. The National Health Service had not yet started.

Lilian Allen (from Harewood), Mrs Lang (the butcher's wife) and Mrs Wigram (the wife of Dr Wigram) helped Sybil Chaffe run the meals-on-wheels service, the four of them working as a team with other local women. 'After the war,' said Sybil, 'volunteers had to cook the meals themselves – an added responsibility.'

'Life was different but you got used to the disruptions and having soldiers around,' said Margaret Foot. 'The pubs did very well. Then the beer got short but we were lucky, being a free house we often had beer when other pubs didn't.'

Bill Legg, of the Oxford and Buckinghamshire Territorial Battalion (the Ox and Bucks), came from Buckinghamshire, where he had worked on a farm, and joined up with the Territorials in March 1939. When the war started the men in the Territorials were the first to be called up:

We were sent to France on Christmas Eve 1939, to the Belgian border to dig trenches to stop the German tanks from advancing. Eventually I came home on leave, but couldn't rejoin my unit because Hitler started his move on Belgium. We were sent to Durham first, then sent down to North Devon and finally ended up in Buckfastleigh. There were three companies in the battalion, one based at Buckfast, one at Widecombe and the third at Broadhempston. C Company was based in Buckfast.

We were the first soldiers to be based in Buckfastleigh. I used to sleep in the Globe. As an NCO I had a comfortable room to myself, but my men had to sleep on straw palliasses, some in behind the Globe, some up at Major Vickers' in Bossell Road and others down at the King's Arms.

THE 1940S: THOSE WHO REMAINED BEHIND

Bigadon House was used as an Officers' Auxillary Hospital during the Second World War.

The reason we were here was to get reorganised. We had lost about 400 men at Dunkirk in 1940 and had to be made up to strength again from different units. We were a holding battalion to be kept in reserve for whoever needed us.

Bill met his wife, Doreen, a Buckfastleigh girl, at a dance in Ashburton whilst he was stationed in the town. Doreen recalled:

I used to sing with Terry Roper's band and we used to go around to Dartington, Staverton, Ashburton and, of course, Buckfastleigh and places like that.

Local people took the soldiers to their hearts and people used to invite them home for Sunday lunch, even though they were on rations.

'The Town Hall was used for our dining-hall,' said Bill, 'but not many soldiers turned up for their Sunday lunch,' he added with a grin, 'most of us soldiers got invited out.'

'The local people took the Ox and Bucks to their hearts more than any other regiment,' Doreen remarked. 'It was probably because the war had just started. They were the first soldiers to be stationed here and the local people wanted to do their bit.'

For well over 50 years Joy and Terry Hallett had been friends with an Ox and Bucks soldier who was stationed in the town during the war. Joy explained:

I was only ten years old at the time and he would ask me to write a letter to his wife, Viola, for him. He would sit me on the camouflage nets on top of his lorry and he would dictate his letter to me whilst working on his lorry.

Of course, I would giggle when he asked me to write 'Hello, my darling,' and 'I love you'. I thought it so funny at that age. I would print out the letter as I couldn't write properly but I was very good at printing and spelling. I used to get letters back from his wife saying thank you for writing Charlie's letters because he would send her letters every day.

Whilst he was in Buckfastleigh his wife had her first baby and Ivy, my sister, knitted her some baby clothes and sent them to her. When he left here he and Viola kept in touch and they often came down on holidays in later years. Charlie was a lovely man and after he died his family continued to keep in touch.

Violet Boon remembered that at this time local people were asked if they would let the soldiers come into their homes and have a bath:

Well, mother, you know, she had three soldiers who used to come in. There was only one bathroom with a gas copper. We would get that filled for one fellow to have a bath, fill the copper up for the second and get it hot for him and the same for the third! After the war had ended one of the soldiers used to send my parents £2 for Christmas and he did that right up to the day my parents died. We always kept in touch. He was ever so good to my mother.

Men with reserved occupations included Fern Cox who originally came from Broadhempston. He moved to Buckfastleigh specifically to take up a job with the mill during the 1920s. Fern said that when the war started and the time came for men to enlist in the Forces, all the men working in the mill who had been in the Territorials, including Ernest Coleman, Freddie French, Jack Nettle and others, were conscripted. 'That was the last time I saw them until the war ended six years later,' Fern said. 'Then Ernest Coleman and Freddie French came back to the mill.' However, things turned out differently for Fern Cox:

As I was only 30 I went in to register to go into the Forces, as I was obliged to do, along with Bill Chaffe and Jack Fouracre. We could choose to go into either the Army or the Navy as too many were opting to go into the Air Force. We were told we would be called up within a fortnight.

The next thing I knew the Regional Officer for Wool Control came to see me. 'What the heck do you think you are doing?' he said to me. 'What do you mean?' I asked. 'Volunteering for the Navy,' he replied. 'Hang on a minute,' I said, 'I went to register and they asked me for my preference, that's all.' 'They're calling you up,' he replied. 'I'm stopping this! I'm going to London. You're in a reserved occupation and you're stopping here. There'll be no more of this nonsense!' So here I stayed. In those days you had to do what you were told, but I would have gone if I had had the chance.

When Ken Fricker was called up aged 18 in 1944 he went into the Coldstream Guards but after two years he was discharged on a Class B release. The government was trying to get industry back on its feet and the mill wanted its pre-war workers back. Ken started work as a pattern weaver but then went on to be a loom turner.

Fred Churchward worked at the Plymouth dockyard, a reserved occupation, during the war. After work he was a volunteer fire watcher. 'Not a fireman,' he explained, ' but someone who watched for fires breaking out.' Fern Cox remembered:

If you did not go away to fight in the war you had to join either the Home Guard or the Air Raid Precaution (ARP) and that meant that when the siren went you had to go out on duty to ensure that no lights were showing in people's windows and often you were out for several hours. The next night you would be at the mill, fire watching, and yet another night you would be down at the report post. When the air raids were on you would be called out quite a bit.

At the report post, one of which was the Town Hall, there would be several men and women on duty. We had to sleep there, as well, and then go to work the next day as usual. We slept on stretchers with one blanket each. The stretchers were so low that the fumes from the coal fire affected us so that we used to wake up with sore throats.

Similarly, Bill Chaffe, manager of the woollen mill, would be fire watching on two nights of the week, controlling the air-raid siren and overseeing petrol rationing in the town. He was based in the old mill office and would hand out the petrol coupons to those who needed them. Wanting to do something more active he joined the Home Guard and eventually received a commission. He ran his own platoon with Reg Coles and Ralph Dunning. Bill Setherton was the sergeant. Their main aim was to defend Dartbridge from enemy tanks. Fern Cox explained:

It was believed that the Germans were going to drop poison gas and, in addition to everything else, I was also the gas identification officer. There were two of us that had this special equipment with which to identify the gas we smelt, which had to be reported the moment it was identified. One gas, I remember, smelt like a geranium.

I went to Newton Abbot to train as an incident officer. If a bomb dropped you had to take charge of the situation. Everybody had to report back to you – the fire brigade, the police, gas and electricity men. We had to coordinate the action. Fortunately only one lot of bombs was dropped on Buckfastleigh – and that was in 1943. It fell to me to coordinate the action. There were two large bombs and six smaller ones. One hit the mill and when we went to work the next morning we found broken windows in the sorting shop and spent cartridges. One went off near Holy Trinity Church damaging it, and another went down through the orchard into Buckfast, hit the road, bounced across the river and landed flat in a field. The bomber probably didn't intend to bomb the town at all, he was just off-loading on his way back home. You can't really believe that you lived through such times.

Margaret Foot worked in the Co-op Offices and was at work when the bombs were dropped on the town:

I was looking out the window and said to the girl I worked with, 'Look at this plane, Esther, there are vapour trails on this one, I haven't seen that before. Oh, my, it's going to drop a bomb!' And with that we got under the table.

Philip Jackson was the captain of Buckfastleigh Fire Service during the war. His father objected to his son being called up to fight and wrote to the War Office to express that Philip was doing essential war work in Buckfastleigh. 'As a builder he was actually engaged in altering the Methodist schoolroom for use as a British Restaurant,' smiled Philip's wife, Nora Jackson. Vic Foot commented:

The fire service was based up at Harewood – previously at West End Garage – and we had a number of firemen who came down to help from Birmingham because they were expecting a considerable amount of bombing in Plymouth. It was 1941 when the blitz was at its worst in Plymouth and it was quite frightening. I came out of The Picture House in Buckfastleigh one night and the skyline was lit with searchlights.

'Very often you would see the searchlights at night,' added Margaret Foot, 'sometimes they would catch the enemy plane in the light and follow it. The Search Light Unit was at Cross Furzes.'

It was a different way of life for everyone. Even those inhabitants who did not venture out of doors had blackout curtains to block out their house lights at night in case of enemy raids. Margaret Foot recalled two old men who had lived in the town all their lives and came to her family's pub one night:

When they left it was so black that they walked up Jordan Street from the Waterman's Arms instead of going down Market Street. It wasn't that they were drunk, it was just pitch black.

My father went to the Globe Inn one night and when he came out he didn't know where he was. In the winter and on a bad night there was no light from anywhere.

Vic Foot added:

It was scary. In the blackness you would suddenly hear footsteps but not see anyone. We had to go to school or work in the dark and there was double summertime – the clocks went forward by two hours to give the farmers chance to plough the fields up to ten at night.

Ann Eales said that growing up in Buckfastleigh during the war and after were good days – much better than they are now:

I used to go down to Edith Higden's shop in Market Street with however much Mum could afford to give me and then, with a bottle of lemonade and a few sandwiches, we'd go out and be away all day in the fields and come back about nine o'clock. You couldn't do that now.

Marian Hoff (née Faxby) came to live in Buckfastleigh with her parents after her school in Plymouth, which was subsequently evacuated to Truro, was taken over as a hospital for the troops. She found Buckfastleigh a very different place from Plymouth:

There wasn't a lot to do but there was the tennis club and The Picture House. All the young people around enjoyed an easy-going relationship with each other. We could hang around quite safely in those days and go into the country and woods for walks.

She met her husband, John Hoff, through her friend, Barbara Searle.

'There were a lot of activities that continued during the war,' said Marian Harvey. 'There were still dances.'

'As long as the blackout curtains were up it was quite safe,' added Esther Taylor.

'Even though most of the young men were away in the war,' said Marian, laughing, 'other young men came to take their place and we had a better social life than young people do now!'

'We had a great impact on Buckfastleigh,' said Ann Smart (née Hegarty), when she referred to the Land Army girls stationed in the town:

We used to have a lot of fun with the local boys. It was dark up at Fullaford House in Wallaford Road where we were living. There were no bungalows up in Ducks Pond then, and the road was one long drive up to the big house, which was beautiful with stables at the back and great rhododendron bushes. The boys used to hide in the trees and jump on us in the dark. Of course, lights weren't allowed during the war. I enjoyed living in the country and never went back to Leeds. In fact, three of us Land Army girls married and stayed here after the war.

Ann married a local man, Horace Smart, who was in the Army. They met at a dance in Ashburton:

We had to walk into Ashburton and walk back and had to be in the hostel by ten o'clock, so we used to leave the dining-room window open and the last one in had to lock it. But we never knew who the last one in was – so it never got locked! There were quite a lot of us who walked back from Ashburton – all of us singing away – you couldn't do that now, could you? It wouldn't be safe.

In spite of the uncertainties of the times, young adults clearly enjoyed the kind of freedom that is missing in today's more violent society, and there is no doubt that Buckfastleigh, because it is rural, further inland and in a sheltered area, suffered less than towns and villages on the coast and cities like Plymouth and Exeter. Children did not have to deal with the anguish of being evacuated and were still able to use the farmland and woods as their playground. When there were shortages, the countryside was a source of food, due to the generosity of local farmers (and poachers).

The men who stayed behind may well have been frustrated by not being allowed to enlist and go to war like their friends. However, they found a worthwhile role in undertaking essential war work which included the protection of Buckfastleigh, which was at risk as proved by the stray bombs.

Many women found the war years exhilarating, especially those who were in the Forces and those who were young and away from home for the first time. But for many housewives life became harder as they strove to keep the home going and waited for husbands, sons and daughters to return from the war, or war work. They also filled the important industrial jobs which the men had vacated.

Dorothy Smith, who was still a schoolgirl when the Second World War ended, remembered vividly the VE-Day celebrations held in Buckfastleigh:

The Mums went out and got all the trestle tables they could find from the Town Hall, the school and hotels, and the tables stretched all the way down Fore Street from the Globe Inn. I don't know where they got the food from but the tables were laden, there was loads of it and we were on rations, mind. Everyone helped and everyone supplied some food and drink. There was music too, and they played all the war songs and people danced in the street. Everybody played their part.

Dorothy neatly summed up the contribution of the people of Buckfastleigh with her final words. Not only for VE celebrations but also throughout the war, whoever they were, everyone played their part.

A group photograph of the Land Army girls in the garden at Fullaford House, 1944. Ann Smart is third from the left in the front row.

Right: *Jan Tarasiuk in the Polish Army.*

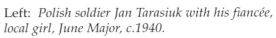

Left: *Polish soldier Jan Tarasiuk with his fiancée, local girl, June Major, c.1940.*

Below: *Jan and June Tarasiuk with their son Robert, 1950.*

Four

THE EVACUEES: A FLUX IN THE POPULATION

At the start of the Second World War the WVS was active in arranging for children from inner cities to be taken to the countryside, where they would be relatively safe from the bombing raids inflicted upon Britain's cities and ports.

Jack Tillyer, who had been living in Buckfastleigh for many years, originally came from London:

In 1939, when I was eight, I was taken away from my parents and, together with my four-year-old sister and another boy relative, we were put on a train at Paddington Station in London, with a group of other children, to be evacuated to Devon. Our parents never knew where we were going. We filed onto those trains at Paddington and off we went. We wore short trousers, a little jacket and a peaked cap and carried a little square, brown suitcase and a brown paper parcel. At the time we didn't think much of it. It was like going away on holiday.

Then, as the train travelled down the line, carriages were shunted off at each station we stopped at. I suppose the children in those carriages were put up in that particular town. Once we reached Newton Abbot our carriage was shunted off and we all piled out of the train and then piled back into waiting coaches, or charabancs as we called them then. The coaches went to villages and towns like Brent, Bovey Tracey, Ashburton and Buckfastleigh.

When we arrived in Buckfastleigh they herded us into the primary school. We had all been travelling for about six to eight hours and then we were told to sit at the desks in the classrooms. We all sat there crying – all of us hungry, all of us tired and all of us missing our parents. Local people started coming around to the classrooms. One would say, 'I'll take that boy,' and another, 'I'll take the maid'. The last thing my mother said to me was that the three of us had to stick together (the other boy, Sid, was a distant relation). Then this lady said, 'I'll take the maid but I don't want the boys.' But we wouldn't let her take away my sister who was screaming and crying anyway and wouldn't budge. In fact we all sat there crying.

Finally Mrs Walters, who lived at Hapstead in the first bungalow there, said 'I'll take the brother and sister.' Mrs Short, who lived next door, agreed to take Sid and we all went off by car to Hapstead.

The Hamlyn family still lived in the big house at Hapstead and Mrs Short's husband was a chauffeur for the Hamlyns, and that's where we landed. Mrs Walters' husband was away in the war. We went to the primary school and walked down and back each day and it was all so very different. We had been living in Elephant and Castle, my father came from Bermondsey, my gran from Walworth and I had aunts living in the Old Kent Road. So we were real Londoners.

My parents didn't know where we were until Mrs Walters wrote to tell them. My mother managed to come down once to see us but had to go back to London because my father was still working there.

'No official records were kept of where the evacuees were sent to live,' said the WRVS archivist based in Newbury. 'The only records kept were by the London Local Authorities who kept records of children evacuated from their borough.'

Sybil Chaffe, from Dartbridge Hill, helped to organise the billeting of evacuee children with Mrs Dunning and Dr Ironsides between 1940 and '41. She remembered the arrival of the children:

We used to meet the evacuees at Buckfastleigh Railway Station. They were poor little beggars. They were all crying and had been on the train for a very long time and their faces were so dirty... I shall never, never forget it. We took the children up to the school and gave them some tea and tried to calm them down.

Phyllis Voisey from Barn Park recalled the evacuees:

I had three children of my own and I was then living in Chapel Street. When I heard that evacuees had arrived in the town I decided that I would go down to the school to see them. I was up at my sister's home being looked after, as I hadn't been very well. When I told her that I was going down the school she tried to stop me. She said 'Now don't go going down there Phyl, you'll be bringing some back with you.' 'No I won't,' I said – and, of course I came back with two brothers and a sister (Ronny, Lenny and Joan Moyse from London) who had promised their parents they wouldn't be parted. Mrs Cranch was prepared to take the boys, and I had the sister.

Their brother, Harry Moyse, used to come down a lot to see them. After the war, when he was married with a little boy, also called Harry, he told me that he was going to move down to live in Buckfastleigh. 'Oh, Harry,' I said, 'it's alright for a fortnight, but you won't like it down here after London.' 'Oh, yes,' he said, 'I will.' And they did settle down and Harry Moyse (junr) grew up here.

Later, Phyllis Voisey was asked to take in a lady from Plymouth called Monica who had a young son and had originally come to stay with relatives. 'I couldn't leave them down in Plymouth, could I?' said Phyllis. 'They had to go out in the road at night when the bombing raids started.' Monica stayed some time and then went back to Plymouth only to return to Buckfastleigh following the birth of her second child – again staying with the Voiseys.

Jack Tillyer recalled his experience as an evacuee:

My mother came down to Buckfastleigh to live and took us away from Mrs Walters and found somewhere to live at Buckfast, near South Gate. Our neighbours were the Pethericks and Jack Birt and his wife. My dad was still working in London.

When we went to Buckfast we had no furniture but Mr Birt and the other neighbours helped us out. We started going to St Mary's School in Buckfast because it was closer, of course. That was an experience too. There were a lot of young evacuees from Ireland who, of course, were Catholic. As Protestants we didn't really know what was going on. We didn't really understand who Protestants were. Religion wasn't important to our family so we didn't understand why these Irish boys would come up to us and spit at us but, of course, it was because we weren't Catholics. Their attitudes were formed already.

Eventually my father locked up our home in London and came down here to live. The next thing we heard was that a land mine had dropped on our flat and we had lost everything. My father went back to see if he could salvage any furniture but there was nothing left. So he came back to Buckfastleigh, got a job in the mill making flying jackets for airmen and we were given a house in Chapel Street which, of course, were tithed houses.

After the war a number of people came and settled in Buckfastleigh. These newcomers were not by any means all from London – some came from Plymouth which had been badly bombed, and many were people who did not have homes to return to; they included: Marian Hoff and her parents; Bill and Doll Jackson, with their daughter, Phyllis (now Phyllis Short); Pat Hedges and her family the Bakers, who initially settled in Buckfast, and the Snowdons.

Ernest Coleman's sister, Doll Jackson, and her family were living in Plymouth at that time. Phyllis Short recalled this wartime period:

We were bombed out of our home three times. On the last occasion we were in the air-raid shelter: my parents and Aunty Edith (Coleman) who was visiting us with Sandra, a baby of a few months old. I was 11. Everyone was outside and I made them come back in. A minute or two later a land mine dropped and there was a terrific explosion. Then everything went quiet. We stayed in the air-raid shelter until the all-clear siren went [off at] about seven in the morning. When we went back in the house everything had been destroyed. Sandra's cot was covered in glass and debris.

We couldn't live in the house because all the plaster had come off the walls and the ceilings were gone so we picked up the stuff we needed and came up to Buckfastleigh and stayed with Aunty Edith at her home in Chapel Street until a cottage became available in Elliott's Plain.

Most people were obliged to take in evacuees. Edith Coleman, was called into the mill to weave khaki for the soldiers' uniforms and was also asked to take a five-year-old evacuee. 'There was no way' said Edith, 'that I could look after a small child and work all day in the mill.' Finally, another local woman took the child and Edith was given a 12-year-old evacuee who proved more than capable of looking after herself and doing household chores after school whilst Edith was still at work. Rene Lewis said:

My mother had two evacuees, a boy and a girl. They came on the train and they were sent up the schoolyard with their gas masks and we had to pick whoever we wanted. It must have been an ordeal for them.

Marian Harvey, who was 11 when the war started, said that her family received an evacuee through the Catholic Church. 'I'm a Catholic and I was attending St Mary's School in Buckfast,' said Marian, 'and we had to move out of the school into the Abbey Tearooms because there wasn't enough room in the school for ourselves and the evacuees.' Sybil Chaffe remembered her family's evacuee:

We had an evacuee whose name was Cynthia and she would only eat marmite – that was all she was used to eating. Cynthia decided to go back because they hadn't had any bombing, at that time, where she came from and she couldn't settle in the town. After she returned home the bombing raids started again and we don't know what happened to her as we never heard from her again.

Many evacuees did, and still do, keep in touch with their host families in the town. Elsie and Fred Churchward's evacuee, Dot, was eight when she came to them. Elsie said:

We loved her very much. If she had lost her parents in an air raid, and if her brothers would have allowed it, we would have adopted her. Dot stayed for five or six years and Fred cried when she finally left.

The population of Buckfastleigh was in a state of flux during the war with people moving in and out of the town. Ann Smart (née Hegarty), who was living at Fullaford where the Land Army girls were billeted, met Horace Smart, a local man, and married him after the war. She has lived in Buckfastleigh ever since. Two other Land Army girls also met and married local men, although they have since moved away.

After leaving Buckfastleigh School Jack Tillyer became an apprentice with Hoskins, the builders. As soon as he had finished his apprenticeship he joined the RAF:

I wanted to broaden my horizons. As a young man I found Buckfastleigh too small, too cliquey, too close, too everything. But after I met my wife and we married I found that the qualifications I gained in the Forces weren't recognised or accepted in Civvy Street, so I came back to Buckfastleigh and went back to Hoskins. Then I decided to go into civil engineering and never looked back from there. We continued to live in Buckfastleigh, we had two children here and we had the sweet shop at Weech Corner, which was leased from Fosters for about nine years until the early 1970s. We have continued to live here and are very settled now. I have travelled around a bit and it has been a good life with lots of different jobs and experiences.

Kazimierz Stryjski, who was in the Polish Army, came to Britain in 1946. He had been serving in Italy but was afraid to go back to Poland because of the invading Russians. He and a group of friends, all in the Second Corps, landed in Scotland and later made their way to Tavistock. From there they moved to Ashburton where they were based in Home Park, a Polish camp. Kaz was then 23 and had been in the Polish Army for two years. He was an ally so he was allowed to stay in the country and become a British citizen. He was demobbed from Home Park and came to Buckfastleigh where his first proper home was in lodgings with Mr and Mrs Prior in Laburnum House, opposite St Luke's Church, with three other Polish men. His first job was at the West End Quarry, Whitecleaves. Most of the other Polish immigrants emigrated to the USA or Canada. Those who stayed in the town have since died.

Kaz met his wife, Marjorie, on a bus going to Newton Abbot. They regularly attended dances at the Polish camp in Ashburton. Marjorie, whose maiden name was Farquhar, recalled this period:

There were hundreds of Polish men around but in those days you felt quite safe walking home in the men's company. Kaz could not speak a word of English then and I could not speak a word of Polish but, in the winter evenings, we used to spend time learning to talk each other's language.

I came from Wales originally. My family came to Buckfastleigh in 1940, just after the war started. My father wanted to get my brothers out of the coal mines. I had three brothers – Douglas, who still lives in the town, and Ken and Desmond who are now dead. Unfortunately the government brought conscription in and my brothers had to choose either to go into the Army or to go back to the mines. So they went back to the mines.

I found Buckfastleigh very different from my home in Wales. There seemed to be much more going on in our home town, with lots of fairs and four cinemas and, of course, we were a mining community. Now I'm so settled here and love it, I wouldn't be anywhere else. In fact my health improved tremendously when I came to Devon. I was so ill before I came that I only had a few years' schooling in Wales.

Kaz and Marge settled down in Buckfastleigh where they raised two children, Denise and Michael, made friends, and enjoyed being part of the local community. 'Kaz felt that the British people had a lot in common with the Poles and used to say how happy he was living here,' said Marge. Both Denise and Michael live in Buckfastleigh.

Robert Tarasiuk's father, Jan, was also Polish and, like Kaz Stryjski, was based at the Polish camp at Home Park when he first arrived in the area. Robert said:

Occasionally the men came out to dances in Buckfastleigh and, at one of the dances, my dad met my mother, June Major. They started going out together and eventually got married in 1948, after Dad was discharged from the Polish Resettlement Unit.

Dad never talked about the war. The Polish had suffered a great deal and he had had a bad time as a prisoner of war in Siberia. He escaped but went through hell. Towards the end of the war he fought at Monte Casino in Italy. He was an ambulance driver attached to the ambulance corps and one of his duties was to go around the battle zone picking up dead bodies.

My father was always polite and taught me to be polite too. If we went to a Polish club in Plymouth he would speak in his own language, but if Polish visitors came to our house they would speak in English. They would occasionally lapse into Polish but as soon as my mother walked into the room they would speak in English again.

Joe Horak, who is part Czechoslovakian and part Polish, was conscripted into the Polish Army in 1942 when he was 17 years old, joining the 17th Battalion of the City of Lwow Sixth Brigade. He spoke fluent Russian so was sent on a convoy as a translator. Eventually, after many adventures, he was sent to Ashkhabad on the Iranian border and from there fought in Iraq, Jordan, Syria and Egypt. After the battle of Tobruk he trained near Tripoli in the Lebanon before taking part in the Italian campaign. When it ended he went as an instructor to a school for the retraining of older officers in newer technology. The officers had been prisoners of war released by the allies from the 1939 campaign. Eventually he was transferred to England with the Polish Resettlement Unit (PRU), finally arriving at the Polish camp near Ashburton.

Joe met Sheila, his wife, in the Golden Lion Hotel, Ashburton and, like Kaz and Jan, settled down locally, finding work with the help of the PRU, and raising a family.

Doreen Franks was a Land Army girl based in Okehampton when she met a Buckfastleigh man called Mick Voisey. Mick had been demobbed in 1947 and was working as a mechanic maintaining vehicles used by the Land Army. Doreen explained:

Franic Protorsjsk (left) and Stefan Derdea (right), two Polish soldiers who settled in Buckfastleigh, c.1940s.

I came from Surrey and had to do something and it was either the Land Army or munitions. Well, I thought, a lovely place like Devon, what could be better? After training in Exeter they put me on pest destruction – killing rats! One day I was driving the van and something went wrong with the horn. So I took it into the garage and that's how I met Mick.

Mick continued:

We started going out and eventually got married and came back to live in Buckfastleigh. The town hadn't changed very much from how it was before I went away but there were a lot of new faces, young faces. A lot of girls met and married Buckfastleigh men, some were in the Land Army and married and settled down here afterwards.

Mick and Doreen Voisey moved into Mick's grandparents' home in Station Road, where they still live in 2003. Doreen recalled:

When he first brought me to live in the cottage I used to look over at the trees in the orchard, on the opposite side of the road, when all the apple blossom was out in spring. It was so peaceful; what a lovely place to live in, I thought.

Perhaps that's what other newcomers thought too. Perhaps that's why they stayed.

Joe and Sheila Horak on the farm, Buckfast, c.1950.

Five

THE YANKS

In 1944 the Allies were planning to liberate Europe. The Americans were now at war with Germany and, trained in amphibious warfare, the US 4th Infantry Division set sail for Britain. They arrived in Liverpool on 14 January and were immediately sent to Devon. Other infantry divisions were to follow. The South West of England and South Wales became the focus of large-scale activity by American troops, particularly Devon, the like of which had never before been experienced. Author Gerald Wasley stated in his book *Devon at War (1939–1945)*:

… ports and harbours were chosen for the eventual embarkation and departure of the Allied forces for the cross Channel attack on the German coastal defences in Normandy. The Devon departure points were, in alphabetical order: Brixham, Dartmouth, Plymouth, Salcombe and Torquay. These harbours also served the Allies for pre-invasion training and for servicing the amphibious landing craft which were to carry 25,000 troops and 2,750 military vehicles.

Lt Robert E. Dennis, 1940s.

The arrival of so many servicemen in the region was a great shock to Devonians. The accommodation of several thousand evacuees throughout the duration of the war had already stretched local resources drastically. This time, however, it was much more of a culture shock as the numerous young Americans burst into action on the hitherto quiet country lanes and sedate seaside resorts.

In South Devon units were based in towns and villages including Newton Abbot, Denbury, Staverton, Totnes, Ivybridge and Buckfastleigh. Not only was accommodation to be provided for the men, but also for their tanks and equipment.

Bill Selley was 11 years old when the war started. He particularly remembered the American soldiers who were stationed in the town during the war. 'Buckfastleigh was very much a garrison town at that period,' said Bill, 'but you got used to having soldiers around.' He added, 'If there hadn't been a war there would not have been the movement of people that there has been.'

Michael Lane and his parents were living at the bottom of Crest Hill where he grew up, and Michael vividly remembered American tanks coming down Crest Hill. 'If you look closely enough,' said Michael, 'you will see marks in the wall as you go down the hill where the tanks scraped the sides.'

Houses in and around Buckfastleigh were used to accommodate officers whilst the white American soldiers camped in Dean, Buckfast and in Victoria Park. The black Americans were camped in fields near Dartbridge and the railway station.

It was the Americans' policy to separate the black soldiers from the white as fights frequently broke out between the two groups. Even the dances that were held were either for the black soldiers or the white soldiers, never for black and white soldiers together.

The problem went deeper, however, than the inability of two racial groups to get along. American racial policies and mores were being imposed on British townsfolk. To the bewilderment and resentment of many, people were encouraged to bar black American soldiers from public places such as restaurants, guest-houses and hotels. Most people were delighted to welcome black soldiers – and their money – as they would any other allied troops.

Whilst the deployment of black American troops in Britain continued to be a problem for the War Department, the majority of people in towns like Buckfastleigh readily accepted both races. Black and white soldiers alike were welcomed into people's homes and many became family friends. At the same time, however, women who went out with black soldiers were often gossiped about and some people would spit on the black Americans as they

Above: *The 459 Battalion, Battery B, c.1940. They were all stationed in Buckfastleigh during the Second World War.*

Left: *Local man Maurice Lane with Major Robert Dennis on his return visit to Buckfastleigh in 1998.*

The gun crews of Battery B, c.1940.

passed by in the streets. Joy Hallett recalled the racial tension:

Of course, we were called names for being friendly with them. But what could you do when they were living on your doorstep? And they were good, they were nice boys. My mother would never ignore anybody. Earlier on she said to us, 'They are human beings and God's children and don't you dare snub anybody – because you wouldn't like it.'

Jack Smith from Barn Park was the caretaker of Victoria Park, at Woodholme, during this period:

I was employed by Buckfastleigh Urban District Council but all my responsibilities stopped when the Americans came and took possession of it. We continued to live in the bungalow in the park and, of course, I was still employed by the council.

The Americans took over the town and used every amenity, including the swimming-baths where hot-water systems were installed so that the men could have showers. A bakery and cookhouse were set up where meals were prepared for all the Americans stationed in the area. Jack continued:

No civilians were allowed in the park except my wife and I but we got on all right with them, in fact they were no trouble at all. Occasionally, after they had been out drinking, they would jump into the swimming-pool fully-clothed, but they weren't very noisy and the officers in charge would make sure that things didn't go too far.

There was only one soldier that got into trouble as far as I can remember and that was a man who had been promoted to corporal. The same day that he had been promoted he went out drinking in the evening at the Globe to celebrate and came out drunk. A policeman saw him and went over, slapped him around the face, and then reported the incident to his commanding officer. His promotion was over quickly as he was demoted the same day he was promoted!

Lieutenant Robert Dennis from Texas served as assistant platoon leader of an anti-aircraft battery with the 459th Anti-Aircraft Unit, which was attached to the 29th Infantry Division. He was billeted in Buckfast and enjoyed evenings out in the local pubs, particularly the Valiant Soldier in Fore Street, which at that time was a popular venue for local people. 'However, as part of my work I was a Military Police Officer,' he recalled. 'I had to go around the town checking that all the public houses closed at the proper time and that no soldiers got into trouble.'

Jack Smith remembered the kindness of the visiting troops:

The Americans were extremely generous to local people, especially the children. They didn't have coppers in their pockets for very long. They would go down to the river and throw coppers to the children standing in Strode Road watching them. They had plenty of anything they needed although we, of course, were rationed. What they didn't have they would send for – machinery or anything. Theirs was a completely different way of life.

When Rene Lewis married her first husband, Leslie Foot, she had a flat at Higher Mill in Buckfast, close to where the American troops were billeted. 'They were extremely nice and very kind to me,' said Rene who, in 1944, was expecting her first child. 'They used to come and ask me to press their trousers, and bring me oranges which we couldn't get during the war.' Fern Cox recalled the relationship between the local people and the troops:

Buckfastleigh was a different place then, with the Americans being stationed nearby. Some of the respectable ladies would be surprised if they knew what I remembered about them and the American soldiers!

Some of the men had a trick of coming up to a house and if they saw a chink of light through the curtains they would open the front door (they weren't locked in those days) and come in, saying, 'Oh, sorry, thought this was a pub!' They just wanted to see who was in the house. Some of the women welcomed the attention from the Americans if they could get cigarettes and that kind of thing.

One woman who didn't welcome American advances was Ann Smart who worked for the Co-op:

The Yanks camped in Victoria Park and had their ablutions in the Co-op Yard – just the first building, with stables next door where six horses were kept. I didn't have much to do with the Yanks as I was going out with Horace but one day, when I was washing out the stables with a hosepipe, a Yank came to the door. I was singing away, oblivious to anything, and he stood in the doorway and said, 'Gee, Red, how yer doing?'
'You're not allowed in here,' I replied. 'Clear off!'
'Oh gee, honey, don't be like that,' he said.
'You put one foot inside this door and you'll be sorry,' I replied, and then I let him have it with the hosepipe! I didn't half get into trouble for dousing him like that.

One of the British regiments stationed near Buckfastleigh had been in North Africa relieving the Americans who had been unable to stand their ground, and had subsequently lost a lot of territory. Fern Cox remembered how some of the British soldiers decided to come to Buckfastleigh one night and threatened to go after the Americans to pay them back. As a result the Americans were shut in for the night – some in Victoria Park, some in Buckfast and different places around. 'There wasn't an American to be seen that night!' said Fern.

Ken Fricker and his family lived in the old Toll House at Buckfastleigh, which was situated between the Ashburton Road and the Totnes Road, before the Devon Expressway was built. The house no longer exists. Ken recalled his memories of the Americans in Buckfastleigh before he was called up:

They were camping in every field available around Dartbridge, waiting to go on the D-Day landings. They always spoke to me and they were always crowding round the house trying to buy my bicycle! Sometimes they used to borrow it – the black soldiers particularly liked to go to the top of Furzeleigh Hill and race down the hill on the bike as fast as they could go!

Joy Hallett, as a girl of 13, was living with her parents and sisters in the house at the top of Station Hill:

One day I was sitting on the step and this face looked over the fence at me from the field beyond and it was black. I don't think that I had ever seen a black person before. I got up and ran indoors and my sisters said 'What's the matter, Joy?'

I replied, 'There's a big black man out there staring at me across the fence!' When they looked out there were lorry loads of them coming into the field opposite our house. We pulled the curtains across and when mum came home she said, 'What are the curtains drawn for, somebody died?'

'No Mum,' said Ivy. 'You can see all those black men out there. They were looking over at us.'

'My dear life,' she said, 'they be helping us win the war, don't ever be so silly. You can't keep the curtains drawn all the time. They're going to have to camp there.'

Of course, as time went on, we got friendly. We talked and we used to go to their dances in the Town Hall. Mum came with us and Cynthia, my friend, and her mum used to come as well. We enjoyed the refreshments that the men prepared at their camp. We used to have lovely doughnuts and all sorts of things.

As a young woman in the 1940s Elsie Foot enjoyed going out:

We had three dances a week including one organised by the black soldiers and one organised by the white soldiers. Of course, we also had The Picture House that had a change of film three times a week. We had a far better social life than the young people seem to have now. And when we had the dances, whether they were American or British, the men would always come over and say, 'May we have the pleasure, please.' After the dance was over they would always return you to your seat. If the American band wasn't playing we would have Syd Myhill's three-piece band. He played the drums and another chap from Ashburton would play the saxophone. As it was wartime there would be complete blackouts and you would have to walk home in the dark. The soldiers would walk you home and they would always be courteous. It was always quite safe.

Joy Hallet continued:

The soldiers were quite young, only about 18 or 19 years old, and used to come into our house to see mum. One of the men, who had the most beautiful singing voice, said 'Mrs Bickford, I don't want the Purple Heart, all I want is my discharge papers so that I can go home to my family.'

We used to go to their choir concerts up in the Town Hall. Cynthia and I used to sit in the front. They had a big band there once and you never heard such a racket in all your life, and all black Americans playing. They had several of these concerts.

In 1940/41 the YMCA opened its premises to troops billeted in the town. It was a new departure for the organisation but the committee had decided that, seeing as the troops were in the town, it was their job to make them welcome. In addition to the recreational facilities already in existence they decided to make the canteen and reading room available.

Many local ladies volunteered to work in the canteen, serving the American soldiers who used the facilities, and Edith Coleman was probably one of many who received a certificate for her efforts.

'The Americans used to hang out at the Waterman's Arms,' said Michael Lane, 'and the YMCA where the men played billiards and generally relaxed.' Michael remembered them giving him candy, of which they always seemed to have plenty.

Margaret Foot, whose parents were the publicans of the Waterman's Arms, said that the American soldiers were very generous with their food allowances:

They had a bakery in Victoria Park where they were billeted and they used to give us a white loaf from time to time. There was a lot of bartering – which was

A drawing by a GI stationed at Higher Mill Cottages during the Second World War.

THE YANKS

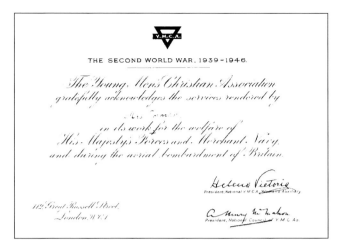

Above: *A certificate which was issued to Edith Coleman by the YMCA for voluntary work during the war.*

natural. You could bargain with some cooking apples from your tree for butter or something.

Local people began to get used to their friendly 'invaders' and the Americans enjoyed a growing rapport with their hosts. However, as increasing numbers of military convoys swept into Devon from other parts of Britain, the reason for the soldiers being in Devon was becoming more evident. Every available space in the towns and in the country lanes was taken up by armoured vehicles, jeeps and transporters. All over the county men were on training exercises as preparation for the D-Day landings in Normandy became more frenzied.

'We used to go down to Plymouth and Dartmouth for Invasion Training and often went on to Dartmoor for training exercises,' said Robert Dennis. 'When it rained we used to spend all our time digging out the trucks that got stuck in the bogs.'

During one of the training exercises at Slapton Sands, near Dartmouth, in April 1944, a German E-boat sank an American landing-craft, resulting in a heavy loss of life.

Devon's coastal areas became the scene of even more frenetic activity and the movement of civilians was strictly controlled. Even in Buckfastleigh the movement of local people was monitored. Ken Fricker's garden was on an allotment by the railway line and his family had to ask permission from the soldiers to go into the allotment:

They were very strict with us, no-one was allowed to go down the Old Totnes Road unless they lived there. However, they were very kind to us and gave us oranges and things which we couldn't get in the shops during the war.

On one occasion Ernest Coleman, coming home on short weekend leave to see his wife Edith, had hitched a lift to Totnes and then walked from Totnes to Buckfastleigh. He was frustrated, however, when having reached Dartbridge he was barred from entering the town that way. Eventually, after proving who he was, two American soldiers took pity on him and brought him the rest of the way home in a jeep. Of course the situation in the town did have its amusing moments as Joy Hallett explained:

One night I had been to see Cynthia and she was walking home with me because it was pitch black because of the blackouts and there was no moon. The soldiers had a sentry-box outside our house and as we were nearing it we heard the barrel of a gun rattle and the soldier cried out, 'Halt! Who goes there?' We clutched each other really scared. The voice came again, 'Halt! Who goes there?' 'It's alright,' said Cynthia, 'it's only Cynthia and Joy.' Then we laughed, we were tickled pink!

The departure of the Americans from Devon for their invasion of Normandy was sudden. It was D-Day, 6 June 1944, and as Gerald Wasley explained in *Devon at War*:

The thousands of American servicemen, the mass of military equipment carried in all manner of craft, had departed to the far shore. News of the Allied invasion was greeted in Devon with considerable relief and hope for the future. Many Devon people went to church and prayed. There had been no cheering, no flag-waving crowds to bid the soldiers 'bon voyage', the invasion forces had sailed amid almost total secrecy.

The 459th Battalion landed on Omaha beach, Normandy, on 10 June 1944, four days after D-Day. In a cassette recording given to the Valiant Soldier, Robert Dennis, who was later promoted to major, described the events that took place as the men fought their way across France and became one of the first units to enter Paris.

Although the Americans' departure from South Devon was as sudden as their arrival, a bond had been formed with the local people that remains apparent. For some of the men who survived the war this bond has been continued through correspondence, visits and by telephone over the past 50 years.

Robert Dennis, described by his British friends the Campbells, who live in Exeter, as a 'gentle man and a true gentleman,' is someone who has a special affection for Buckfastleigh. He returned to the town in 1998 and, during his visit, went to the Valiant Soldier pub, now a museum and heritage centre, in Fore Street, where he was warmly welcomed. One wonders what memories this brought back for Robert, and for other British and American soldiers who have visited Buckfastleigh in the last few decades.

Certainly there can be no finer accolade for the town than Robert's comment in a recent letter to the Campbells that 'Buckfastleigh will always be my second home.'

The Half Moon Inn, West End.

The Salmon Leap Café, 1940.

Left: *Ready to serve. This picture includes Messrs Gomm, Foot, Coleman, Henle, Voaden, Roberts and Northcott.*

Below: *The cover of the 'Welcome Home' souvenir programme.*

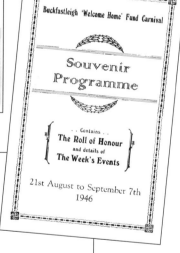

Left: *Ann Smart as carnival queen with Lady Astor, MP, at the 'Welcome Home' carnival for the Armed Forces, 1946. The attendants are Joan Setters (left) and June Setters.*

Six

WELCOME HOME!

During 1945 and 1946, thousands of cities, towns and villages around Britain welcomed home the men and women who had fought in the Second World War. It was more poignant, perhaps, for smaller towns like Buckfastleigh where those people lost, and those returning from the conflict, were all well known locally.

In December 1945, during the interval of a variety show produced by the Buckfastleigh Amateur Dramatic Society, Mr L.R. Dinwiddy, chairman of Buckfastleigh Urban District Council, presented savings vouchers of £3.15s. to 50 of the town's ex-servicemen and women. He was assisted by Mr R.W. Cole, the honorary secretary, and Mr Hugh Symond, the honorary treasurer, of Buckfastleigh and Dean Prior Welcome Home Fund. Before making the presentation Mr Dinwiddy asked the town to stand in silent gratitude to the memory of those Buckfastleigh inhabitants who had died on active service. He then went on to make a moving speech, recorded in the *Western Guardian* on 20 December 1945, which began:

We have gathered here this evening to do honour to and welcome home our own men and women from the Forces, and it is my privilege and pleasure on behalf of Dean Prior and Buckfastleigh Welcome Home Fund to extend to these men and women our sincere and cordial welcome home and to make this preliminary presentation to them...

Mr Dinwiddy expressed great appreciation for all that the servicemen and women had endured during the previous six years, he listed the far-flung places they had travelled to and named each individual as they mounted the platform to receive their voucher.

In a small country town like Buckfastleigh, festivals and carnivals were often the highlight of the year, so it was natural that Buckfastleigh and Dean Prior Welcome Home Committee should organise a 'Welcome Home' carnival.

It was an event for the whole community and people eagerly awaited the carnival. The austerity of the war years meant that there had not been a carnival for some time. Activities started on Wednesday 21 August 1946 with a ballot for the choosing of the carnival queen at Harewood. Ann Smart was selected – she was living in the hostel at Fullaford House where the Land Army girls were billeted.

The dance at the Town Hall was packed on 21 August and, from the crowning of the queen by Mrs Holdsworth on Friday 30 August, there was something on every night for the next week except for the Sunday. Ann was kept extremely busy; she opened the CWS fête on the Saturday, attended another dance in the Town Hall that same evening and was present at various events throughout the week, including the furry dance through the town on the Tuesday. The finale, was the grand carnival procession on 7 September and the carnival dance in the Town Hall that same night. Ann remembered:

The dance was packed, people had a job to get in if they weren't there early. Everyone had supported the carnival and other activities throughout the week and, although people couldn't afford a lot, everyone gave something. My carnival queen dress was a borrowed wedding dress made of satin. [She laughed.] *We had very little after the war – even my bouquet was made up of chrysanthemums from someone's garden!*

It was a hearty welcome home for those men and women who had served in the Forces – men like Bob Voisey who served six years in the Navy. Phyllis Voisey recalled:

He worked for the DEMS (Defence Equip Merchant Service) and was paid by the Navy. He travelled all over the world and in all that time they only had one accident. Before he joined the troop ship he was on a collier ship that got sunk in the North Sea on his birthday when another ship cut the collier in half. He had only just gone back from Buckfastleigh after being on leave and, after the accident, returned home immediately. There was a knock on the door one night and there was Bob. 'What are you doing here?' [I asked]. I thought the beggar had run away!

Letters were often censored. I wrote and told him about the bombs that went off in Buckfastleigh – but that was returned to me.

Bob's cousin, Mick Voisey, was 19 years old when the war started. A year later he was called up and joined the Air Force. After training in various camps, which included acquiring skills as an electrician, he was drafted to Mons in Belgium. He belonged to a workshop unit that sent men to service diesel engines in radar stations in small groups. As the war progressed Mick found himself working with the American Army increasingly often.

There were five radar chains, all in the highest parts of the country, and five units to a chain. As the British and Americans advanced so the service units advanced with them. 'We were on the move all the time,' said Mick, 'and the equipment we had was specialised and very valuable.'

Mick was in Bonn when VE Day was declared. 'All I saw,' he said, 'was one plane flying over and some Very pistol lights!' He was demobbed in 1947 and missed Buckfastleigh's 'Welcome Home' carniva. Mick was sent to work for the Devon War Agricultural Committee, servicing the vehicles used by the Land Army girls. He was based in Okehampton where he met his wife, Doreen, who was in the Land Army. Joyce Blank was in the Army from 1942–45:

I was stationed in Bournemouth but my old billet has gone now. I did my initial training in Honiton. I wasn't demobbed but came out on the unemployed list to look after my mother who had a stroke.

Joyce's husband, Graham Blank, who originally came from Ashburton, became a prisoner of war after being captured in the desert and was sent to a farm in Italy. When the Italians surrendered, the prisoners had more freedom but continued to live and work on the Italian farms. Each time the Germans arrived the farmers would warn the British soldiers who would then hide in the fields. One day, however, the Germans came to the farm early in the morning and caught the men asleep. They were taken down to the Gestapo headquarters and, after questioning, were driven in cattle trucks through the Brenner Pass to Czechoslovakia where they ended up working in a coal mine. They were liberated by the Russian Army and flown home to Britain by the Americans.

Maurice Lane remembered his time as a serviceman during the war:

I was in the RAF. My wife Joan and I married in 1939 and I volunteered in 1940 and I did three years here and then went abroad. Before I was posted overseas I was sent to the Isle of Man to control aircraft as Liverpool was being bombed considerably at the time. I was there for nine months and Joan was allowed to come with me. We hadn't been married long and that was our honeymoon! We were so happy there and there wasn't any food rationing. From there I was sent to Ireland and Joan and I had to part. Then I got 24 hours leave to come home and see her before being sent overseas. After that I didn't see her for three and a half years. Parting was terrible.

I went to Ceylon first because the Japanese were invading all the islands and Ceylon was the next one they wanted. I got out there just as they started to bomb the island and we had a couple of bombing raids but they never invaded in the end. When the danger receded I was put on to combined operations and sent up to India and Burma where I worked in Further Operations Control.

I was at school with a local man, Eddy Beer, and we were good friends, but I didn't know his whereabouts during the war. I was based seven miles from the airbase at China Bay (Ceylon). One day a sergeant from Exeter came into my unit and said, 'Maurice, there's a chap from Devon at China Bay.' My wife had already written and told me that Eddy Beer had gone to India and the sergeant confirmed that this man's name was Beer and that he worked in the Met Office.

After listening to Eddy's voice on the radio for days I decided to ring the Met Office to get their weather report for flying purposes. So I plucked up courage and rang up and a broad Devon voice replied, 'Met Office here.' I replied, 'Can you give me a forecast for Buckfastleigh?' And Eddy said, 'That's Maurice!'

We met each other afterwards and discovered that we had played together in the same inter-section football match and hadn't realised it! Of course, we were on opposing teams, but both of us played in defence. Anyway we started to play tennis on our days off and once went down to Colombo together on leave.

Reg Gill was in the Navy for six years and spent much of it away:

I saw an advert in the papers for volunteers to join the Light Anti-Aircraft so I went to Exeter to enlist and they tried to get me to join the heavy artillery. After I enlisted I just went straight to Aldershot from Exeter. Gwen, my wife, was with me when I went to enlist that day and she had to go home on her own – just like that. I didn't see her for six years! From Aldershot we went abroad: Freetown, Durban, Mombasa and Madagascar, and back to Mombasa. I was fortunate that I didn't see a lot of action except for some bombing.

Gwen Gill added:

It was six years before I saw Reg again. I had no idea

WELCOME HOME!

where he was! One night in 1946, about 8p.m., a knock came at the door and when I opened it a policeman was standing there. 'Oh, God, whatever is it?' I asked. 'Don't worry,' the policeman said, 'I've good news for you. Your husband landed in England this afternoon.' When Reg did arrive home he just walked in the door and things went on as normal!

Terry Hallett shared his memories of the war:

I joined the Navy. One day, after returning to barracks from leave, I got roped in to do a job. We got on the back of a lorry and [were] taken down to the docks where we boarded an ocean-going tug. The tug was going into the Channel to bring back a merchant ship, which took us a week. At that time I didn't have a clue about ships. I didn't know one end of a ship from the other. Anyway, things progressed from there and eventually I served on mine sweepers. It was a dangerous job and I did it for two years. On one occasion we had to go and rout out a German radar station. We completed the task and brought back German prisoners. Sadly, there were a lot of men killed on both sides.

I was away from Buckfastleigh for two and a half years. When I arrived home I rang the front door bell and my father came to open it. When he saw me he just looked and didn't say anything, but the tears were streaming down his face.

John Henle, who had been brought up at Dartbridge Farm from the age of six, went into the Territorials in 1939 and, after he was called up, eventually found himself in charge of a tank destroyer:

The tank gun was a very powerful one. It was an American gun which was supposed to knock out German tanks as they were coming towards you. Anyway, we were sent over to Normandy towards the end of June 1944. One day I shot at two German tanks, both of which caught fire so that the crew had to bail out.

After some time we were ordered over the radio to move forward because it was reported that enemy tanks had been seen in an orchard. We were slowly moving forward, feeling very exposed, when, suddenly, there was an extremely loud bang and our tank burst into flames. We bailed out and ran for dear life to get somewhere to shelter because we were in the middle of a battlefield. When I looked back I noticed that two crew members had got out but there were still two in the tank. So I thought well, I'd better go back and see, so I went back and got on top of the burning tank and looked down into it. The driver and the wireless operator were in this part, right up the front, where the guns are manned. The driver was pulling himself up, but looked up and said, 'My leg's trapped'. I got in the burning tank – but the rest I can't remember. The next thing I can remember is that I had his body stretched out across the tank. He was a big bloke and it was at least eight feet down into the tank so, somehow, I must have dragged him up. I didn't know what to do with him because he was obviously in a bad way. But there was nobody else around and I couldn't leave him there. My biggest worry was that the tank would explode. If that had happened that would have been it for everyone within 20 yards – so I rolled him off.

He was unconscious then, although he was conscious at first because he spoke to me when I first looked into the tank. I was sweating buckets by then. Anyway, I rolled him off and tried to think where I could take him as it was too risky to go into the town or outside the area. Then, suddenly, I just keeled over and fainted. After a while I came round and found myself lying next to the driver who was awake and in a lot of pain but he wasn't groaning or anything. If you read any stories about battlefields the wounded are always moaning and shrieking, but he never murmured even though he had lost his leg. It was smashed off and all that was left were jagged bits of bone. He was in awful pain and I had to get back in the tank again to get the first aid kit.

The second man in the tank was dead and still in his seat. My mind was racing trying to work out how to get us both away. Of course, we had no stretchers and no stretcher-bearers, but what you can do in that situation is to make a stretcher with two rifles. A rifle has a sling on it for slipping over the shoulder and if you slide these slings under the wounded person you can actually pick that person up. One of you is holding one end of the rifle and the other person is holding the other end and the body is lying across the slings in between. It's very awkward but a soldier I dragged out of the trenches and I did just that with this wounded man.

When we eventually got ourselves away I remember looking at my hands and there were great lumps of skin coming off the back of them, and from around the wrists, which was just hanging on. Until then I hadn't realised that there was anything wrong with me, and I thought I can't carry on like this I must put something on them. I went to the nearest first aid post where they bandaged me up and it was just as if I had two boxing gloves on. They just left one thumb free on the right hand so that I could hold a spoon or fork. I was in a shocked state and we had been in action, on and off, for a good week and a half. We hadn't washed or shaved, we were all a bit of a mess really.

To cut a long story short, all the wounded were taken to the ship – many far worse than I was of course. We were lying in rows and rows with some men in a terrible state, and some, like me, nothing much wrong with them. But I couldn't do anything for myself and there was always this dreadful thought that the Germans would bomb the ship.

When we reached England we were put on a slow train to Scotland. I was rather worried because people in Britain hear news quickly – a telegram from the War Office and my wife and family would be worried, you see. So I said to this chap next to me, 'I've

Left: *A street party, c.1940s. Margaret Joint and friends.*

Below: *The King's Arms men's outing. Including: Fred Truscott, the landlord (front left), Jack and Dougie Harvey, Bill Jackson, Freddie Hawkins, 'Trapper' Wicks, Arthur Honeywell, Alf Hayman, Fred Hoare, Jack Polkinghorne, Bill Brown, Larry Waters, Eddie Willis, George Harvey, Bob Bartle, Henry Spear, ? Rice, Arthur Tonkin, Bill Groot.*

Right: *Buckfastleigh Garden Association Committee, 1949. Left to right, back row: I. Prowse, W. Wallcocks, H. Ford, J. Harvey, W. Hayman, L. Lane, W. Thompson, I. Ford; front: R. White, J. Hannaford, Mrs Thomas, K. Badman, H. Foster, A. Ballard.*

got an airmail letter' (very much like you'd get now) 'and I am going to write a note on one half and you can have the other half. When we get to the next station where we slow up, but don't actually stop, we'll chuck the two halves out of the window.' And that's what we did in the hope that someone would pick them up and post them. And, believe it or not, someone did pick up my half of the airmail letter and it arrived safely. Not only that but it was redirected to Buckfastleigh where Gertrude, my wife, was staying at Dartbridge Farm with a cousin of mine. She was thrilled to get those few words saying 'Just a line to let you know I am in England and I'm o.k. Hope to be seeing you and Frances very soon. All my love to you, John.' The letter arrived just a few days after I posted it. I couldn't tell where it was posted from, or who picked it up.*

John Henle was awarded the Military Medal inscribed with his name, rank and number:

I am quite proud of it. I used to dread being thought of as a coward because that's something you can't wipe out. That is, if you don't do something you know you should have done, someone you could have saved, you'd regret that for the rest of your life. I know that other people have said their biggest fear was being a coward.

Charles Coulton Stewart, whose mother came from Dean Prior, was Officer-in-Command to the 21st and 22nd Bomb Disposal Sections in 1940. The 22nd Section was attached to the 1st Battalion Scots Guards. On one occasion in Norway the battalion had been forced to retreat from their position when the sappers, who had mined the bridge, were killed by gunfire and no one knew how to set off the explosives.

Charles recalled, 'I was asked by the Scots Guards Commanding Officer to train his troops in the use of explosives and did so in open country at Foots Cray.' Charles Stewart's experience came from Bulley Cleaves Quarry where, as co-owner with R.W. Coles, he had become experienced in the use of explosives. In 1940 he undertook a bomb-disposal course at RAF Mawby in Lincolnshire:

The area covered by section twenty-two extended from Erith and Woolwich in the north, on the Thames, to Surbiton and Esher in the south. I was the only officer and only officers were allowed to extract fuses. Because of the balloon barrages in central London the first air raids, which were in daylight, took place in my area and, to put it mildly, I was slightly over-worked.

In 1943 Plymouth was bombed and three 500 kilo UXBs were discovered with unmarked fuses, known to us as 'Y' fuses. Since we had prior knowledge of them, and they were designed to deal with BD personnel, I blew up two in [a] fairly open position at Efford. Major Andy Polsen arrived from London with X-ray seedlings and we X-rayed the bomb which lay in a dungeon in Devonport affecting naval instalments and movement. We had to freeze the bomb to make the batteries inert, which took hours in a dark dungeon working by torchlight. I had taken sandwiches and morsels were fed to a little mouse that kept on appearing and did much to lift our morale.

The operation was successful and we left for a supper, cooked by my wife, at Buckfastleigh, she had hoped for some offal (off ration) but Gerald Lang slapped down three large steaks.

The Roll of Honour taken from inside the 'Welcome Home' programme.

Jack Setters volunteered for the Air Force and was trained in the North. He was fortunate in getting transferred back to Dorset for 18 months before going overseas to India and Burma in the Far East. He was due to go into Malaya when the bomb was dropped at Hiroshima, 'So I spent the rest of my time in Kuala Lumpur,' he said. Vic Foot recalled:

I went straight to Dorchester Infantry Training Corps 149C. Then I went to Colchester for two months followed by Yarm, in County Durham, and three months later we were sent to Durban and Bombay. I joined the battalion there and in less than three months we were in Burma.

Many other men and women were not as fortunate and Buckfastleigh grieved for those who did not return alive. For those who did return home there were street parties in different parts of the town to celebrate the end of war.

One has to wonder whether it was easy for those who had served in the Forces to settle down again in the town in which they had grown up. And what did their families and other local people want now that the war had ended? Vic Foot described his return:

When I came back to Buckfastleigh on leave the main thing I noticed was how green everything was. Buckfastleigh itself did not seem to have changed very much, even though I was away for five long years. There were very few new buildings, with the exception of the houses built by Mr Pickles (brother to Mr Pickles who ran The Picture House). He was building as fast

Above: *VE-Day celebrations in Buckfastleigh, 1945/6.*

Left: *Scouts camping at Wallaford Down. Left to right: Noel Downie, Barry Goss, Raymond Hill, Ian Tankard, David Dodd (behind).*

Above: *The Buckfastleigh bandstand, Victoria Park.*

Left: *VE-Day celebrations in Buckfastleigh, with ladies of the town including 'Bobby' Smerdon, Mrs Gill and Jessie Tucker, 1945/6.*

as he could. I had no difficulty in settling down. I got a job quite quickly. I helped to lay the water mains that extend from the top near the waterworks over into Buckfast. A firm called Foster Deacon laid the waterworks. I was glad to be home as my mother was blind and I felt I wanted to look after her for as long as I could. I didn't want to fly off again.*

'You wanted to settle after the war,' added Margaret Foot. 'You wanted to come home. Many men came back and settled down. In fact, Vic and I married in 1947.'

'I had no difficulty slotting back into local life after the war,' said Jack Setters, who had been away for five and a half years. 'I was tired of the Air Force by then. My business needed to get back on its feet and we had to work hard.'

Audrey Coulton went to her parents' home in Kingsbridge during the war and came back to Buckfastleigh in 1946 when her husband, Guy, was demobbed:

It was a difficult time for some men when they came back especially if, like Guy, they came back to find an established family. My son, Nicholas, was 18 months old when his father went away and my second child, Susan, was three and a half years old before she saw her father for the first time.

The children were excited to see their father at first but when he tried to discipline them they didn't like this strange man! It took about six months before they really got to know each other. One summer afternoon the children went up to the caves to play and Nicholas succeeded in tipping a big tin of oil that was on the shelf in the stables over himself and Susan and they came home covered in the stuff. I took Nicholas, Guy took Susan, and we put them straight in the bath. Susan said, 'I want Mummy.' 'Well, you've got me,' said her father, smacked her bottom and put her straight in the bath – and that was that. Everything was fine and she followed him around like a puppy dog.

Maurice Lane talked of his return from the war:

Coming home? Well a lot of men didn't come home. My mate, Billy Chaffe, was one who died very early on in the war. I was fortunate in surviving it and was content to come back to Buckfastleigh to live. Joan and I were very happy and I slipped back into the way of life very easily really. I missed the activity of the war years, though, you were on the go the whole time. Joan and I did consider moving away to get work but we felt we made the right decision to stay. My job had been held open but it wasn't easy to get back into it, but I still stayed and worked for the Co-op for some years after that.

Reg Gill commented on his return:

I didn't find it hard to settle down when I came back. I had worked in the mill before I went to war, starting in the spinning mill, then in the mill house, followed by the packing shop and then in the mending department. When I got back I went straight into my packing job in the mill. Coming back didn't seem to affect me very much.

We used to work long hours in those days. We needed the money and if you didn't want the extra work somebody else would jump right in. You didn't always want to work. I had an allotment, but many nights I had to work until eight in the evening, Friday nights until seven, Saturday mornings and Saturday afternoons until four.

My allotment was up at Jordan Street. We lived in Jordan Street in the old days, opposite the Royal Oak. Not many people knew about the allotments, as it was mostly the people who lived in the street who had them. A lot of families had allotments in those days.

Nick Tiratsoo, in 'The Attlee Years Revisited', said:

... when people in Britain started to think about what they wanted from peace their choices tended to be fairly prosaic – a home with a garden, steady employment and some relaxation and quiet... How did this mood shape the outcome of the 1945 election? Most working class people, of course, voted Labour; they did, not because the party promised socialism but rather it spoke of new houses and full employment. Nevertheless, plenty of ordinary voters, even in 1945 liked the Conservatives better.

'It was a great shock to everyone when Labour got in after the war,' said Vic Foot. 'It shocked the nation. After all, Churchill was the man who saved us.'

'It was the soldiers who came back from the war who put Labour in,' said Margaret Foot. 'But conditions gradually improved and we are reaping the benefits now,' she added. But, as T.O. Lloyd said in his book, *The Short Oxford History of the Modern World*, 'The Labour government came to office in a world that had changed much more than people realised.'

BIBLIOGRAPHY

The quotation at the end of this chapter is taken from: 'The Post-War World – Dream and Reality: 1945–1949' (page 239), *The Short Oxford History of the Modern World, Empire, Welfare State, Europe: History of the United Kingdom 1906–2001* (Fifth Edition), T.O. Lloyd (2002). Reprinted by permission of Oxford University Press.

Above: *A waitress race from Damarell's Bridge during carnival time, c.1950. Left to right: Phyllis Jackson, Pam Jones, Doll Jackson (in the background), Maureen Jeffery, ?, ?, ?, ?, Mrs Lock, Mrs Leather, ?, Sybil Chaffe.*

Right: *The Buckfastleigh band, c.1900.*

Fore Street, 1952. This double-decker bus was one of six buses given by the city of Leicester in return for six single buses from Devon General, it is negotiating the original bus route through the town. Bob Major and Annie Lane are on the left, Miss Scoble is stepping onto the left-hand pavement and Mrs Tonkin is to the right.

Seven

THE 1950S: AN INDUSTRIAL TOWN

At the start of the 1950s, five years after the declaration of peace, Britain was still in an age of austerity. The hope that had swept through the country at the end of the Second World War – that Britain would again become a prosperous nation – had dissipated. Rationing was in force and Britain had no financial reserves. At the beginning of the decade the Labour party returned to power but with a small majority. At the General Election in 1951 the Conservatives returned to power with Winston Churchill as the prime minister. With his success as a wartime leader behind him many people looked to him to lead Britain out of the slough of despond.

The death of King George VI on 6 February 1952 must have saddened the nation but, equally, the accession to the throne of the young Queen Elizabeth II marked a new era and thus brought renewed hope to many.

In hindsight it is interesting to consider how the events that were taking place on the world stage, and indeed in Britain, might have affected small communities like Buckfastleigh. Certainly the Cold War with Russia, the start of the Vietnam conflict and Churchill's decision that Britain should build a hydrogen bomb, must have affected the mood of local people.

However, Buckfastleigh, a community that was still close-knit with its own Urban District Council (BUDC), worked quietly to better its lot – and sometimes not so quietly! Carnivals were still taking centre stage each year and local people celebrated both the Festival of Britain in 1951 and the coronation of Queen Elizabeth II in 1953 with events that spread over three weeks.

Clubs and organisations were well attended, including sports teams such as the cricket club, which generally had two matches a week on the Recreation Ground, and the local rugby team, the Buckfastleigh Ramblers, which reigned supreme in the early 1950s. They held the junior cup for three seasons and, after one defeat by Cullompton, held the trophy for the next three years.

Panto time! Margaret Truscott (left), c.1950.

The well-supported annual race meeting, held on Whit Sunday evening and Whit Monday with a day meeting in August, was organised under National Hunt Rules and was always eagerly anticipated by local people, many of whom took part in the running of the event. The races were organised by voluntary committee members, some of whom belonged to the Coulton family who had helped to establish the races 60 years previously.

On a national scale, attending church services was no longer the focus of people's lives, but in Buckfastleigh the churches were still well attended and provided a lively social life that permeated the community.

Bill Chaffe was chairman of BUDC at the beginning of the new decade and it was during his chairmanship, and that of Revd John Timms, that the town saw the development of new housing. Housing estates such as Glebelands were built between 1948 and 1950 under the Essential Works Act. On 29 September 1950 permission was granted by BUDC to build five flats at Glebelands. A further 12 were permitted in 1951. Since 1945, 70 council-houses have been built.

With Elm Bank, Gipsy Lane and Fairy Lane already established, permission was granted in 1953 to build Tweenaways. Church Street flats with garages were started in the late 1950s. Oaklands Park

Above: *Old Totnes Road, Buckfastleigh.*

Right: *The Salmon Leap Café Dartbridge, 1951. The Little Chef now stands on this site.*

Above: *A photograph of Station Road showing Buckfastleigh Picture House, c.1940s.*

Right: *Mr Lock and Mrs Pickles outside The Picture House. Mr Lock was an usher and Mrs Pickles ran the ticket office.*

Donald Joint and colleagues at work in the foundry, c.1950.

and Barn Park did not yet exist. Eventually Buckfastleigh had more council-housing than anywhere else in Devon. There were just fewer than 300 council-houses in total and a population of 2,460.

Councillor Donald Joint remarked that there was building work undertaken from 1926 until the 1950s, and it was more likely that houses were built for people coming to look for work in the town than for local men coming back from the war. He also noted that many people came to look for work in the town and then stayed. 'The council-houses built were far superior to other houses in the town at that time,' he said.

In 1954 the caravan site at Buckfast brought more visitors to the area. This benefited local tradespeople to some extent as ration books had been abolished and, for the first time since 1939, people could buy whatever they wanted, in the quantities they desired, provided they had the money. What a sense of freedom that must have given to many people.

In 1954, after initially being declined, consent was given for Bakers Pit Quarry to be used as a refuse site. The prime concern was for the caves and how best to protect them from the damage and pollution which would inevitably occur if precautionary measures were not taken. Permission was granted by the County Council, subject to a retaining wall being built which would prevent the access to the prehistoric caves from Bakers Pit Quarry being blocked or obstructed.

The woollen mill at Buckfast, owned by John Berry & Sons and famous for its woollen blankets, was not doing well and ceased to function; the business was taken over by Buckfast Spinning Company. Many of the mill's workers, by then old-age pensioners, lived in tied cottages and were alarmed by the changes, but Miss Calmady Hamlyn purchased all of the cottage property and handed it to the council to administrate, together with a considerable sum for maintenance.

Gertrude Weekes, Buckfastleigh's own resident journalist, writing in the *Western Morning News* in December 1950, observed that the town was 'fortunate in having three resident doctors (Dr Eva Ironside, Dr Williams and Dr Wigram), a chiropodist, a masseur and a visiting dentist.' She also went on to say that:

> ... postal deliveries were made twice daily and there were several telephone kiosks around the town. Homes were equipped with gas and/or electricity for lighting and cooking and in general Buckfastleigh is considered to be an exceptionally well-equipped, well-centralised and progressive country town.

Town is the operative word in the above quote as Buckfastleigh is frequently mistaken for a village by visitors and tourists. However, it possesses a fine Town Hall which was donated by the Hamlyn brothers and was built in 1887 to celebrate Queen Victoria's jubilee. It boasted a 'fine hall used for concerts, a billiards room, club room, library and reading room' (*Buckfastleigh Western Guardian*, c.1930s). In 1924 money raised by public subscription enabled a wing to be added with the main benefactors being the Hamlyn brothers and John Furneaux.

The Town Hall and institute, however, had been a constant source of financial worry for the trustees for some years. In 1951 there was a deficit at the bank and no prospect of reducing it. The Town Hall had no proper sanitary accommodation and, in view of public health standards, it was becoming a matter of urgency to provide it. In addition the premises required internal and external decoration. It was finally agreed to ask BUDC to take it over. As it was run as a charity the charity commissioners were involved in the decision-making at every step of the way and, with their active participation, the Town Hall was transferred to the care of BUDC in 1952.

Built by John Furneaux, who had been in partnership with James Hamlyn in 1868, Harewood House at Bossell was purchased by the council for use as an administrative centre because the Town Hall was being used most of the time.

'The surveyor and the Town Clerk had an office at Harewood,' said Bill Chaffe, 'and it was such a good atmosphere because the staff were so

Left: *The swimming-pool in Victoria Park, Buckfastleigh.*

Right: *Hapstead House Children's Home.*

Left: *Mrs Markus with one of the children at Hapstead House, c.1960.*

The children and their donkey at Hapstead House.

The Buckfastleigh Fire Service, c.1950. Left to right, back row: Les Carne, Ned Voisey, Stanley Harris, Charlie Eales, Norman Manley, ?, Brice Pinney, ? Roberts; third row: ?, ?, Charlie Short, ? Willcox, ? Cleave, Les Lane, Pat Spiller, ?, ?, Jim Gill; second row: ?, Jean Heywood, Lil Bulley, Beryl Heywood, Vera Pickles, Doreen Shute, Eve Stuart, Muriel Northcote; front: Stanley Paxman, Charlie Manell, Philip Jackson, ?, ?, Betty Bray.

capable and interested in what they were doing.'

Donald Joint's father worked for the council for 40 years. The family lived in Harewood House and Donald's father was the caretaker there when it housed the welfare clinic, the food office and the local branch of the Devon County Library. The library had over 5,000 books and Margaret Dawe was the part-time librarian; most readers in the town will remember her with great affection.

Margaret met her husband, Lew Dawe from Buckfastleigh, when he was stationed as a soldier in Hull where Margaret lived. They were married in 1945 and moved to Buckfastleigh in 1946 when the Army discharged Lew under a Class B release. Following the war rebuilding was considered to be essential work and Lew was in the building trade. Margaret talked fondly of Buckfastleigh:

It was rather a joke to come and live here after living in a large northern town. There were no shops to mention compared with what I was used to. It was so quiet here but Lew's family were kind to me and we got on well and I enjoy living here now – after all I have been here for 54 years.

My job as librarian helped me to get used to Buckfastleigh. I wasn't a trained librarian but I applied for the post when it was advertised, and was invited to an interview. The man who interviewed me had worked in Yorkshire and was so pleased to meet a Yorkshire woman that all we did was talk about the county and then he gave me the job!

Before I started there were a few boxes of books in the school and the librarians were voluntary. I was the first paid librarian for the town. The library moved to Harewood House in 1947 and we were situated in a room that had been a bedroom previously. Few people had seen the inside of the building before and so many people started to come that the library became very cramped. There was a beautifully polished banister on the side of the stairs leading down from the library to the ground floor and I frequently had to go to the door and say to the children, 'Don't slide down that banister!' I was always worried that they were going to hurt themselves.

Catharine Sparkes (née Peters) and Carole Millman (née Honeywell) remembered visiting the library as children. Cathie recalled how 'the library bookcases had deep wooden shelves and held a large number of books. I had read all the books in the children's section at one stage.' 'Mrs Dawe was so good to us,' recalled Carole. 'She was consistently helpful and always remembered what each of us had read and wanted to read.'

Eventually, in 1952, the library was moved from Harewood to the Town Hall where there was more room, and it was open on three nights a week until eight at night.

'I used to hear all sorts,' laughed Margaret, who was often treated as a confidante. 'One of the things I developed was a magazine exchange. Readers used to bring magazines in and others would take them away. That was very popular.'

Margaret enjoyed the readers coming in with their books and asking her advice about different authors. 'The children used to come in with their homework looking for reference books, I enjoyed that too.'

In spite of improvements to the town and the new housing, Dr Derek Moore and his wife, Marjorie, said they were horrified at the poverty and the standard of living that they found when they arrived in Buckfastleigh in 1958.

'I had been working in the Luton and Dunstable hospital in Luton, home to well-paid Vauxhall workers,' said Derek, 'but I had lived in the countryside during the war,' he continued, 'and when we first drove into Buckfastleigh I thought we had taken the wrong turning and ended up in an East Yorkshire mill town!'

By October 1959 the Town Council had drawn up plans for a slum-clearance programme in Buckfastleigh as several houses were deemed unfit for human habitation. There were still many houses belonging to private landlords and the council that had no bathroom and an outside toilet.

Buckfastleigh was very much an industrial town during the 1950s. The mill chimney-stack, standing proud and tall, dominated the town and the siren, which sounded at regular intervals throughout the day to signal workers to come to work or to finish, reminded Derek Moore of northern industrial towns.

'Our lives were regulated by the mill siren!' exclaimed Catharine Sparkes whose father, Henry Peters, was a manager at the mill. 'Even those of us who did not work in the mill were reminded of the time.'

Mill employees worked long days, including Saturday mornings. The average wage was four to five pounds a week, and often workers worked one week on and one week part-time.

'We were very concerned when we first came,' said Marjorie Moore, 'as it seemed that people were being exploited.' But despite long working hours and low pay the static population was very close-knit. Marjorie noted:

We observed that everyone was from a large inter-related family of grandmas, grandpas, uncles, aunts, cousins, and everyone was nearby for advice and support – next door, round the corner or up a hill! Now, at the beginning of the twenty-first century, the population is larger and more diverse but the individual families are smaller and more isolated.

By the mid-1950s the national population figures had already started to increase whilst the death rate had remained steady. The crime rate was low in Britain during that period and this was reflected in Buckfastleigh where families were still close and there was a strong network of support.

Derek Moore came to Buckfastleigh to work as a trainee doctor with Dr Eva Ironside. After 18 months he was offered an 'assistantship with a view to partnership' in the practice of Dr Ironside, whose surgery was at Redmount, Old Totnes Road, and Dr Wigram who had a surgery in Bridge Street.

'We remember the surgery at Redmount very clearly,' said Marjorie Moore. 'With Mrs Evemy sitting in her little entry vestibule whilst the patients sat in a hut in the garden.'

'So,' added Derek, 'you came in with an ingrowing toenail and went away with tonsillitis!

'Dr Ironside had strict ideas about social structure,' smiled Derek. 'She was very Victorian. She would refer to her staff as servants and call them by their surnames. It was like turning back the clock to pre-war years'

Derek and Marjorie remembered with fondness Dr Michael Wigram, with whom Derek Moore got on well and admired, and Dr Sidney Rice Williams, living in retirement in Plymouth Road – 'a lovely man'.

After making the decision to stay in Buckfastleigh the Moores built their own house. There were seven building plots between Fullaford Lodge and Fullaford House in Wallaford Road and they took the one right next to Fullaford. The first house to be built was Bob and Sylvia Northcott's. Marjorie recalled:

We built the house thinking it would be for life. We had four children born between 1958 and 1964. As they grew bigger so the house seemed to grow smaller. We were happy living in Wallaford Road, but plans by Fullaford to build on our boundary changed our plans to extend and in 1972 we moved to Hawson.

I used to go down [to] the town every afternoon to meet the children from school. I remember pushing the pram around the town and also pushing my bike up Wallaford Road with all the groceries in the basket. It did mean that I met local people but no one ever called me by name, they always called me Mrs Doctor, which I hated!

When Dr Derek Moore first arrived in Buckfastleigh, Dr Michael Wigram had been in the town for 12 years with an established practice at Toll Marsh in Plymouth Road and then in Bridge Street in Higher Town. Margaret Wigram commented:

Michael was a partner in a practice at Trowbridge when we first married and then we came to Devon on holiday in 1946 and stayed at the Church House Inn at Holne. Sidney Williams and my father were great friends and it was through my father that Michael first met Dr

Williams. It wasn't long before he asked Michael if he would like to come to Buckfastleigh as a junior partner in the Buckfastleigh practice. So we moved into Toll Marsh just before Christmas. It was a great barrack of a place with 12 bedrooms!

Michael got on very well with Sidney Williams and with Eva Ironside. Michael had two surgeries at Toll Marsh which we rented until the lease expired. Eventually we bought three fields up at Oaklands Road and built a house there.

Michael worked very hard and was well liked. There was a terrific care for patients by the doctors and numerous home visits in those days. Now doctors have so much paperwork to do. Not long before he was killed, Michael and another doctor, from Teignmouth, were voted the best GPs in the South West.

He was a very fast driver and could be a good driver but, apparently, if the mothers in the town were out with their children and saw him coming they would grab the children and pull them aside saying 'Old Wigram's coming!' If he was out at night I could never go to sleep until I heard him come in.

Sadly, Dr Michael Wigram was killed in a car accident on 23 November 1973. There was a thick fog and he was driving along the dual carriageway which was still in the process of being built. Signs to indicate that the road was narrow were not in place and Dr Wigram collided with a lorry that was coming from the opposite direction. 'Death was instantaneous,' said Margaret, 'and it was not his fault.' The whole town was horrified by the death of the capable and much-loved doctor.

During the 1950s parental influence was on the wane and young people began to rebel in a way that had previously been inconceivable. Before the war young people had been more dependant on their parents and employers and there was concern for safety and future security. The war had changed the social order and, with the release of the record 'Rock around the clock' and the advent of rock'n'roll music, young people everywhere began to enjoy a sense of security. The Teddy-boy cult emerged with their Edwardian frock-coats, drainpipe trousers, suede shoes and sideburns – causing havoc in every cinema they entered!

In Buckfastleigh the changes were considerably slower. Young people, like their parents before them, enjoyed the company of their peers and took advantage of the few facilities the town boasted. The well-patronised town cinema, The Picture House, was especially popular with children and young people. Richard Pickles, whose parents owned the cinema, would help his mother on two or three evenings a week when she was working in the pay box; 'Unless it was an X-rated film, of course,' laughed Richard. The Picture House had matinées after school on Mondays as well as on Saturday mornings before moving to a Saturday afternoon slot. There was the gripping *Jungle Girl* and *Flash Gordon* series of films, with a fresh instalment every week, and the inevitable cowboy-and-indian films. Richard described working at the cinema:

I did a memorable show with Alan Tolley once. Alan was the 'rewind' boy who used to wind the film back after the film. One day, as my father was away somewhere, we worked the projector and did a matinée between us. He was about 14 and I was eight or nine. Well, the reel broke down six times! I shall never forget that day.

The swimming-bath in Victoria Park was also very popular with children and young people. Carole Millman recalled using the pool:

You waited for the baths to open at two and the first thing you did when you got in was to see what the temperature was. The pool was not heated then. In those days the changing rooms were very basic and at the back behind the seating area, and there was just a thin partition between the boys and girls section. The boys used to clamber over this partition and make the girls scream!

As with previous generations, young people in Buckfastleigh enjoyed going to the dances in the Town Hall. Carole continued her reminiscence:

They were wonderful and we had a proper band with a superb drummer. I also remember going to dancing lessons in the room above the King's Arms. It was brilliant. Then there was the youth club run by Eric Jones which was so well organised. Eric used to arrange barbecues and evenings in one of the fields where we used to have a big fire. We used to have great fun. On Sundays small groups of us used to go down by the weir. We used to have a lark and it was so innocent. Young people don't know what it is like to have such fun today.

'I used to go out to the Queen of the Dart to pick daffodils to sell,' said Richard. 'I would sell the daffodils to people living in Grange Road because that was where the money was!'

'I used to go picking primroses with Stella Pinney and Vauldene Boon every spring,' said Carole. 'We would count out ten primroses and four leaves to a bunch, then hang all the bunches on long sticks and go around selling them, like Richard.'

An environment which provided children and young people with the opportunity for a free and happy childhood was probably what Kit and Fritz Markus had been searching for when they bought Hapstead House, Buckfastleigh, and turned it into a children's home.

During the Second World War Fritz Markus had escaped from Nazi-occupied Austria and fled to

England, via Switzerland, eventually reaching Torquay. In 1942 he and his English wife, Kit, set up home at Hillaway, a house they had bought in Stoke-in-Teignhead, and started to take in evacuee children.

Although they had originally intended to take in only two or three children, the family somehow grew (including the birth of their own son, John Markus). Eventually the Markuses bought a second house at Manaton to accommodate the growing number of children and then opened two other children's homes, one of which was at Hapstead House.

The majority of the children the Markuses took in were simply in need of fresh air and, during the war, a safe haven from bombing raids in Britain's cities and ports. However, at least a quarter of the children were unmanageable, having suffered from child abuse or neglect, or were chronically ill. The children's ages were wide-ranging, as were their backgrounds, but, somehow, the quite disparate group of youngsters at Hapstead House blossomed under the genuine love and care of the Markuses. The additional bonus for the children was, of course, the freedom to enjoy the Devonshire countryside, Hamisher the donkey and the swings and tree-houses that the Markuses provided in the grounds of Hapstead House.

David Evans, a 15 year old from Birmingham, was sent to Hapstead because of failing health. He already knew the Markus family from having stayed at their other home in Teignmouth. Nevertheless, it had still been difficult for him to leave his home and family to go into care.

He described his first glimpse of Hapstead House as he approached it by car: 'It was a big house on a hill, a cold white house, but with windows that gleamed warmly.' Inside the initial welcome was cool and brisk rather than warm, as he submitted to having his head searched for nits – 'My hair was always clean and healthy!' – and his case searched, 'for what? I wondered.' Then he was taken to the bathroom where he had to strip under the gaze of a young female staff member who was barely older than himself.

'I shall never forget the indignity of that first day,' said David but, fortunately, the remainder of his stay at Hapstead was happy:

Auntie Kit and Uncle Mark, as we called them, had their faults but you could feel the genuine love emanating from them. There was discipline but it was not harsh, and we were allowed to play and enjoy ourselves in the big playroom or in the garden with Hamisher, the donkey.

The Markuses did not replace our parents but they did all they could to be uncle and aunt. They were a little out of touch with the rock'n'roll era that had begun but they were fairly liberal. One of the girl residents had a record player and they let us bop away on Friday nights in the playroom to her pop records.

David, who went to King Edward VI Grammar School in Totnes when he was well enough, often walked down into Buckfastleigh:

I liked Buckfastleigh, although some of the Hapstead residents didn't think it was lively enough. It had a particular charm, especially for a city boy like me. Local people were very nice and I enjoyed being called 'm'dear'. I remember Mrs Waller's shop and the fish'n'chip shop at Weech Corner where we used to buy fish and chips and eat them as we walked back to Hapstead after a cinema show in Newton Abbot.

We often used to go out walking in the woods and just being in the countryside was wonderful. It was not only physically healthy for us but mentally healthy too.

David's health improved considerably whilst he was at Hapstead and he stayed for about four-and-a-half years, during which time Auntie Kit and Uncle Mark retired and, in the early 1960s, Hapstead was taken over by the Devonports.

The ethos on which Kit and Fritz Markus based the running of Hapstead was considered original and unorthodox in its day: 'There's no way of explaining it, really,' Kit Markus would say, 'because no two children are the same... but call it a mixture of affection and common-sense.'

Whatever 'it' was, it was a successful method and many children eventually returned to their homes from Buckfastleigh as fitter, happier and very well-adjusted people.

Left: *Children playing in the grounds of Hapstead House.*

Eight

CARNIVALS AND CARNIVAL QUEENS

Carnivals were always a popular event in Buckfastleigh with most of the townspeople wanting to participate. A number of the clubs and groups in the town would enter a float and take part in the carnival-day procession.

Jill Yolland (née Pearse) was chosen to be carnival queen in 1949 – she was 17 years old. Local girls paraded at a fête or dance for the selection of the carnival queen and, in the early days, were elected by those people who turned up for the occasion. 'If you bought a ticket you were entitled to vote,' said Pat Hedges, an ex-carnival committee member. On this occasion 15 girls paraded at the fête and Jill received the most votes.

Bill Searle's coal lorry dressed for the carnival, c.1930.

Like the earlier 'Welcome Home' carnival held for the men and women who had fought in the war, this carnival was preceded by a week of events in the town. 'The best part of the week for me,' said Jill, 'was the furry dance. As we danced through the streets everyone stood on their doorsteps to watch. I also enjoyed the carnival night dance,' she added. 'It was lovely to think that all the boys were there for me to dance with!'

It was a busy time for everyone as many of the dresses were made by mothers and the floats would be decorated with whatever people could find. 'Today people go and buy what they want instead of making things. So it is not so much fun,' Jill said.

The Setters family have long been associated with the carnivals – the queen always having ridden on one of their lorries. Jack Setters recalled:

We were always ready to help with the carnival. Father used to say on carnival day 'No work today, the lorry has to be cleaned up, and we have to find something to decorate it with.' We used laurel leaves and firs and that kind of thing for decorating. Lots of people came to help. The only thing was no one came back to help with the cleaning up afterwards! We didn't mind really. Father always said, 'We have got to look after Buckfastleigh.'

Jill remembered her carnival queen experience:

The year I was carnival queen was the first time that the queen faced the direction of travel whilst on the float. Before that she used to sit over the cab with her back towards the direction of travel. It was Ken Setters' idea, it meant that everyone could see her coming.

Phyllis Short (née Jackson) was carnival queen in 1950 at the age of 18. She recalled that her white dress with its royal-blue cape and her crown were borrowed from the carnival committee. Her attendants bought their own dresses.

Everyone spent the Saturday morning before the

Above: *Buckfastleigh carnival, c.1900.*

Right: *Carnival Queen Phyllis Short (née Jackson) with attendants, 1950.*

Below: *Carnival queen Ann Williams (now Eales) with attendants Joan Joint (left) and Beryl Deakin (right), 1954. The prince is Barry Honeywell and the princess Hilary Blank.*

Left: *Carnival queen Jill Pearse (now Yolland), 1949.*

The Buckfastleigh Amateur Dramatic Society carnival float, c.1950.

parade finding greenery for the lorry. They decorated the vehicle in the 'ope' way at Setters' old yard, which was between the King's Arms and the National Provincial Bank. The parade started at Station Tree, by the road that originally led down to the railway station, and continued along Station Road into Buckfastleigh. 'I was nervous when the float crossed over Church Bridge in Station Road,' Phyllis said. 'I was so high up and thought I might fall off!' Ann Eales had memories of one carnival mishap:

Carnival floats used to visit different towns and villages and one of the villages was Staverton. One year we used one of Mr Searle's coal lorries for a float. We had an organ on the lorry, one you turned with a handle. I don't know what he did but as we were going over Hood Bridge (now Riverford Bridge) the lorry nearly turned right over into the river. An organ on a float would make it top heavy, wouldn't it?

Joyce Kerswell, carnival queen, 1930.

Ann Eales (née Williams) was elected carnival queen in 1954 when she was 15. Carnival week ran from 13–18 September that year and the proceeds were in aid of the Town Hall Improvement Fund. Her attendants were Joan Joint and Beryl Deakin, the prince was Barry Honeywell, and the little princess was Hilary Blank. Joyce Blank recalled:

I can always remember taking Hilary up to the Town Hall on the election night. Carolyn, my younger daughter, was still a baby and I had to hurry home before the elections started to see to Carolyn. When I went back to pick up Hilary people were coming down the road from the Town Hall saying, 'She's got in! She's got in!'

Hilary, now Hilary Hammond, remembered the carnival well. 'I was four-and-a-half when I was chosen as the princess,' she said. 'Barry Honeywell was the prince and, of course, Ann Eales was the queen. The float was designed as an incredible ship in the style of the *Golden Hind*.'

Ann still has copies of the two speeches she had to make. 'I remember shaking in my shoes,' said Ann, whose speeches had been written by local journalist, Miss Weekes, who lived nearby.

Arthur White was chairman of the carnival committee and Mr A. Sproston was the organising secretary, with F. Tankard, Eric Midgley and Ken Setters working with him to organise the week's events. These events included a waitresses' race, children's sports, a tug-of-war tournament, a talent-spotting competition, a variety concert and a furry dance starting from Damarell's Bridge. It was, apparently, the best furry dance the town had seen with hundreds watching and many couples taking part. Ann and Joan Joint ran from work and arrived at the dance hot and breathless.

The town band provided the music for these events. The band was composed of local men and played an integral part in the life of Buckfastleigh. Regular band practices took place at the King's Arms and the band was prepared to play at carnival events and at Christmas time when they would go around the town playing carols – mostly outside the local pubs. Local band members included the Yolland brothers, Freddy French, Fernley and Wilf Petherbridge, Ginger Miller, Frank and Graham Lock and Freddie Coombes.

As mentioned before, the carnival processions originally started at Station Tree. This only took place, however, until the tree was removed, at which time the procession started at West Point Corner Field in Buckfast and stopped at the top of the road leading down to the railway station to pick up the walkers in fancy dress. Bill Selley could remember the excitement of preparing for the procession:

Carnival days were great and the preparation for them was wonderful. If you were going to have a float in the carnival procession you would decide what the theme of your tableau was going to be and then decide what costumes you wanted. We had a Victorian tableau on a mill float once and we had several lovely costumes, some of which we made and some which were given by Major Vickers' daughters who were interested in theatricals. We used to enjoy everything, especially the carnival procession and the town band. Then, of course, you had the carnival dance at the Town Hall to look forward to.

In 1951, when a carnival was organised to celebrate the Festival of Britain, Major Vickers was the chairman of the council and Bill Chaffe was vice-chairman. The organisation of the event demanded considerable time and hard work. Bill Chaffe recalled the team responsible for the arrangements:

That was real work. We always went to town in those

days. We had a very good Town Clerk, called Bruce, who was a good organiser. Arthur White was chair of the carnival committee and the carnival queen was June Tarasiuk (née Major). We even had Dudley Savage, the organist, who played his organ in the Town Hall.

Another memorable carnival was the one in celebration of Queen Elizabeth II's succession to the throne in 1953 which was held between 15 May and 7 June 1953. Events were spread over three-and-a-half weeks and included the crowning of May Francis (née Wicks) as carnival queen. Other events were: a dance; a cricket match at the Recreation Ground; a variety concert organised by the Buckfastleigh Amateur Dramatic Society; and a special service in Holy Trinity on coronation day itself, followed by a sports afternoon at Victoria Park. A children's pageant at Harewood, a football tournament, a swimming gala, an over-60s tea party and the carnival procession, which started in Buckfast, completed the celebrations.

At the time of writing Buckfastleigh does not have a carnival, although carnivals are held in other surrounding towns and villages. The 1986 and 1987 carnival committee were Mike Tolchard, Pat and Derek Hedges, Marian Harvey, Bridget Soper and Joan Mason. Pat Hedges recalled:

In the early days everyone wanted to join in the fun of the carnival. All the local clubs and the mill were represented. Nowadays it is too much trouble. Being on the last couple of carnival committees was hard work and there was very little joy as it was so difficult to raise money for worthwhile causes and the carnival events were badly supported.

Marian Harvey explained:

It was apathy. Like everything else, people would criticise but would not be prepared to join in and help. After the last carnival to be held in Buckfastleigh we arranged, as usual, for a presentation evening when we were going to hand over the money that had been raised. The money was to be divided between St Mary's School, Buckfast, and Buckfastleigh School, and the only people who turned up other than the carnival committee were the teachers from the two respective schools. No one else bothered to come. The committee felt that they had had enough, gave all the money away and closed the carnival account.

It had been hard work for some years. We were reluctant to let the carnival drop because we knew that once we had done that it would be difficult to revive it again. It is a shame. This apathy seems to be peculiar to Buckfastleigh as other towns still have their carnivals. We used to call them the Moorlands carnivals – South Brent, Buckfastleigh, Ashburton, Newton Abbot and Chudleigh. Each town had their set dates each year.

Will the carnivals return? Will local people want to organise something that will bring the populace together in this way? Or are carnivals outdated? This seems a sad ending for what had once been a popular and joyous annual event for local people.

Buckfastleigh carnival day, 1976.

Nine

The South Devon Railway

A view of the railway station from Dartbridge Road.

The Buckfastleigh, Totnes and South Devon Railways started on 1 May 1872 under the chairmanship of John Hamlyn (1816–78) who contributed considerably, financially and personally, to the building of the railway. The fact that the main railway from Exeter to Plymouth had been constructed by Isambard Kingdom Brunel, the famous engineer, for the South Devon Railway Company in the early 1800s must have excited local businessmen who saw the railway as a means of expansion. Eventually, after a considerable amount of hard work and many disappointments, including a shortage of finance and difficulties with land acquisition, the 9½-mile branch line that ran from Totnes through Staverton and Buckfastleigh to Ashburton was built. However, it was never a viable concern and in 1896 the organisation went into liquidation and was amalgamated with the Great Western Railway Company.

The Buckfastleigh line ran throughout the two world wars. In 1948 the railways were nationalised but the gradual decline of the service came to a head during the 1950s and the last passenger train ran on 3 November 1958. Richard Elliot, manager of the South Devon Railway, explained the closure:

There was a lack of passenger traffic. The only people using the train were a few students going to school, shoppers going to Totnes and workers going to Staverton. Sunday school trips, which usually went to Teignmouth or Dawlish with six coaches and two engines, and race day trips carried on until 1962, so there was some passenger traffic until then. The freight was very busy, however. The freight was mainly sheepskins for the Buckfastleigh tan yard and general farm produce and coal. The market days at Ashburton were also extremely busy, so busy in fact that often the wagons had to be left at the Buckfastleigh yard and a bus was run into Ashburton because Bulliver couldn't make it up there.

Buckfastleigh was one of the busiest freight yards in Devon – really busy. Eventually, however, that started to slow down as well and closed in 1962. Cars, buses and lorries all took the freight off the railways and on to the road. It was nothing to do with the government minister, Dr Beeching, who started to close down the railways in 1963. In fact Dr Beeching came to open the branch line when it reopened privately in 1969.

In 1965 the Dart Valley Railway Company started to restore the railway line to working order. Volunteers were recruited to help with the restoration. I was among the volunteers.

The company agreed to buy the line from British Rail – which they did. They also applied for a Light Railway Order to run it as a light railway with restricted speeds

Left: *Buckfastleigh Station, c.1950.*

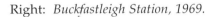

Right: *Buckfastleigh Station, 1969.*

Above: *A view from the train as it arrived at the platform, 1969.*

Above left: *The staff, c.1950. Left to right: Sam Doidge, George Siddal, Leonard Dinwiddy, Dick Joint, Harry Leigh.*

Left: *S. Goffin, Town Mayor, at the railway, 1977.*

up to 20 miles an hour, which still applies, instead of 40 miles an hour which was the previous case.

We can't run big engines, only smaller ones. When the line was open in 1969 we couldn't run the line to Ashburton. The Ministry of Transport decided that they wanted to use the railway route for the new A38 dual carriageway.

We were never allowed to use the mainline at Totnes because we didn't have our own line into the Totnes Station. Previously, Bulliver used to share the mainline with the express trains and used to dodge in and out of the platforms as required, it was rather an operational nightmare. Dart Valley was only allowed to run trains down to the junction and back again. That was how it was for years and years.

Initially the project was set up as a tourist attraction, using volunteers to make a profit, and it was certainly a viable concern. Some 120,000 passengers were carried in the Dart Valley Railway's opening year in 1969. To begin with the service was a novelty but over the next ten years there was a decline in use.

New directors joined the board who saw the railway as more of a commercial enterprise and were unenthusiastic about the number of volunteers involved. They wanted to run the railway commercially in order to prove that steam trains could be made to pay. So, in 1972, the Dart Valley Railway Company accepted the offer to take over the Paignton to Kingswear line. From then on the line went from strength to strength, whilst the Buckfastleigh line remained the poor relation. Consequently, the traffic and the volunteer input went down. This trend continued well into the 1980s with a dwindling income and fewer volunteers participating in the running of the railway. Richard Elliott described this decline:

In the mid-'80s we fought really hard for a contract to build a footbridge over the river at Totnes, to give us access to Totnes. Just as the contract was approved British Rail gave permission for our trains to run into the station at Totnes and for the following four years that is what we did. Unfortunately, it proved financially disastrous because it meant that the Dart Valley Railway spent more money on the cost of running trains into Totnes Station than was generated in additional revenue. There were the costs of daily inspections of the stock – to make sure we had the same number of wheels as we did the day before [said with a wry smile] and BR had to provide a crew for a quarter of a mile from the station to the junction, including a guard. We had to run the trains at the times they permitted and also two sets of crews were involved. BR sold tickets for our trains in the railway booking-office at Totnes and kept ten per cent commission. The whole arrangement was a complete and utter disaster.

So, in 1988, the Dart Valley Company decided that enough was enough and decided against running the line anymore. I said we would run the line for them using volunteers. My role as a director at that time was to represent the volunteer workers on the railway and maintain relationships between the volunteers and the Dart Valley Company Director. In 1990 the company allowed us to run the railway for them. They gave us a budget and let us loose!

Richard was given the challenge of arranging a complete roster of volunteers to run the railway for the whole summer:

It was a tall order because they gave us such a short time to do it in. But there were so many volunteers beavering away in the background on their own little projects that we managed to put together a roster of qualified people to drive, fire, guard and manage the ticket office for the whole summer. We did all the marketing and the traffic went up by 25 per cent by the end of the year.

Nevertheless, the company still decided to close the railway:

I said, 'Over my dead body! We'll run it as a charitable trust.' So in 1991 we were given a 25-year lease from the Dart Valley Company. They leased us carriages for the first year and we turned the £100,000 loss into an £86,000 surplus in the first year!

The Dart Valley Company were extremely helpful. They allowed us to have the use of the railway virtually rent-free in the first two years. Now the turnover has risen by 85 per cent in the last few years without us having to put the fares up. The railway is doing very well and now we are trying to get back the coach business.

We have succeeded in having a bridge built over the River Dart at Totnes, as a result of a partnership project with the Countryside Commission, the local councils, the Rural Development Commission, the British Railways and the Dartmoor National Park Authority. Through these organisations we raised £200,000, including £86,000 through our own membership. Another £40,000 from profits went towards the bridge, footpaths on either side of the bridge and to improve the station.

We couldn't keep the name of Dart Valley Railway so we have had to change. The railway has been known for many years as the Dart Valley Railway. So we have gone right back to the beginning and called it the South Devon Railway, as it was known in 1892.

Richard had always been interested in railways:

I used to live in Braunton in North Devon in a little lane. At the end of the lane was a railway line and I used to watch the trains go up and down. It was always quite something to see the trains in an evening when it was dark. The Pullman coaches would be brightly lit –

and the big engine was quite something. Trains have always been in my blood.

When steam began to disappear I became aware that there was a preservation scheme in Buckfastleigh to preserve the railway line. So, in 1964, I became a volunteer, working in Totnes. Then in 1965 I came up to Buckfastleigh, actually travelling in the first of two trains to come up the line. In 1969, when working parties were being organised, I made sure I was in one of them. I have been involved with the railway at Buckfastleigh ever since.

In 1967 Richard was elected to the committee of the Dart Valley Railway Association where he undertook various jobs such as sales officer and magazine editor (three times), before eventually becoming chairman. He had been working for Lloyds Bank in various branches around the county and had a good grounding in finance, accountancy, budgeting and marketing. He then represented the association as a director of the Dart Valley Railway Company on the board of the Dart Valley Light Railway:

I was there when the proposition was made to close down the Dart Valley Railway, then I took on the job of running it and handed in my notice to Lloyds Bank. They all said, 'We knew you would run the railway someday!'

Jill Elliott, Richard's wife, commented:

I thought that, although it might be a difficult period, it was one of those opportunities you have to take. Otherwise you would spend the rest of your life wondering what would have happened if you had taken the job. After all, it's not often that a job like that comes along.

Richard added:

I feel that I am part of a crusade and I am determined that we shall succeed. We only had a short lease on the workshop and the aim is to acquire the freehold, which will cost us a lot of money. Once we do that we shall be secure. Then I can retire and I shall have to find another railway to offer my services to! But the railway will have to rely on volunteer support – without volunteers it would not work because the labour needed to maintain the railway is so enormous that it would swallow the entire takings.

In September 2001 the South Devon Railway was able to float a public company to raise the funds to buy the railway from the Dart Valley Railway Plc. As a result, the line and all the various buildings were purchased, in March 2002, for the sum of £1,100,000, which will, hopefully, give it a more secure future than at any time in the past 130 years. Richard explained:

Although we have enough volunteers it is sometimes difficult finding the right person for the right job. The volunteers come from a variety of backgrounds. Some come through volunteer recruitment days, others hear about the railway by word of mouth. All are thoroughly trained over a period of time, medically examined to see that they are fit, and examined in various skills, like engine driving, by those qualified to do so. Anyone can drive a train, it's knowing how to stop the train in the right place!

All our volunteers love what they are doing and this comes across to the customers. It is a very time-consuming interest and some come and spend their whole holiday period with us. There are a lot of retired people who come from all over Devon, but only a few from Buckfastleigh, except on the buffet which Jill runs.

Jill remembered joining the team:

When I married Richard I followed the principle 'if you can't beat them join them', so I offered to help at the railway. Richard offered me the chance to work in the ticket office, which is extremely busy as the telephone rings all the time. I wanted the opportunity to meet the customers more though, and doing the catering for party bookings on the line gave me that chance.

At first pasties were served, now the catering team, led by Jill, provide a more varied buffet. Occasionally groups like the Rotary Club make a party booking but it is mainly church groups that flock to join the train for the evening specials such as 'Carols Down the Line' at Christmas time, or on one of the summer evening trips. The money made on the buffet goes to charity and is split between the National Children's Home and the Gambia Fund with which Jill and Anne Kenyon, a local Methodist, are involved.

And what do Richard and Jill think of Buckfastleigh? 'We think it is a nice little place,' said Richard, 'and I'm happy that local people accept the railway as part of the community so much more than they used to.'

Buckfastleigh Station, 1997.

Ten

THE RACES: A STIRRING SIGHT

One of the most important events in the town calendar was that of the Buckfastleigh Races. The event was started by the Coulton family, together with local sportsmen, and the races were initially held at Wallaford Down. Joseph Hamlyn was the first president of the Buckfastleigh Race Committee and in 1883 the races were moved to land belonging to Dean Court. Charles Stewart, a member of the Coulton family, recalled:

A year or so prior to that Thomas Hamlyn and Farmer Hoare of Caddaford were arguing in the King's Arms on the merits and speed of their respective mares, and my grandfather, W.R. Coulton of Dean Court, suggested they should race on his marshes. Others in the town got to learn of the challenge and a fête was held which included other races, one of which was for pedestrians.

The headmaster at Buckfastleigh School was Mr ('Clicky') Abbott. The May 1883 log-book recorded:

This has been a very broken week on account of Buckfastleigh Races. On Thursday we had 105 boys in the morning but only 20 came in the afternoon… I find that the races exercise a very evil influence on the morale of the boys. Today in the playground such expressions as, 'Two to one on Harebell, six to four, etc., etc.' This I promptly checked. I cannot help but think, however, that the gambling and betting carried out at such times will help undo what little good one may try to do in the short school life of the boys.

The Buckfastleigh Races, under National Hunt Rules, commenced in 1884 and, apart from the war years, National Hunt meetings were held regularly until August 1960. Then, in 1960, Lord Churston sold his lands, including Dean Court on which the racecourse was situated.

The Coulton family were tenants of Dean Court for well over 100 years. The Coultons, who were landowners in their own right, acquired land around Buckfastleigh including the quarries, Church Hill,

A picnic at the races.

Russets Lane and Common Field in Old Totnes Road.

Helen Harris, the writer, who now lives in Tavistock, was born at Dean Court. Her mother was a Coulton, one of seven children of Edward Coulton who farmed with his brother Walter. Helen remembered Dean Court as a lovely place which the family would visit often. Her grandfather, Edward, died when Helen was seven. She was the oldest grandchild and the only one who knew him.

Helen's father, John (Jack) Warren, was the son of the Buckfastleigh saddler, John William Warren. His sisters Marjorie Warren and Edith Walters were both well-known and respected local women. Helen described her family:

In the eighteenth century members of my family were respected wool combers and they worked from Warren's Court, in Fore Street, which they owned. Then the industry became mechanised in the middle of the nineteenth century and many smaller manufacturers, no longer able to compete, diversified. So my great-grandfather, John, became a saddler and harness maker, with my grandfather, John William Warren (1859–1940) continuing after him. The work of a saddler was very important in those days with so many working horses.

Since both my parents had their families in the Buckfastleigh area we visited frequently in the 1930s, although we lived at Tiverton where my father worked. My father used to play cricket for Buckfastleigh and we came here nearly every weekend, especially in the summer, and stayed at Dean Court – so Dean Court was as much my home as anywhere else and I have very clear memories of those days.

My maternal grandfather, Edward Coulton, was very much the leading light in the early days of the races. He was secretary. I remember the days when the races were held and the teas we had after and my grandmother entertaining and presiding at Dean Court. It was a great occasion.

After grandfather Edward died, my youngest uncle, Guy Coulton, became hon. secretary and his brother, John, who lived at Dean Court, clerk of the course. My uncle Eddie and my father were on the committee and my father was also clerk of the scales. It was a busy, exciting time. I remember huge horseboxes coming into the courtyard of Dean Court. Then, as things progressed, they built more stables at Dean Court Hill, on the right. Many horses would be stabled in the town including at the King's Arms.

Audrey Coulton met her husband, Guy, at a dance at the Seymour in Totnes, in the late 1930s. They were married just after war was declared in 1939, on September 16, the last night before the official blackout was declared.

Audrey came from Kingsbridge and her first memory of Buckfastleigh was when her father took her to High Beara to see family friends, Donald and Joan Warren:

We walked through some fields to see some cattle and Donald said, 'That's Buckfastleigh down there.' That was my first memory of Buckfastleigh. Not long after I was married it became my turn to entertain visitors at West Rock for the Whitsun Week Races. This would be 1940. I had made all the cakes – and I was pregnant too. I was only 22 and this was the first time that I had entertained in this way. But the night before the races were due to be held they were cancelled! What a blow! They were then stopped for the duration of the war. As soon as Guy was demobbed in 1946 the first thing he did was to apply for the dates for the races. At that time they were held at Whitsun and August Bank Holiday. He had to be quick with the application so that other race organisers wouldn't claim the dates.

Charles Stewart also reminisced enthusiastically about seeing the horses arrive by train again:

It was a stirring sight to see the racehorses being led in a string down Station Road to the loose boxes of the Coultons at Dean Court, others through the town to those at Fullaford, the King's Arms, the Globe, Rose Cottage in Silver Street and other stabling in the town now used as garages or turned into workshops.

A few horses would come by horsebox, the use of which was beginning to catch on. The passenger seat would often be occupied by a jockey who would be pleased to accept a free lift. Their riding fees would be two guineas a time. They did not travel by Jaguar or in a helicopter in those days.

The timber grandstand was erected each year by the Millman brothers and tested by the Buckfastleigh Urban District Council surveyor, Lionel Williams, and Dr Sidney Williams who was the honorary medical officer for the day. Audrey Coulton remembered:

Everybody had a job at the races. We needed stile operators, car-parks attendants, lavatory attendants and people to man the entrance gates. Others watched the jumps or accommodated the jockeys – everyone had things to do. On one occasion, when the stewards were being entertained in the stewards' room, the man who helped with the fences came running in saying that Nora had run out of toilet paper in the men's lavatories! Information not appreciated at the time!

Over the race meeting family and friends needed feeding for tea and late supper so I used to cook large joints of meat. I enjoyed it but it was a tremendous amount of work. It was really a way of life.

The races were run by a committee and what they made they put back into the races. When the racecourse was eventually put on the market, prospective purchasers from Torquay could not believe that the races had been run just for the pure love of the sport – and that no one had made anything from running them.

Between 1963 and 1977 point-to-point racing took place until the land was again sold and race meetings stopped. However, in 1998 Dart Vale and South Pool Harriers initiated plans to bring back point-to-point racing after a break of 21 years.

Above: *Princess Margaret at the races.*

Eleven

THE 1960S: A BETTER QUALITY OF LIFE

The mill and chimney in Buckfastleigh.

The 1960s was a decade of achievement and disaster, personal tragedy and personal accomplishment, both internationally and nationally. A *frisson* of excitement ran throughout the decade and the world opened up for young people breaking away from the established order. Space was opening up too and, in 1961, both the Russians and the Americans put a man in space. At the end of the decade Neil Armstrong walked on the surface of the moon.

In 1961 John F. Kennedy was inaugurated as the president of the United States. He was inspiring and attractive and the world warmed to him, in spite of bringing the West to a near-nuclear war with Russia. However, the bubble burst when he was assassinated in 1963, a year after Marilyn Monroe committed suicide. The relentless Vietnam War, which began in 1964, and the murders of Martin Luther King and Senator Robert Kennedy, both in 1968, caused the sense of progress and excitement to deteriorate.

In Britain industrial unrest was escalating, Beeching closed half of the country's railways in 1963 and the situation in Northern Ireland worsened. Despite all this, the political and economic situation was softened by several events: Princess Margaret's marriage to Anthony Armstrong Jones in May 1960; the triumph of Francis Chichester who won the first single-handed transatlantic yacht race; and England beating Germany at football in the 1966 World Cup.

Stuart Barker, former Mayor of Buckfastleigh, recalled the decade:

The 1960s were a good time to be living in Buckfastleigh. There wasn't any significant unemployment in the town. People still looked out for each other and probably wanted for little. I was actually a civil servant in the late 1960s, for the Department of Employment, and worked in Birmingham for a short time. It involved going into factories where there were problems. You do see huge contrasts when you move around. It is true that the quality of life in the South West was significantly better than in the highly industrial areas of the country.

This does not mean Buckfastleigh was an affluent town. Wages were still low and at the bottom end of the scale rather than at the top end of the scale, people worked long hours in the mill and there was still more rented accommodation than private housing. It was the quality of life that differentiated the industrial areas like Birmingham and a rural area like Devon.

Where you have areas where people don't want to be, like some of the big cities, you are paid more money to be there or to go there, so you may have more money but not that quality of life.

In his annual report of 1960 to the Buckfastleigh Urban District Council, Dr F.T. Hunt, medical officer of health, stated that the population was 2,450, having dropped by ten from the previous year. The birth rate had risen to 16.7 from 14.3 in 1959, and the death rate had fallen from 11.2 in 1959 to 9.7.

Concern was expressed about the sewage effluent and the slaughtering facilities and slaughterhouses in the district. Slaughterhouses were beginning to comply with new regulations which were outlined in 1958 under the Slaughter Houses Act. Dr Hunt said that, although the meat (staining and sterilisation) regulations were welcomed, he was still concerned

Above: *The Buckfastleigh Amateur Dramatic Society, c.1960s.* Left to right, back row: *Evan (Dick) Scoble, Fred Seager, Reg Burington, A. Sproston, B. Lee, Pat McNaughton (top), ?, John Hoff, S. Fuller, Donald Hayman, Mrs Bray, Josie Peters, Henry Peters, ?, ?;* third row: *Jean Fleming (?), Donald Warren, Edith (Babs) Scoble, May Lee, ?, ?, Muriel Bracher;* second row: *Pauline McNaughton, ?, Edith Walters, ?, Kitty Fuller;* front: *Arthur White, ?, ?, ?, Mrs White, Margaret Truscott, ?, ?, Alf Bracher, Mrs Hayman, ?, Fred Walters, Molly Luscombe.*

Left: *The town band, c.1960.* The photograph includes: *Reynold Lock, Bill Hayman, Freddie French.*

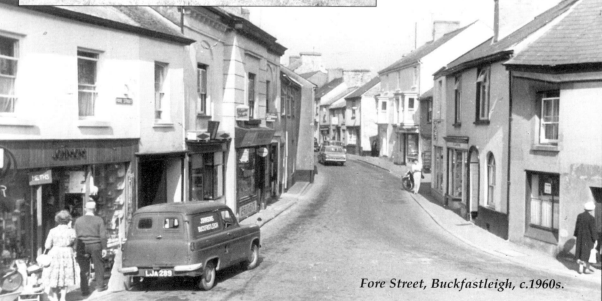

Fore Street, Buckfastleigh, c.1960s.

that no arrangements had yet come into force whereby all meat unfit for human consumption must be both sterilised and stained before being offered for sale for animal consumption.

He further mentioned that the Noise Abatement Act had come into force in November 1960, which conferred powers on councils to deal with nuisance arising from noise or vibration. The Caravan and Control of Development Act of 1960 conferred on local authorities 'effective means for controlling caravan sites' thereby raising the standard of caravan sites including sanitary conditions.

The BUDC was still concerned about the number of houses that were unfit for habitation. Housing grants were available but had mostly been taken up by owner-occupiers in the town. By 1960 no decision had been taken by the council to clear the houses and build new ones.

There were 885 dwelling-houses in Buckfastleigh, 309 of them owned by the council. There were 41 food premises made up of 15 cafés, hotels and restaurants and 26 retail food premises. One local shop, which closed during the 1960s, was Peachey's at Weech Corner. Amy Peachey recalled:

When we started I thought we would sell a few sweets and groceries and open from nine to six. But each day customers would come earlier and earlier in the morning, so then we opened about six-fifty. The men would be going to work then and would call in for cigarettes on the way. We worked it up ever so well but it was hard work and, on Saturdays, it would be nine in the evening before we closed and then we had orders to prepare. I hadn't really expected that! I enjoyed it, though. Of course, there were no supermarkets then – I wouldn't like to do it today. It must be very hard for a small shop to make a living.

In 1963 Mary Blair came to Buckfastleigh with her parents. She bought 'a derelict little shop at the bottom of the town next to Johnson's hardware shop:

There was no trade there at all, just 50 empty sweet jars and a chill cabinet and that was about all. I built it up from nothing and it became a thriving little business and, to my mind, that period was when Buckfastleigh was at its best. I recall Mrs Owen who owned the dress shop opposite the Post Office, Mr Penney who ran the Post Office, Frank Johnson's hardware shop by Damarell's Bridge, Hunts the bakers, Mrs Tillyer's sweet shop and Miss White's, near Weech Corner, who sold knitting wool and things like that.

Together with other businesses the Buckfastleigh Traders' Association was formed. Mary continued:

We met once a month. We all agreed, as an association, to do up the shops and put flowers outside. The Dart Valley Railway then started up again and the caravan

The Over-60s Club, c.1960. Left to right, front row: Revd Timms, Father Christopher, ?, Hartley Bowden (Mayor), Revd Long. Club members include: Kathleen Abbot, Mrs Barnes, Clara Widdicombe, Mrs Ham, Annie Lane, Lucy Lane, Doris Nolan.

park in Buckfast was doing well – Buckfastleigh became a thriving little town.

We had the best of the business years. We brought the community into the events we organised. Whatever we got from the town we put back into the town. We organised events for the health centre, the swimming-pool and Ashburton and Buckfastleigh hospital.

The traders were the group of people who held the town together. There was also the Traders' Association Ladies Committee and I was the chairman. We got on well and enjoyed ourselves tremendously. All the shops seemed to have a lively atmosphere and traders used to go out of their way to make their customers feel special. It was a wonderful time.

We enjoyed dressing the windows at Christmas, even the hardware shop. The traders arranged a Traders' Carol Service and we would go around carol singing and give the money to a local charity.

Mary laughed as she talked about Mrs Green from Rill Farm in Colston Road who used to go shopping on her horse:

She remained mounted on the horse and the horse's head used to poke through our shop door. She gave us her basket and then called out what she wanted. We would put the shopping in the basket and the horse would carry the basket for her!

Paul Dove and his family came to live in the town in 1968:

Our first impression of Buckfastleigh was of a dirty, smoky, little mill town which was incredibly run-down, but Fore Street was full of little shops which seemed to thrive. I remember particularly the Co-op, which had shops spread around the town, Johnson's, Stark the watchmaker, and the fish-and-chip shop. It was in the days when lard was used and this gorgeous smell

Left: *Fore Street, 1962.*

used to waft around Plymouth Road. They were the most wonderful fish and chips, especially eaten out of a newspaper.

Jim Searle was brought up in Buckfast and joined the Navy during the war. When the war ended he came back to Buckfast, did a course at Devonport Technical College in Radio Servicing, and then went to work in Edinburgh where he met and married his wife, Betty. They spent 20 years in Edinburgh before coming back to Buckfast to live:

We had been to the Lake District on holiday and then I realised how much I missed Devon and living in Buckfast. I missed Buckfastleigh as well, I think the town is genuine and the people are genuine. In the city people appear very clever but Buckfastleigh people are honest.

It was at that time that he decided to buy the electrical shop at Weech Corner in Fore Street, then owned by the Manns:

Every time we went to the shop, there would be a notice on the door saying 'Back in 20 minutes' because Arthur Keen, the electrician, was running the business single-handedly and would be out on a job! There was much more competition then as there were three other electrical businesses in the town.

Just under 40 years later, in 2003, J. Searle & Son is still thriving and is managed by Gordon, Jim's son, with a second outlet in Ivybridge.

One of the biggest challenges for local doctors was the building of a new health centre on the site where High Holly stands. The prime mover was Revd John Timms, vicar of Buckfastleigh, who was chairman of the Urban District Council in 1951 and 1952, and chairman of the Health Committee of Devon County Council.

The proposals to build the new premises were submitted to the County Health Committee during 1963 and were approved by the County Council in January 1964. Building began in 1965 and the official opening of the new centre took place in May 1966. It was named after Revd J.W. Timms.

Derek Moore explained that at this time health centres were a new concept. He pointed out that to have all the health services, like the health visitor and midwife, under the same roof was quite revolutionary and, in fact, Buckfastleigh's was one of the first purpose-built health centres in Devon. Derek said, 'Other doctors in Devon later learnt from our experiences and made improvements to their buildings.'

Fullaford House on Wallaford Road was built by John Hamlyn, the son of Joseph Hamlyn (senr) in 1876. As benefactors of Buckfastleigh in the latter part of the 1800s, the Hamlyns were instrumental in the development of the town and its community life. John himself is remembered especially for his financial contribution and commitment to the building of the Buckfastleigh, Totnes and South Devon Railway (as it was then known). Born in 1816, he lived to enjoy Fullaford House for only the last two years of his life, and was 62 years old when he died.

The lives of many local residents have been bound up with Fullaford House. Vic Foot went to work there in 1939 when he was 16. One of his many jobs included looking after the horses. The family who lived there had about seven horses and Vic stayed there until he was called up in 1942.

For several years during the war Fullaford was used as a hostel for Land Army girls and, during the late 1940s, it was also run as a guest-house by Captain Martin and the Greenwood family. Captain Martin described Fullaford as a delightful country estate of 7 acres with large gardens, tennis courts, garages and stabling, and the Greenwoods emphasised the 11 bedrooms, three baths, putting green, children's amenities and good food.

In December 1959 the council granted permission for Fullaford House to be used as a remand home. At that time the remand home was situated in Ashburton with George Thorogood as superintendent. Jim Elliott had started working at the home whilst it was still in Ashburton and five years later he moved to Fullaford House in Buckfastleigh. 'I enjoyed working with the boys,' said Jim, 'and was always able to find something good in them.'

Rene Lewis' first husband, Leslie Foot, worked there and she recalled the home having lovely Christmas parties to which all the staff, their families and friends were invited. She also remembered it being a beautiful house. Dr Derek Moore and his wife Marjorie lived next door to the remand home:

They used to have superb Christmas parties to which we were invited. George Thorogood, the superintendent, told me that if the remand home had stayed in Ashburton they would never have been able to have parties like that because in Ashburton people did not mix so easily. But in Buckfastleigh everyone was invited and everybody went – and it didn't matter what job you had, you all mixed in. It was interesting how the social structure of the two towns differed.

Elsie Churchward worked at the remand home as a cook and remembered the boys helping out in the kitchen. She also recalled the wonderful parties held at Fullaford:

The Thorogood family were well thought of in the town. Some local people got up a petition to stop Fullaford House being used as a remand home as they were afraid for the safety of their young daughters. But the scheme went ahead and was successful.

Derek Moore continued:

Fullaford was a most unsuitable house for a remand home really, but the staff managed to maintain a well-structured, disciplined lifestyle for the boys. They used to do marvellous gardening under the supervision of Leslie Foot. Most of the boys came from homes where there was no discipline. Every Saturday the boys went down into the town in a crocodile to buy sweets. Then they used to come back and tell us how many cars they could have stolen! The chap I liked was about ten years old and used to drive his father's Bentley. He drove all the way down from the North to Cornwall and didn't even dent it!

During the early '60s George Thorogood invited a group of girls from Buckfastleigh Methodist Church to do some country dancing with the boys. Gillian Limb, daughter of Revd Eric Williamson, the Methodist minister at that time, and Sandra Coleman laughed as they remembered their weekly visits to the remand home.

'I am not sure what I was expecting, but I didn't think the boys would be that interested,' said Sandra. 'But they all turned up and my outstanding memory of them is that they all wore short grey trousers and smelt of carbolic soap.'

Following the closure of the remand home, the fortunes of Fullaford House changed. Having stood empty for many years, it was finally taken over by squatters who lived there between July and September 1987, after which it was demolished to make way for the development of new private housing.

Paul Dove lived in Mount Pleasant in Plymouth Road:

I was a tea planter in Malawi for some 20 years. We came back to England in October 1968 and arrived in Buckfastleigh in the November. It was one of the coldest winters that England had seen, I think. We stayed at the Globe for a week. They made us very welcome and very comfortable.

We had come back to give the children a better education, but I came back without a job. As I am an engineer I decided that a garage business was probably my best bet and we decided to come down to the South West because it was warmer. There was no way we could live in the cold North. So we searched, but most garage businesses were supplied with a two-bedroom bungalow, which for a family of five was no good. Mount Pleasant, in Plymouth Road, was the only business we found which had adequate accommodation for my first wife and three children.

However, Mount Pleasant, which then had petrol pumps outside, was incredibly dirty. The yard was just a mass of oil and the workshop was dark, filthy and very oily. It needed a lot doing to it. We were fortunate that we had the support of Brian Kelsey, a wonderful man, who was working for the Mount Pleasant Garage when I first arrived. He knew a great deal about running a garage as a business and he was extremely good. But there wasn't enough work here for the two of us so, finally, he left and took over the fish-and-chip shop.

Above and top: *The River Dart in winter, February 1963. The river was completely frozen.*

Above: *Silver Street, Buckfastleigh.*

Above: *A well-known local man, Bill Prowse.*

Left: *Furzeleigh Mill, 1966.*

Right: *Kingston Minerals' Christmas party for the quarrymen's children, 1964. Standing at the back are: Kas Stryjski, ?, Marge Stryjski, Gwen Laity, Mrs Drew, ?, ?, Phyllis Wilcox, ?, Joan Butler, Mrs Vennings, ?, Mary Nicholls.*

Jennifer Dove, Paul's wife, described Mount Pleasant as an interesting house. She talked of how the house spoke to her when she first visited it, saying, 'Come and live in me and make me beautiful.' Jennifer and Paul have been working on the property ever since.

Originally Plymouth Road was mainly fields and orchards and much of the land around was owned by the Earl of Macclesfield. Mount Pleasant (not known by that name at the time) also belonged to the Earl of Macclesfield who leased it in 1803, together with an orchard, garden, barn, stable and outhouses, to George Arscott, a builder, dairyman and pig farmer. Jennifer explained that this was when the land became leasehold for the first time.

Stockabrook, which flows through Plymouth Road, continues underground through part of the property belonging to Mount Pleasant. Stockabrook was at one time known as Sages Mill Leat and, in 1884, an agreement was made between George Arscott and James, John, Joseph and William Hamlyn and John Furneaux to allow them access, as mill owners, to the Town Mill Leat when it was required. Jennifer explained:

There was a requirement of the leaseholders to build a wall with a door in it in the corner of the yard, going through to what is now the next-door premises. We assume that this was to give security and privacy to people who lived there, but also to give access for the maintenance of the leat.

The garage closed in 1998 but the premises are still used by Paul as a workshop. Both Paul and Jennifer are keen gardeners and, in 2003, the wonderful array of flowers in tubs and hanging baskets on the forecourt are admired by all those passing by.

As far as young people's interests were concerned, life was changing fast during the 1960s. Conscription had been abolished and young men were now free to make their own decisions about their immediate future. Contraception was widely available and young people were never freer or more independent. The arrival of television in most homes, and a youth music culture that was becoming big business, made for brighter leisure time. There was also a radical change in fashion, including the introduction of the miniskirt, making for a 'swinging' lifestyle, which emanated from Carnaby Street in London.

In Buckfastleigh, however, concerned parents and other interested people held a meeting in the school to decide what they should do to provide some kind of leisure-time opportunity for young people. The local cinema had now closed, and the town youth club which Eric Jones, the curate of the Anglican church, had run for many years, had also closed.

Jim Elliott, who worked at the remand home, had been leader of the Roman Catholic Youth Club for some time and he resigned when Father Christopher took over. The club attracted young men with motor bikes in particular and, in 1961/62, Buckfast Abbey reluctantly closed the club because of complaints from neighbours about the noise of the motor bikes.

Buckfastleigh Methodist Church ran a small youth club but a larger town youth club was needed. A committee was formed and Brenda Hale was appointed leader. The club was held in the National Schoolroom on two evenings a week, and Brenda was assisted by Jim Elliott until she left to have a baby. Jim was then asked to be leader, he recalled:

My idea for a youth club was to provide a place where they could do as they pleased with nothing too structured because school was structured. Give them things they wanted to do or just let them sit and talk if they wanted. Elsa, my wife, used to come down and run the bar, serving soft drinks and sweets. There was only one rule: they could do as they pleased as long as they didn't annoy anyone else.

At one time we were getting a hundred kids coming in from as far away as Yelverton, Bovey and Chudleigh and there was always a double-decker bus going back to Ashburton at 11 at night, full of kids that had been to the youth club.

The age group we were asked to take was 9 to 21, but that was too wide an age group so we took them from 13 years old. We had a members' committee and a lot of kids who were on the committee went on to other committees in the town as they grew up. It was in the youth club that they got their experience.

It seemed that, in spite of the exuberance of the youth culture that was sweeping the country, life went on as usual for young people locally. However, they did want something different. Old-established organisations, such as the YMCA, only appealed to the few. The pride of belonging to a town sports team gradually dissipated over the next decade. Pay was still low for those young people who worked. It seemed that the sophistication and glamour of the new youth culture raised young people's expectations and, somehow, life in a small country town did not match up. This became a problem which intensified over the next 20 years for adults as well as young people.

Above: *School group, c.1875.*

Right: *School group, 1895.*

Below: *School group, c.1890.*

Twelve

THE PRIMARY SCHOOL: A PRECIOUS RESOURCE

The National Schoolroom in Chapel Street, the venue for the youth club, was originally the site of a school for local children. It was built through the efforts of the great-great-grandmother of the writer Helen Harris, whose family came from Buckfastleigh:

My maternal great-great-grandmother, Helen Worrall, was a very interesting person, she came from a well-to-do family in London who were associated with the Royal Court. When her parents died her uncles sent her to Buckfastleigh to recuperate as she was failing in health. Why they chose Buckfastleigh I don't know. However, Helen came to the town and lived in the vicarage in Silver Street and, being a very cultured person, she gave lessons to many of the town's children. She was concerned about the state of the children who lived in the town at that time as there was very little formal education and not all the children had access to education anyway.

During the 1830s Helen Worrall started a fund, to which she herself contributed, to provide a schoolroom for local children. She would travel around on horseback and collect money from wealthy people. The National Schoolroom was built using the funds she raised.

Sadly, Helen died at an early age, apparently from consumption. She had married a local doctor, an Irishman, called Owen McKiernan who was practicing in the town. He was a good man and looked after his ailing wife with devotion. Helen Harris owns a poem written by her great-great-grandmother about her husband's kindness.

William Parker was the first certificated teacher at the school, intially teaching both boys and girls together. Later on in the development of the school the boys and girls were separated after their first few years. Although in the 1800s facilities were basic and materials inadequate, discipline was strict. School inspectors regularly examined the school premises and syllabus.

Buckfastleigh School, 1918.

In 1875 a new school was erected at a cost of £2,959 and the master in charge was George Abbott, also a certificated teacher, well known to many older inhabitants as 'Clicky' Abbott.

Some 55 years later, in 1930, Nora Jackson (née Shillabeer), who trained as a teacher in the late 1920s, started teaching in Buckfastleigh Primary School. At that time Mr H.J. Jeffrey was the headmaster. Other teachers included Miss De La Rue, Dick Tarring, Tommy Blight, Win Midgley (née Tozer), Marjorie Warren, Mr Ford and Miss Seeds. Nora recalled:

I didn't want to come to the town to start with but all the teachers got on well together and we had a good social life. We would go off picnicking together, go for long walks across the moors, or go to the Queen of the Dart to pick daffodils. We even started a country dance club in the school.

Nora taught at Buckfastleigh Primary School for about eight years. During that time the school was rebuilt and pupils and staff were based at two different places. Nora continued:

I was in the Methodist schoolroom sharing the space with another teacher and her class. It was impossible to work. The deafening noise with so many children in the room really got me down.

At playtime we took them into Bossell Lane. I stood at one end of the lane and the other teacher stood at the other end of the lane and they played in between. Later,

Left: *School group, c.1947. Left to right, back row: Richard Perkins, Raymond Hill, Bill Tucker, Fred Prior, Godfrey Horsman, Michael Parsons, ?, Ian Davey, Gethin Wilcox; third row: Miss Marjorie Warren, David Badman, ? Hooper, Errol Pinney, ?, Dorothy Wakeham, Paula Bonathan, Cyril Doidge, Timmy Reed, Michael Smith; second row: Jill Hext, Betty Finch, Margaret Barnes, Valerie Pope, Joan Setters, Gloria Routley, Joan Walters, Sylvia Powell, Marcella Valance, Shirley Hannaford; front: Cyril Short, Lionel Pearse, George Hill, Russell Pearse, Michael Lane.*

Right: *School group, 1926. Left to right, back row: Jim Gill, Ivor Thorne, Percy Head, Alan Lane, W. Maddick; front: Dick Joint, Charlie Boon, Mr Abbott (headmaster), ? Barnicote.*

Left: *Miss Norah Shillabeer's class, c.1930s.*

Right: *School group, 1926. Left to right: Amy Lane, Edith Higden, Ede Weeks, Rose Dunne, Margery Dodd, Loveda Knott, Joan Morris.*

THE PRIMARY SCHOOL: A PRECIOUS RESOURCE

Left: *The woodwork class, c.1930s.*

Below: *School group, c.1930. Left to right, back row: Royston Selley, ?, Joan Coaker, Marian Hill, Frances Cox, Betty Bartlett, Betty Sibley, ? Honeywell, Arthur Millman; middle: Jack Knowling, Harold Fricker, Terry Lambell, Mary Prowse, ?, Enid Crouch, ? Short, Horace Smart, Royston Millman; front: Edgar Willcocks, Donald Hayman, Miss Tozer, Arthur Tonkin, ?, Henry Spear.*

Left: *School governors, including Charlie Hoare and Bill Chaffe (senr), at the opening of Buckfastleigh School after rebuilding, 1937.*

Right: *School teaching staff, c.1930s. Left to right, back row: Mr Blight, Mr Tarring, Mr Les Ford; front: Miss Marjorie Warren, Miss Nora Shillabeer, Mr Jeffrey (headmaster), Miss Enid Seeds, Miss Tozer.*

PE demonstration in Victoria Park, c.1930s.

Mr Joseph Hamlyn rented the bottom bowling-green to us so that we could take the children there to play.

In 1936, with 232 children on the registers, finding alternative, temporary accommodation whilst the school was being rebuilt would not have been easy. The church Sunday school rooms (the National Schoolroom), the Town Hall, the Congregational Sunday School hall, and the Wesleyan Sunday School rooms were all used as temporary classrooms until the beginning of May 1937 when the school reopened again. Its official reopening day was in September. The Town Hall continued to be used by the children for some years.

Vic Foot, who was born in 1923, attended Buckfastleigh Primary School. His teachers were Miss Shillabeer (Nora Jackson), Miss Tozer (Win Midgley) and Miss Blight (Edith Scoble):

In 1938, with 20 minutes to go before leaving school for good, I was whacked across the face by a teacher for talking to a lad sitting behind me. Miss Tozer was the music teacher and one day in her class I did something wrong and she called me out to the front and went to hit me with a stick. I withdrew my hand and she broke the stick on the table. Of course, I got hit twice as hard then! In those days the stick was out as quick as lightning!

His Majesty's Inspector, Mr D.M. Simmonds, visiting the school in June 1938, presented a different perspective on school life. He wrote that:

… an extensive reconstruction of the building carried out in 1937 has greatly improved the teaching conditions and, in particular, has provided the seniors with the facilities necessary for work in modern times. This is a full range school with seven classes: one infant class, three junior classes and three senior classes. A midday meal is provided daily by the canteen and about 90 children partake of a meal which is well conducted.

This is a thoroughly good school. Much of the credit for the good behaviour and industry of the children, the sensible schemes of work and the effective manner into which they are put in operation, must be given to the headmaster. But every member of staff has contributed to the school's success. The two senior assistants deserve special consideration.

[Subjects included] English, arithmetic, history and geography, art, gardening and science. [There is]

PE demonstration in Victoria Park, c.1930s.

instruction in housecraft and handicrafts given by visiting teachers and this year a course in poultry and dairy work is given by a member of the staff of the County Agricultural Committee.

Kenneth Badman was appointed headmaster in November 1938 and started work in January 1939. In September 1939 war was declared and the school was closed, it reopened two days later when ten official evacuees and 17 unofficial evacuees arrived in Buckfastleigh and registered at the school.

In June 1940 evacuees were received from Southwark, in London, and Gravesend. This meant almost twice the number of children in the school with 258 children from Devon and 247 children from London. Not only did the children have to be accommodated in the school, but also the teachers who came with them. This situation necessitated meetings to discuss how best to cope with the influx, which affected both teachers and pupils alike.

From then on there were frequent disruptions to school life and the logbook recorded that the opening and closing of the school varied for the duration of the winter months, owing to the blackout restrictions.

Although the evacuees were now under the care of Buckfastleigh Primary School, the London County Council Authorities still had a responsibility for their pupils and, as well as the Devon County Health Visitors, the LCC Authorities sent their own health visitors to inspect for scabies and diphtheria, as well as the more common hazard of nits.

In 1941, two years later, pupils were still being accommodated in the Town Hall and the school had an agreement with the Town Hall Institute Management Committee for the use of two rooms on a temporary basis. The school was now having to deal with a different kind of difficulty as illustrated in this extract from the Town Hall Institute Management Committee minutes:

November 26th 1941: A letter was read from the caretaker calling the committee's notice to the obstruction caused by the military, from the main gate to the billiard room entrance daily, by some score of men peeling potatoes, this being somewhat of a nuisance to the schoolchildren and teachers complaining of the same... It was agreed to write to the CO.

At the beginning of 1943 the school acted as a rest centre for 14 townsfolk from Church Cross whose cottages had borne the brunt of the only bombing attack to which Buckfastleigh had been subjected. Finally, however, the war came to an end and a farewell party was held for the evacuees on 21 June 1945, with the children finally departing by train from Totnes on Sunday 24 June. One wonders what impressions the children took home with them of life in Buckfastleigh and the children with whom they had made friends. What happened to them when they got home and how hard was it for them to settle down again?

In the school garden, c.1930. Left to right: Miss Marjorie Warren, ?, Miss Tozer.

In April 1953, eight years after the end of the war, Kenneth Badman left Buckfastleigh School and Robert Emmett succeeded as headmaster. He stayed one-and-a-half years and, in January 1955, Arthur Thompson was appointed head teacher.

The year 1958 saw one of the biggest changes in education for a long time. Up until this point children remained at school until they were 15, unless they passed the 11-Plus examination, qualifying them for entry to a high school or grammar school. Suddenly, with secondary education a priority, Buckfastleigh Primary School ceased being an all-age school after 83 years and became an infant and junior school.

In practical terms this meant that, in addition to pupils over 11 years old attending the secondary modern school in Ashburton, many of the teachers lost their jobs as the school population went down by more than 100 children to 223. The remaining teachers at the school were Marjorie Warren who was deputy head, Miss Denning, Miss Kelly, Miss Luscombe, Mrs Vicary and Mr Cullen. However, Marjorie Warren retired the following year after 27 years as a teacher at the school.

In 1975 a successful fête was held to mark the centenary of the school. A request for local people, both adults and children, to come to the school in Victorian costume was met with an overwhelming response. An exhibition of records and photographs was well attended. Michael Lane, a keen amateur photographer, held on to the cine-film he made of the occasion. When he showed the film a number of years later, it provoked a lively response from those watching as to the identity of those dressed up in Victorian costume.

Arthur Thompson retired as headmaster after 20 years and two terms in August 1975, and John Shinner was appointed as headmaster at the start of the autumn term in the same year.

The school at which John Shinner became head in 1975 was a very different place from the wartime school run by Kenneth Badman. Although there were frequent disruptions, and adjustments to be

Above: *The school, c.1930s.*

Right: *Domestic science class, c.1930.*

Left: *School group, 1951. The headmaster is Mr Badman and the teacher Marjorie Warren. The picture includes: Sheila Pickles (fifth from left, back row); third row: Faye Kerswell (third from left) and Jennifer Line (fifth from left); second row: David Miller (second from left), John Reed (second from right), Cedric Hard (far right); left to right, front row: Brian Joint, ?, Cyril Pearce, Peter Hawkins, ?.*

THE PRIMARY SCHOOL: A PRECIOUS RESOURCE

Right: *The class of 1953 including John Coleman, Margaret Furneaux, Hockley Brooking, Margaret Chambers, Colin Bray.*

Left: *School netball team, 1955. Left to right, back row: ?, Heather Weeks, Ann Petherbridge, Janet Spiller; front: Denise Goss, Pauline Watts, Gillian French.*

Right: *School group, c.1940. Left to right, back row: Lionel Pearce, ?, Peter Miller, ? Dawe, Raymond Hill, Errol Pinney, ?, ?, Fred Prior, ?, Brian Woodley; third row: ?, Timmy Reed, David Badman, ?, ?, Guy Miller, ?, Derek Wallace, Bryan Maddocks, Godfrey Horsman, ?; second row: Wendy Pearce, ?, Honor Voisey, Anne Medland, Crystal Way, Miss Warren, ?, ?, Medora Ham, Julie Baker, Arlette Daw; front: ?, ?, Shirley McCarthy, Joan Stacey, Joyce Voaden, Margaret Jones.*

Left: *School group, c.1950. The photograph includes: Doreen Lee, Geraldine Kerswell, Carol Giles, Barbara Jones, Pat Chapple, Barbara Axford, Graham Davey, David Hayman, Terry French, Bobby Pearn, Edward Soper.*

made, school life was relatively secure and happy during the 1940s. During the 1970s, however, society was changing rapidly and at the beginning of the 1980s the staff at Buckfastleigh School recognised that the number of family units breaking up, and the dominance of television in everyday life, was reflected in the school classroom by behavioural problems and language deprivation.

Additionally, unemployment hit the town hard and many families moved away to seek employment elsewhere, resulting in fewer pupils on the school roll at the beginning of the 1980s.

One of the first tasks John Shinner and his staff had to undertake was to improve the reading standard and to raise the standard of education generally within the school. An HMI report notes the 'children now have a short attention span and have to be trained to listen.'

As public awareness of violence in society increased so measures were taken in school to raise children's understanding of the dangers outside school. The log-book recorded the showing of the film *Never Walk with Strangers*. The school building became more vulnerable and was subjected to frequent break-ins.

Through the staff's efforts and the support and concern of parents, a working partnership developed and a number of new initiatives were started. Reports from HMIs were encouraging and they wrote that, 'the school was moving forward.'

One big blow to the school was the death of John Timms, the vicar of Buckfastleigh, in February 1980. John Timms had been very much involved in the community as chairman of Buckfastleigh Urban District Council and the chairman of the Devon Council Education Committee. He was also a governor of Buckfastleigh School. John Shinner wrote movingly about John Timms who, he said:

> *... was a man of great intellect, gentle humour and a wry sense of humour. The school will greatly miss his influence and I, personally, regret the loss of a man whose words and thoughts were invaluable at governors' meetings.*

One of the most satisfying results for school staff, and the pupils, was the Home Reading Scheme which was, in John Shinner's words, 'pursued with vigour.' In 1975 very few of the children in the top infant class could read according to their chronological age, ten years later over two-thirds attained the appropriate reading level for their age.

In 1986, to celebrate the 900th anniversary of the Domesday Book, the BBC undertook a survey to update the Domesday Book for future historians. Buckfastleigh School took part in the exciting project and the children were given 12 square kilometres of land in the area to survey, photograph and describe. The area to be surveyed included the caves, Buckfast Abbey, the Steam Engine Railway, the Butterfly Farm and the quarries. This was quite an undertaking for the pupils as the area had to be looked at from various high points and a land survey completed. The 20 pages of results were recorded on computer disk and stored for posterity.

In October of the same year a presentation was made to the Town Mayor of a computer printout of the Domesday project completed by the children of Junior 5. Some 17 children attended the presentation which was received with pleasure by the Town Mayor and councillors. The computer printout was then placed in the town's archives.

In October 1985 five members of the National Union of Teachers went on strike for the afternoon in support of a pay claim. It was action that both the teachers concerned and the head teacher regretted. Action by teachers in schools across the country resulted in widespread disruption at this time.

By the end of 1987 there had been numerous disputes, and the bad publicity received by the teaching profession meant that teaching staff were dispirited and disgruntled. The Minister for Education forced an agreement on the teaching profession and a Bill went through Parliament which prescribed exactly what would be taught in schools. It became known as the National Curriculum.

A unique occasion earlier in 1986 had resulted in three generations of Buckfastleigh head teachers meeting together in the town. The occasion was the Devon Association Annual Reception, held in the Town Hall, and Kenneth Badman and his wife and Arthur Thompson were invited by John Shinner to see the school as it now was. 'It was a unique occasion,' said John Shinner. 'Kenneth Badman enjoyed... remembering their life here during the war years.'

Another unique occasion was the retirement of Mr Windeatt, the secretary of the school governors. He was presented with a gift as a token of appreciation for his service to the school for over 50 years. Not only was Mr Windeatt's length of service remarkable but also the fact that a member of the Windeatt family had held the position of secretary to the governors since 1870!

Deputy head, Miss Kelly, known and loved by many children, retired in July 1988 after 30 years' service in the school. 'She will be remembered as a warm and caring human being,' said John Shinner. 'Her enthusiasm and interest and love of the children here has been characteristic of her teaching methods.'

For those teachers remaining in the profession the demands of the National Curriculum, and in particular the testing of children, became almost overwhelming and many staff were depressed. In addition to the burden of the National Curriculum, Buckfastleigh School staff were faced with a badly needed building programme for the school that took 20 months to complete.

The official opening of the redeveloped school was held on 26 November 1992. Mrs Edith Walters, sister of schoolteacher Marjorie Warren, was guest of honour. She was 97 and had been a pupil at the school at the beginning of the 1900s. She thoroughly enjoyed her visit and played an important part in the school's reopening. Sadly, Edith died just under six weeks later.

At the time of writing the headmaster was Robert Freshwater who continued to maintain the high standards set by previous head teachers, with a teaching staff behind him that were equally dedicated as in the past but facing different problems.

Throughout the years headmasters have faithfully recorded the academic and sporting successes of their pupils and have remarked on the dedication of their teachers in the school log-books. The log-books have also included descriptions of Christmas plays, school outings, visits by the nurse and inspectors – everything that contributed to the daily running of the school.

Records of achievements, special occasions and school visits have continued and it is clear that successive headmasters and teaching staff have taken great delight in their pupils' achievements. They have also taken care to assist and encourage less able pupils to reach their potential.

The teachers work very much in partnership with parents and staff. Those doing the catering and cleaning, the teaching assistants and volunteers who help children with reading, all have a part to play in the education and social awareness of local children.

At the time of writing, Ann Eales, who had been at the school for 30 years, played her part as a dinner lady well – she was responsible for the children whilst they had their dinners (although not involved in any cooking). 'There are five of us who do it,' Ann said, 'and there are now 500 children – and I know all the children. When I go down town it's, 'Hello, Miss. Hello, Miss'.'

Margaret Coombes was a teacher's assistant. She saw an advert in the local paper for an infant helper for the primary school in 1965. She was engaged for two terms and stayed for 21 years, mostly under the direction of headmaster Arthur Thompson. Margaret, who comes from Paisley in Scotland, said:

I thoroughly enjoyed the work and was proud that no one ever said they could not understand my accent. There were a number of changes over the years but things didn't change too much in the infant department. In fact, we were lucky to have such nice children. Most of the ex-pupils who were at the school still speak to me even now. Some, of course, have children of their own.

When John Shinner retired at the end of August 1994, after 19 years, he said that it had been a pleasure to work in the school. He went on to say that he had been headmaster of a marvellous school in a country town with a village environment. 'Buckfastleigh school,' he said, 'is a precious resource in the development of human potential for both child and adult. Long may the school continue.'

Senior class of 14 year olds, 1950. Left to right, back row: *Mr Badman (headmaster), Joyce Lee, Ann Medland, Shirley Pickover, Crystal Waye, Maureen Coaker, Joan Stacey, Barbara Eales;* middle: *Brian Woodley, Shirley McCarthy, Joan Setherton, Sylvia Tillyer, Miss Amor, Pat Boyer, Frances Horsman, Margaret Jones, Martin Hayman;* front: *Allan Hoare, Brian Deacon, Rodney Perkins, David Crannaford, David Dodd, Noel Downie, Donald Joint, Roy Boon, John Bragg.*

Above: *Hamlyn's Mill, c.1890.*

Left: *Mr James Searle, a wool comber at Buckfast, 1880.*

Below: *The engine room at Hamlyn's Mill.*

Thirteen

THE WOOLLEN MILL: PART OF DAILY LIFE

As one of the main employers in the town Buckfastleigh Woollen Mill has been an integral part of the life of local people for almost 200 years. However, the development of Buckfast and Buckfastleigh as wool manufacturers began nearly 1,000 years ago with the Cistercian monks. They were followed by the Benedictines of Buckfast Abbey, who farmed and bred sheep and engaged in the wool trade as members of the Guild Merchants of Totnes. It is likely that Buckfastleigh developed as a result of the success of the Abbey with local people in its employ. After the Dissolution of the Monasteries by Henry VIII in 1539, the trade continued with local men and women spinning and weaving at home.

The climate of South Devon is soft and humid, suitable for the production of fine yarns. Soft water is another advantage and, with Buckfastleigh situated between the River Mardle and Dean Burn, two tributaries of the River Dart, the town is especially suited for the wool trade.

Even in Europe, Devon cloth has been famous for hundreds of years. Exeter alone exported more than 300,000 pieces of cloth annually at the height of its success. In Buckfastleigh it was due to two men, Joseph Hamlyn and Benjamin Hayman, that weaving as an industry gained prominence in the West Country. In 1806, the Hamlyns bought a tannery and started wool combing.

Bill Chaffe, whose family have been associated with the mills for over 100 years, recalled:

Opposite the Waterman's Arms, on Crest Hill, there was a smithy. One day Mr Joseph Hamlyn went into the smithy to have his horse shod and saw a notice advertising a property for sale. It was part of the old mill, which they used as a stannery for the tin mining business. So Mr Hamlyn went to the auction and bought the building and that was the start.

In 1818 Benjamin Hayman went out of business and the Hamlyn brothers continued without him. In 1842 the Hamlyns rented the West Mill factory and later bought the Town Mill, formerly Sages. With the introduction of a wool-combing machine they effectively put all master combers in the town out of business. Machinery revolutionised industry throughout the country and without it the wool trade in Buckfastleigh would not have survived.

There were five woollen mills in the immediate area: the West Mill and Town Mill run by the Hamlyns, and Churchward's Mill (destroyed by fire in 1906) in Buckfastleigh. In Buckfast there was Higher Mill belonging to the Hamlyns and Berry's Mill. These five mills ensured that Buckfastleigh and Buckfast together became a flourishing wool centre.

In December 1891, however, a dispute over wages and the right to join a union led to picketing of the Town Mill in Buckfastleigh, followed by similar trouble at Berry's Mill in Buckfast. Rates of pay in the country were then, as they are now, much lower than in towns and cities, but the mill owners had to pay for expensive fuel (coal), costly rail transport and faced severe competition from other parts of the country.

Even at that time almost as many women as men were employed in the wool trade. The women worked as sorters and wool pickers and earned 9s. a week. The older women performed a variety of tasks and earned between 7s. and 10s. a week. Weavers, chiefly girls and young women, earned from 9s. to 12s. a week, whilst young men over 17 years old and older men, many of whom were elderly, earned between 12s. and 20s. a week. Although the threatened lock-out at Hamlyn's Mill by union members collapsed, Berry's Mill owners decided that they would remain a non-union firm and that those employees who insisted on belonging to the Gasworkers and General Labourers Union would be dismissed. This decision, taken without any consultation at all with the workforce, only served to exacerbate the situation and made the workers all the more determined to stand against their employers. Workers from Ashburton who had decided to end their association with the Labourers Union were conveyed in brakes to and from their homes, arranged by Mr Berry, to avoid confrontation with the pickets.

A meeting of the district members of the Gasworkers and General Labourers Union was held in the Town Hall club room in Buckfastleigh on 2 December 1889; it was attended by 250 people. The speakers were Mr W. Gardner, the district secretary of the National Labourers Union, based in Plymouth, and a Mr C.A. Millman.

In January 1890 several of the workforce had capitulated and the dispute had almost collapsed. However, the disagreement served to highlight several facts about Buckfastleigh and Buckfast at that time. The main problem, which was a genuine grievance, was that there was inadequate housing for the workers in the town settlements. There was neither enough housing to accommodate the workers, nor housing that was suitable for anyone to inhabit. The mills, particularly Berry's Mill, employed workers from Ashburton who walked in six days a week, and home again, in all weathers. Many, no doubt, would have moved with their families to Buckfast or Buckfastleigh had there been houses to rent.

Furthermore – and this may well have contributed to the breakdown of industrial action – Messrs Berry gave those workers who had joined the Union not only notice to quit their employment but notice to quit their homes as well. It was the middle of winter. As a *Western Morning News* correspondent indicated in an article about the workers' dispute, they could not leave their homes as there were no other houses to move to – except the workhouse.

Messrs Hamlyn, Berry and Churchward were well aware of the lack of decent, affordable accommodation for their employees, as were other employers in the area. The Hamlyns had already built numerous workers' cottages and Mr Simeon Berry had adapted a building to house some workers. However, there was still insufficient housing and, although several meetings had been held to discuss the situation and consideration had been given to suitable land on which to build, there had not been sufficient will among the employers to do anything about the situation and the scheme had fallen through. Despite this, as proved over time, the Hamlyn's were one of the greatest benefactors in Buckfastleigh, providing cottages and other amenities for the townspeople.

Bill Chaffe's father left school in 1895 and went to the Hamlyn's Mill office. That was the start of a long tradition of the Chaffe family's association with the wool trade. Joseph Hamlyn (junr), who lived at Fullaford, was chairman of the company at that time and took an immediate liking to Mr Chaffe's father who was a brilliant mathematician. Bill remembered:

Everything was done by telegraph in those days and my father used to receive a telegram from Thomas Hamlyn to his brother, Joseph, and, as usual, Joseph was out hunting all over Dartmoor. My father had to get his horse and go off and find him and then bring Joseph's answer back as quickly as he could and send off the telegram! That's how they used to do business then and it took nearly all day!

Joseph Hamlyn (junr) was a useful man and he was always out looking for water. I give Joseph Hamlyn the credit for the River Mardle. He used to dig up the rivers and run them in little streams into the town.

The most unique aspect of the development of the wool trade in Buckfastleigh was that, unlike many northern towns, the Buckfastleigh mills undertook all the different processes of cloth manufacture from start to finish – they worked with the raw wool until it became a piece of cloth.

The Hamlyns had a good reputation for high-class woollen cloth and serges. In 1927 *The Wheatsheaf* noted that most of their trade consisted of:

… plain, blue and black botany coatings, striped tropical coatings, white and grey flannels, checked and striped mixture suitings, Devon Admiralty serge and women's costume coatings in fancy self colours.

The dyeing of material was Buckfastleigh's speciality, the credit for which goes to the rivers which flowed from Dartmoor. The cloth was steeped in indigo dye and kept in a vat for a considerable amount of time. It emerged a whitish-yellow and then, through oxidisation, became green and then indigo blue, after which it was dried naturally.

Terry Hallett, who worked in Buckfast Mill and later in Buckfastleigh Town Mill, described how the well-ventilated weavers' cottages in Chapel Street were used for drying cloth:

When Hamlyn's started their trade the cloth they turned out had to be put somewhere where the top of the cloth would pick up the pile. The loft inside the weavers' cottages was ideal.

A walk around the loft in the first cottage, which is two cottages knocked into one, reveals a large room with beams and louvres that would have opened out into Chapel Street before they were boarded up. The louvres can be seen from the street, running the length of the four cottages as far as the double doors above the first cottage. These horizontal slats (louvres) opened by means of vertical wooden poles. 'The loft actually runs the entire length of the row of cottages,' said the present owner of the first cottage. 'Now, of course, the loft has been partitioned off at the end of each cottage.' Terry Hallett continued:

The cloth would have been pleated down and then stretched over and under several rollers, suspended from the roof, from one side of the loft to the other where

Left: *Mill workers in the rug room, c.1920. Left to right, back row: Mr Seager (foreman), ? Routley, ?, Frank Murch, ? Seager (junr);* middle: *Maria Chaffe (forewoman), Rene Saunders, Winnie ?, Winnie Coombes, Rene Furneaux, Alice Wakeham;* front: *Edna Bartle, May Weeks.*

they would be weighted down. Hundreds of sharp tentering hooks, jutting out from the beams at each end of the room, would hold the ends of the cloth so that it did not slip. Then the louvres would be opened up and the damp air would come in and raise the pile. After a certain time the cloth would be taken back to the mill and cut up according to the size wanted.

'Most probably they would hoist the material up and down through the double doors above the street,' said the owner of the first cottage, 'but the workers doing the job must have had to walk through the tenant's cottage to get up to the loft.'

In 1920 the Co-operative Wholesale Society bought Hamlyn's Mill for £270,000, thus ending over 100 years of the family's involvement with the industry. The purchase was completed on Friday 19 March, after which a meeting of the workforce took place so that the old employers could say goodbye and introduce the new owners. In his farewell speech Joseph Hamlyn said that the time had come when he and his colleagues on the board of Messrs, Hamlyn Brothers Ltd felt they were entitled to stand aside from active management of the affairs of the company and, as he and Mr Furneaux had no sons to succeed them, the board, considering the whole of the circumstances, had decided to dispose of the business.

Having come to this decision, the Hamlyns felt anxious to find successors who would maintain the pleasant relationship which in the past had existed between the firm and the workforce, a relationship which had always been ideal, founded as it was on mutual trust and confidence. They had decided that the CWS should succeed them as owners of the premises and whilst, naturally, he and his colleagues felt the parting intensely after spending their business lives amongst their workpeople, they were glad to think that they were handing over the destiny of the firm to an organisation whose reputation as employers of labour was unimpeachable.

The CWS transaction comprised the weaving mill, woollen warehouse and the tan yard in Buckfastleigh and later the carding and spinning factory in Buckfast. There were also 16 acres of land attached and 94 cottages inhabited by the workers. Mr Douglas Hamlyn, the son of William Hamlyn, and Arthur Ridgeway, both of whom had been trained at the mills, were retained by the CWS to manage the businesses on their behalf.

When the CWS took over the business there were about 100 looms working in the town, turning out 200 pieces (50 yards each) weekly. There was an ample water supply for both mills and the Buckfast mill was run by water turbines for most of the year.

Many local people worked in the woollen mill; it was here that the cloth was manufactured and passed through many different processes from blending, carding, spinning and warping to weaving and mending, after which the cloth would go into the wash house and then to the finishing department.

The CWS saw the mill as an opportunity for development in order to provide for a greater range of goods to meet the demands of the Co-operative Movement. The author of an article in the movement's magazine, *The Wheatsheaf*, wrote:

[Buckfastleigh's serge's] *reputation is every bit as good today. There is no doubt that as soon as Buckfastleigh Mills can manufacture solely for the Co-operative Movement, the several CWS distributive departments will be able to dispose of all the cloth, as the CWS produces less than ten per cent of the woollen goods it can sell.*

With the arrival of the CWS there was a boom which was followed soon after by a slump and, although the CWS recovered and made a great impact on trading in the town, Buckfastleigh never regained its former importance as a centre for the wool trade.

Most local people have memories of the mill, particularly those who worked there. Bill Selley started his working days up at Heywards, the bakers, during the 1940s. Then, after Mr Heyward died, Bill was invited for an interview at the mill by Ernest May.

'Mr May said, 'You will be starting on Monday.' In those days you weren't asked when you wanted to

Above: *The mill office, Chapel Street, c.1970.*

The mill chimney being prepared for demolition, c.1976.

Below: *Mr Gill working in the mill.*

The end of the mill chimney, 1976.

THE WOOLLEN MILL: PART OF DAILY LIFE

start,' said Bill, 'you were told.' Unsure that he wanted to work in the mill, Bill said he would start the following week and would take the job for three months. He stayed for 25 years until the mill closed.

Bill Chaffe recalled:

In about 1936 we heard that Robert Cox, at Victoria Wharfs in Plymouth, was closing down and that they had half a dozen men sorters in Plymouth. Harold Coaker, foreman of the sorting department, and I were sent down to Plymouth to find suitable men. We had only had women sorters before.

One of the men was Ernest Coleman who came up to Buckfastleigh with his wife, Edith, and settled down happily in the town.

Marian Harvey started working in the mill when she was 14. She left at 22, and then went back again after she had married. Along with the other employees she worked 48 hours a week – 8a.m. to 6p.m. on Mondays to Fridays and 8a.m. to midday on Saturday mornings. 'We used to long for Saturday dinner times,' she said, 'but the weekend went so quickly and then it was back to work again on Monday.' Vic Foot recalled:

I went to work in the mill in 1937 when I was 14 years old. I shall always remember receiving my first wage of 11s.10d. for a 48-hour week. I stayed there for two and a half years but didn't like it at all.

In the early 1920s Fern Cox came to Buckfastleigh from Broadhempston to work in the mill. His sister was already employed there and through that contact he was taken on as an apprentice for five years by Mr Ridgeway, the manager, in order to learn the wool trade from wool sorting onwards. When Mr Ridgeway left, Bill Chaffe, who was running the tannery, took over as manager of the whole plant, just before Fern's apprenticeship ended in 1930. Fern was then made under-manager of the sorting department with Mr Coaker as foreman. 'After a while I became a buyer,' said Fern, 'until I was ill and went to Hawkmoor Sanatorium for several months.'

The Second World War saw most of the male employees called up for active service. The wool trade was considered essential work and more women were employed at the mill. Of course, as it had been agreed that those called up for active service would have their job back after the war, many of the women then found themselves unemployed when the men returned. Edith Coleman recalled:

The majority of local people worked in the mill and after Ernest and I came up to Buckfastleigh to live and he went into the mill to work, we felt more part of everyone's daily life. When the war started Ernest enlisted with the army and I went into the weaving shed. It was a new experience for me – going into a factory. But I didn't take long to settle down. The mill gates were opened each morning at eight when the siren went. Everyone who worked there had to be ready to clock in, if they weren't there when the doors closed they had to wait about ten minutes outside which meant losing some of their earnings.

The mill, 1921.

'Each day the workers would congregate outside the Co-op Grocery Dept entrance on the opposite side of the road waiting to clock into the mill,' said Bill Chaffe. 'Usually all that remained after everyone had gone into the mill was a load of dog-ends,' he added, smiling.

During the war huge quantities of cloth were made for the Navy. Officers' uniforms were also made through the Worsted Spinning Department which was finer than the ordinary khaki. The ordinary khaki included puttees which were made at Fox's in Wellington. Fern Cox recalled:

We had to collect skins from the abattoir and keep them clean because they were perishables. We dressed a lot of skins for 'bovver' gloves for the Air Force – thick wool inside and leather outside. Then it would be creased on the outside to make it supple – and we were quite busy with that.

We were short-handed during the war. There was no buyers's job as the price of wool was fixed. I had to grade the wool as it came in. Things remained like that until the Ministry of Supply took us over. Then the Ministry of Agriculture and Fisheries took us over and we were passed from one department to another. That's how we stayed until the war was over. Even then they did not release us because they still carried on until 1951 when the Wool Marketing Board was formed.

It took quite a while for things to get back to normal after the war. One of my jobs was to salvage the wool at Cook's in Plymouth. There were incendiaries, glass and other things all mixed up in the wool and we had to pick it out. Women would be doing it as well as men.

Another job I had to do was sort out bales of wool stored on a ship which had been sunk in Liverpool harbour during the war. It was underwater for about six months before they could do anything about it. The ship was from South Africa and there were bales and bales of wool aboard it. When the bales were recovered they were sent to me and I can still see them in my mind now, all this wool just left out in a field. When they were cleaned up a bit you would never believe that with the wool being pressed so tightly the water hadn't even reached the centre.

Bill Chaffe remembered how things gradually returned to normal after the war:

Ralph Dunning was running the woollen mill and I ran the fellmongering – the chamois, the rugs and wool combing in the old part. We carried on until, finally, it was decided that the old wool-combing building was in such a state that a new place should be built. When we got our new building we transferred up there and left the woollen mill on its own.

Fern Cox added:

When we moved from our old premises in the mill to our new building I was made under-manager responsible for the wool-combing department by Bill Chaffe. After a year or two the Wool Board Agency bought the premises from the CWS in 1972 and I was made manager of the Wool Board until I retired.

Both Bill Chaffe and Fern Cox retired in 1974. The end of another era in the wool trade in the town.

In 1975 the woollen mill and the old weaving shed closed down, causing shock and bewilderment among the workers and the townspeople. It was as if the heart of the town had been removed as the long-established trade of the manufacture of cloth ended. Now Hamlyn's Way council-flats stand where the mill once was and the old weaving shed has been made into several units and is now used by H. & K. Sims, the sawdust and wood merchants.

Then, in 1976, the one remaining symbol of the manufacture of cloth, the mill chimney, a striking feature in the town, was blasted. Many people stood and watched with tears in their eyes as the tall chimney swayed and finally disintegrated.

In 1955 when Bill Chaffe's son Alan was 17, he started working in the wool-combing department, in the fellmongery and the wool agency B merchants, grading fleece wool:

I switched into the fellmongery full-time in 1957. I then did my National Service but was soon discharged as being medically unfit. So I came back to the fellmongery and there I stayed until 1960. Then I went to Loughborough College to study industrial management for 12 months, after which I came back to Buckfastleigh and worked for 10 years throughout the fellmongering, and wool-combing industry.

I later went back into the fellmongery when I became a management trainee for the CWS Fellmongery Group, which included Buckfastleigh, Pontefract and Northampton. I have never worked in any other industry but I am sure that if I had my time all over again I would do the same thing.

When Bill Chaffe retired in 1974 Alan succeeded him under the CWS. He later became group manager for the CWS which included Pontefract and was responsible for the hide markets at Beeston, Northampton and Newcastle which involved considerable travelling. 'I enjoyed it,' said Alan, 'but I was always glad to come back to Buckfastleigh because Newcastle is such a long way away and it's a lot of travelling.'

There were several other changes over the next few years. Hillsdown Holdings, who at the time were the owners of the FMC Fellmongeries at Yarm and Leeds, took over the Buckfastleigh fellmongery, together with the hide market at Beeston and Northampton, in the early 1980s. Alan recalled:

My role changed then, I became involved in the fellmongeries at Leeds and Yarm as well as Buckfastleigh. Two or three years later a company called Strong and Fisher, who had fellmongeries at Newtown and Retford, were also taken over by Hillsdown and I was on the committee that looked after the five factories.

Those factories were closed in the early '90s but the Buckfastleigh plant remained until 1997 when it was taken over by a subsidiary company called Skins International, which comprised 50 per cent Hillsdown and 50 per cent Marshall Farmer:

When the fellmongery closed there was no one unemployed within six weeks of the factory closing. When I started working there were something like 45 to 50 fellmongeries in Great Britain. There are only four now in the UK. Many of the skins that would have been processed here previously in the original fellmongeries are now sent to China or Turkey where they can be processed more cheaply because of low wages.

In 2003 Axminster Carpets owned the plant. They tanned sheepskins from the UK and made a variety of products. And the state of the industry? 'It is as good now as it has ever been,' declared Alan Chaffe.

Les Coombes, a weaver, on Northropp Looms, CWS Mill, 1952.

Fourteen

THE 1970S: REORGANISATION & DETERIORATION

The 1970s were a politically turbulent decade. In June 1970 Britain had a trade imbalance of £31 million. A long, cold shadow loomed over the country in the form of high unemployment which continued to rise from 500,000 in 1970 to well over 1.5 million towards the end of the decade. Successive Labour and Conservative governments were held to ransom by the trade unions demanding higher pay for their respective workers, which resulted in national strikes by the dockers, the postal workers, miners, train drivers and refuse collectors over the first half of the decade.

In 1972 official blackouts were imposed and 12 power stations were closed down. In 1974 a three-day week was instigated and television programmes finished at 10p.m. in order to conserve electricity. It was a period of misery for people all over Britain. Paul Dove, an engineer from Plymouth Road, recalled:

In 1974 the Co-operative Society installed a generator on the Co-op premises in Chapel Street in case of emergency. It was an old, wartime, diesel generator which had been done up. I was asked by Sid Goffin, who was manager of the Co-op then, if I would be prepared to start it if they needed to use it and it was agreed I would get ten shillings each time I did it. There was always a warning when there would be a blackout and then my son and I would go around and start up the generator. It meant cranking the handle and then going through the shop switching on all the switches. Sid Goffin told us that if we didn't get the generator going before the main lights went off the shop would be plunged into darkness, some customers would start stealing things and would race out of the shop with whatever they could get away with! You wouldn't think that would happen in a place like Buckfastleigh.

Mr S. Goffin, the Town Mayor, 1976.

I also remember Geoff Tall, who had a shop in Fore Street, telling me that one day during the blackouts a lady came in to buy some candles from him. Geoff Tall knew she was the wife of someone who was on strike and said, 'No way! You go and get those lights on first then you can have the candles!'

There were four major events in Britain that would have affected local people: the decimalisation of Britain's currency in 1971 (causing confusion to many older adults, although more easily adjusted to by younger people); the new age of majority in 1970 which meant that men and women became adult at the age of 18 (the law that lowered the voting age from 21 to 18 years came in 1969); Britain, Ireland and Denmark joining the European Community in January 1973; and, in 1977, the celebration of Queen Elizabeth II's silver jubilee, in which Buckfastleigh took part.

Internationally, the decade saw chaos in major wars and a new wave of terrorism which alarmed the whole of Europe. The threat of nuclear war was great as Russia and Britain played cat-and-mouse games.

In Buckfastleigh, which was undoubtedly directly affected by the economic situation in Britain, there were three events which set the town on a new course for the future – major events which altered the lives of local people considerably.

In 1975 the Buckfastleigh Woollen Mill closed down. The mill, where the cloth was manufactured, and the old weaving shed were demolished. Suddenly, a way of life for most of the families in Buckfastleigh came to an end and unemployment faced many who had only ever worked at the mill. The mill chimney, a landmark for the whole town, was razed to the ground in 1976. It spelt the end. Marian Harvey commented:

Losing the mill was one of the worst things to happen! It took the heart out of the place. Working with all those people you could not help but be involved with each other and with what was going on.

Margaret Foot added:

When you walked down the town you knew everybody, if only by sight. Everyone in the family worked in the mill. Dads worked there, mums worked there – all of us in the mill. Our lives were dictated by the siren calling us to work! Buckfastleigh started to deteriorate when the mill closed and the commercial life started to go down. Some men found work but a lot of men never worked again. Some of them had been there all their working lives.

It seems that the people of Buckfastleigh became disorientated after the closure; their employment and way of life was gone and they were left feeling uncertain about the future. The old camaraderie, which had been so much a part of the town, gradually disappeared. Unemployment, with little or no prospect of work for the older men, must have been an unbearable prospect – especially for those who had grown up thinking that they had a 'job for life.'

In 1972 work began on a new dual carriageway which would accommodate the increasing volume of traffic coming into the West Country. Starting in Exeter the dual carriageway bypassed Ashburton and Buckfastleigh only to virtually cut off Dartbridge from the rest of the town. However, the increased number of workmen living in and around the town did bring more trade to Buckfastleigh. Mary Blair (previously Mary Mitchelmore), whose delicatessen was at the lower end of the town next to Johnson's, remarked:

We did well out of the men who worked on the new dual carriageway. Passengers on the Dart Valley Railway used to come in as well. But once the road was completed and the big supermarkets were built within easy travelling distance, that was the beginning of the end. The old A38 was limited to restricted traffic so we lost all the passing trade and the caravans coming down to Devon came loaded with food from their own local supermarkets.

Derek Moore:

We were living in Wallaford Road when work on the dual carriageway started and we used to be woken up every morning by these massive earth movers! I have never seen anything like the size of them before or since. Then we were told that the road-building men were coming and to lock up our wives and children as they were all drunken Irish men! When they arrived they were a very mixed bag. Of course, there were a few colourful characters but there were several people who had been in very poorly paid jobs previously and could not believe their luck at landing such well-paid work.

The first day they arrived on the site at Furzeleigh I went to see the man who was nurse for the site. He couldn't get over the fact that on the very day they arrived, the ambulance crew came to visit, the police came and I came. Some of the men wished not to be traced, and refused to register even as temporary residents, but offered whisky as currency!

Marjorie Moore continued:

The primary school became overcrowded with children of the families who came with the men, but this was a wonderful enrichment for the town because they were folk from many different backgrounds and with vastly different experiences.

'They set themselves up on a caravan site, a temporary 'town', in the fields around Furzeleigh,' said Ken Fricker who had lived in the toll-house at Dartbridge, near Furzeleigh, for over 40 years. 'I had been happy living there undisturbed by neighbours,' he said, 'but as the years went by, however, the noise of the traffic increased until it was continuous.' Ken lived there until work on the new dual carriageway began. He remembered the time at the beginning of the '70s when a petrol tanker overturned at Dartbridge, spilling all the fuel into the road. Thousands of gallons of petrol were spilt. He was outside when he heard the squeal of brakes:

I looked out of the back gate and saw this thing turn over and the driver scrambling out. I went to my mother and said, 'Dinner ready?' 'Yes,' she replied. 'Well,' I said, 'I think that we had better have it as we're going to have to leave soon.' When I told her what had happened she couldn't eat a thing. The front door [bell] rang and the policeman came to the door and told us we would have to evacuate the place because there was petrol everywhere. He told us to turn off all the lights and anything else that was electrical. The front doorbell was electrical. That would have been enough to send anything up!

In 1969 Suzanne Manley came to live at the Cott Orchard Tearooms, Dartbridge, with her mother and sister, just up the road from where Ken Fricker lived:

My grandparents, Doris and Douglas Hallam, who moved from Birmingham, owned Cott Orchard then and I was only two when we came to live with them. It was a wonderful place to live in with all that land and space around us and I can't think of a better place to grow up.

It was beginning to develop as a restaurant when McAlpines started to build the dual carriageway and, whilst the road was being built, the inside of Cott

THE 1970S: REORGANISATION AND DETERIORATION

Cott Orchard, Dartbridge.

Orchard was being completely refurbished. Although I wasn't very old I remember clearly that there were workmen everywhere outside. Some of them used to lodge in the White Hart pub.

One of Suzanne's earliest memories is of Neil Dalgleish delivering bread and cakes from the bakery he managed in Fore Street to Cott Orchard. 'My sister and I were allowed to choose a cake from the back of the van,' she said, 'and we always enjoyed that.'

The bakery in lower Fore Street was originally owned by the Shutes and then by the Hunts who sold it to Neil Dalgleish's parents in 1969. Neil and Rose Dalgleish managed the bakery and coffee lounge, which was a popular venue in the early 1970s. When his parents retired in 1978 Neil bought it outright. His van would often be seen parked outside the bakery and in the summer a brightly-coloured awning would extend over the width of the pavement to protect the cakes and bread from the sun.

One summer afternoon in 1975 the bakery was the scene of an awful accident when a heavily-laden CWS lorry lost one of its bales of wool as it was negotiating Fore Street. The bale severely injured a lady who was walking along the pavement by the bakery. The awning and the van prevented the 200lb bale of wool from crashing through the bakery window where Edith Coleman was reaching for some cakes whilst serving a customer. The van was pushed further down the road.

Edith would have been badly injured if the wool had crashed through the window. The bales piled on top of the lorry rose higher than the bedroom windows of the Chapel Street terraced houses which the lorry passed as it drove slowly down through the town. It had already negotiated the difficult corner coming out from the tan yard into Chapel Street. Edith was shocked but unhurt and helped Rose to tend to the injured passer-by after the emergency services had been contacted. Three days later Edith collapsed in the shop, probably a delayed reaction to the accident. The injured person was a stranger and it is not known how serious her injuries were.

It was an accident waiting to happen in the narrow streets of the town centre which were, at that time, the only available route out of the town for articulated vehicles and coaches full of tourists on their way back from a day-trip to Dartmoor. It was a problem that was to become more serious over the next 20 years, making Fore Street hazardous for pedestrians and drivers alike.

Another accident, which wiped out a landmark in Buckfastleigh, was the fire that destroyed the Salmon Leap Café at Dartbridge in August 1975. Suzanne Manley remembered watching the café by the River Dart, with its 'olde worlde' charm and thatched roof, go up in flames:

My grandparents owned the land on the other side of Totnes Road down to the River Dart and so we were watching the flames from there. It was a chilling experience. The flames were burning fiercely but everything was silent.

Both Cott Orchard and the Salmon Leap Café were an established part of Buckfastleigh. Cott Orchard was originally a country house with stables and a swimming-pool. The Salmon Leap Café was owned by the Watsons who offered bed-and-breakfast accommodation at a reasonable price and ran a successful tearoom specialising in cream teas in the daytime and salmon fish dinners in the evening. The fish were caught at the weir further along towards Austins Bridge by fishermen who often stayed at the Salmon Leap Café.

With the Cott Orchard Tearooms developing successfully, Furzeleigh Mill guest-house and restaurant nearby on the Ashburton Road (the old A38), and the Salmon Leap Café by the River Dart between the two, local people and visitors to the area were well served. There was one café missing, however, and that was the popular Dartbridge Tearooms on the corner of Buckfast Road, opposite Dartbridge Manor, which had closed earlier. The author recalled the fresh smell of the café and the ice-creams they sold – a treat to look forward to on a walk to Buckfast.

Cott Orchard was renamed the Dartbridge Inn during the period that the Devon Expressway was built and at the time of writing, where the Salmon Leap Café stood before it burnt down, the Little Chef restaurant stands. It serves motorists and their passengers who have driven off the dual carriageway for a break.

Derek Moore reflected:

There was quite an influx of people into Buckfastleigh in the '70s. Many were elderly couples who had moved down here from the North leaving their families behind. When one of the couple died the other was left isolated.

Oaklands Park, which was newly built, was one of the estates on which you could buy a place cheaply, and buying your own home was becoming the thing to do.

Left: *Dartbridge Tearooms, c.1950s.*

Right: *The CWS wool lorry accident outside Barnes' bakery in Fore Street, 1975. The force of the bales of wool pushed the baker's van down the road.*

Left: *Buckfastleigh's drum majorettes, 1974.*

Right: *Buckfastleigh Fire Service, 1976.*

THE 1970S: REORGANISATION AND DETERIORATION

But prices zoomed right up, I know one place which was bought for £5,000 and sold within three months for £10,000. So there was this great shift in population at Oaklands. Many people came from the London area but decided after six months or a year that they had made a mistake.

The third major change to affect the town was local government reorganisation. Margaret Foot recalled:

Everything changed overnight when local government reorganised in 1974. At the beginning of April Buckfastleigh Urban District Council closed on the Friday night and on the following Monday the town came under Teignbridge District Council. It was a massive shift as there was no gradual change over. Staff from Teignbridge came out to Buckfastleigh and picked up the account books we were working on and we never saw the books again. Then they would ring us up to say – what was this and what was that? Can you remember where that's gone and what does this mean? It was 12 months of aggravation.

When Teignbridge took over there were no plans. It was all in the heads of local people. Buckfastleigh went from having a local authority who knew the area well to a vast authority which had no records about Buckfastleigh and didn't know it well at all.

Buckfastleigh was not the only town which lost its autonomy. There was local government reorganisation all over the country. Mike Tolchard remembered the period:

I served on Buckfastleigh Urban District Council from 1969 until the local government reorganisation in 1974. There was Sid Goffin, Revd John Timms, 'Bud' Thompson the headmaster, Bill Rucker the chemist, Dr Michael Wigram, John Willcocks, Eric Pinney, Miss Axford, John West, Ken Setters and Clarence Northcott. It was an interesting time because we went from being autonomous Urban District Council to being under a council where we had little autonomy.

Under the old system you had 12 people who used to walk around the town and who could be buttonholed by local people so that they could complain to us or inform us about something. Once I was stopped because the rates had gone up by a halfpenny! Everyone had easy access to BUDC.

Leslie Lane, who was foreman of the BUDC workforce, used to walk every footpath once a year to see what needed doing. We had our own workforce and if they weren't collecting rubbish they would be doing something else!

Margaret Foot, who worked for BUDC, agreed:

We ran a good water supply to the town. Leslie Lane would go and turn it off at night so there was never a water shortage then. There was more of a personal, hands-on approach to caring for Buckfastleigh.

Mike Tolchard continued:

In the old days BUDC was responsible for practically everything – the sewage works, the rubbish collection, public footpaths, most things in fact. With reorganisation we became a Town Council. I served on the Town Council until 1977 when I resigned for personal reasons, having moved away from Buckfastleigh for a short period of time.

Betty Northcote worked for the council from 1969–92:

I have seen a lot of changes. When I first started Mr Stokes was the Town Clerk and we came under BUDC. That was in 1969 and I was responsible for the rents and the housing side. Then I went full-time and worked with Margaret Foot.

Margaret and I were given the chance to organise and run the elections at Buckfast. Margaret was in charge and I was poll clerk. You met so many people – and, of course, we knew everyone. Margaret used to say that when we worked in the Town Hall we knew everybody in the town.

We used to enjoy the elections for BUDC. There were just three of us running things: Eric Midgley, Margaret and myself. We would set out the booth – get everything set up, put up the posters advising people what to do, and then I would do the marking off on the register and Margaret would do the stamping. People used to crowd outside the Town Hall, so many that they had to let them in a few at a time. All the candidates would be up at the Town Hall and everyone would be going for the candidates – there was a real sense of community then. Elections used to finish at 10p.m. and after that we would have to fill out the forms and take the results into Totnes, often not getting back until 11.

'It made a difference when we had our own council,' said Marian Harvey. 'We used to wait outside the Town Hall after the elections had finished until 11 or 12 at night waiting for the results.' Betty Northcote recalled:

After the reorganisation of local government came in 1974 there was a vacancy for Town Clerk in the Buckfastleigh office and, being so familiar with the work, I applied for it and got the post. I started in May 1974. Dr Wildman was the medical officer of health at the time and I combined a part-time job working for him with the job as Town Clerk.

Then Dr Wildman retired and I continued with the Town Clerk post. There were a lot of business people on the Town Council. I think you need people like that with local knowledge. They were all good councillors.

Stuart Barker, former Town Mayor, added:

Right: *In 1977/8 the BBC came to Buckfastleigh to film a scene from the television drama* A Horseman Riding By, *by R.F. Delderfield. This photograph shows the action taking place in Chapel Street.*

Mr Jim Searle, 1941.

Above: *The filming of* A Horseman Riding By, *outside the mill office in Chapel Street, 1977/8.*

Left: *Chapel Street appears crowded in this view of the BBC's visit to Buckfastleigh in 1977/8.*

THE 1970S: REORGANISATION AND DETERIORATION

The Local Government Act of 1974 changed the status of the Urban District Councils. Buckfastleigh lost its status and was swallowed up into a District Council. Before then all Buckfastleigh's greatest benefactors were Town Councillors and the council was made up of churchmen, businessmen, eminent dignitaries and factory managers – they all had a genuine interest in the welfare of the town. Then that power base was taken away. I believe they thought the District Council would be as great a benefactor as they had been but it wasn't. Local people lost the will to get involved in any decision-making and lost the will to be an influence. Those on the newly-formed Town Council thought that all they had to do was to write to the District Council and make recommendations and things would get changed – and, of course, they weren't.

Mr Jim Elliott.

The situation in Buckfastleigh deteriorated over the next six years and into the next decade with little or no investment. Mary Blair commented:

As far as the traders were concerned the downfall came when Cash-and-Carry started about 1974 and people started to use other people's discount cards to get goods from Cash-and-Carry. Local customers who used to come into my shop and those of other traders every day now started to come in once a week because they had borrowed a friend's card and had gone shopping at Cash-and-Carry.

When Frank left his business we could see the writing on the wall. Gradually the local traders sold out because they could see what was happening as large supermarkets had already opened and in about 1975 the Traders' Association disintegrated.

Jim Searle, who owned J. Searle & Sons Electricians, was the chairman of the Buckfastleigh Traders' Association in the early 1970s:

We used to have regular meetings and we tried to encourage traders to look after their shop fronts and improve their appearance. Compared to today trade had been very good but the large supermarkets eventually saw the demise of local trade.

In 1972 the Congregational Church in England and the Presbyterian Church of England had combined to become the United Reformed Church. Eventually the local Congregational church ceased to be and the few remaining members joined with Buckfastleigh Methodist Church to form the Methodist and United Reformed Church of Buckfastleigh.

It was a sad day when the Congregational church closed but in 1975 it was reopened as the John Loosemore Centre for Organ and Early Music by John Wellingham, an organ teacher from Dartington Hall, and Bill Drake an organ builder. It was a positive and fruitful partnership that added a new dimension to the town and placed Buckfastleigh on the map for musicians and organ builders on the Continent.

One event which helped to distract local people from their concerns was the filming, in 1977/78, of the BBC television production *A Horseman Riding By*, from the book by R.F. Delderfield, starring Nigel Havers. The old mill office in Chapel Street, now replaced by the Hamlyn's Way flats, was decorated with bunting and used by the actors as a political party headquarters for a scene in the play.

In 1979 Hapstead House, originally owned by the Hamlyns and after the war run as a convalescent home for children by the Markuses, and then as a children's home by the Devonports, became home for the Camphill Devon Community for adults in special need of care, including those with Down's Syndrome.

The first Camphill Community was founded in 1939 by a group of people which included Dr Karl Konig, a paediatrician from Vienna, and was based on the principles of Rudolph Steiner. Eventually, the need arose to develop adult communities. The first one opened in North Yorkshire and was followed by others in different parts of the UK, including Devon; the community in Buckfastleigh started in 1979. It was a learning experience for both the villagers at Camphill and the townspeople of Buckfastleigh – an experience that benefited all, as the next 30 years were to prove.

Surrounded by rivers, parts of Buckfastleigh were still vulnerable to flooding and in December 1979 more than 70 properties were flooded. But like everything else local people weathered the storms.

By this point, however, a new national leader had emerged who was determined that Britain should do more than 'just weather the storms!' On 4 May 1979 Margaret Thatcher became prime minister.

Bossell House Hotel.

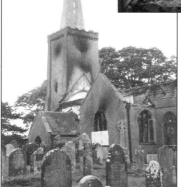

Top, above, left and right: *The ruins of Holy Trinity Parish Church, 1992. The 800-year-old church was destroyed by fire on 21 July 1992.*

Above left and right: *The flower festival at old St Luke's Church, Plymouth Road.*

Fifteen

THE CHURCHES: LOOKING OUT TO THE COMMUNITY

Buckfastleigh's churches have belonged to three main religious traditions over the past 800 years – Roman Catholic, Anglican and Nonconformist (the Methodist and Congregational Church). During the 1990s the town welcomed The Christian Community, which is based in the old YMCA building on the corner of Chapel Street and New Road.

The Parish Church, Holy Trinity, is the oldest church in Buckfastleigh; it was built in Gothic style and dates from the thirteenth century. Now in ruins, but with the spire still intact, it is situated on the outskirts of the town and, to quote from the report by English Heritage to the Parochial Church Council (PCC), it is 'spectacularly sited' high up on the edge of Bulley Cleaves Quarry – with the spire a distinctive landmark as you drive into Buckfastleigh.

Built prior to the Reformation, Holy Trinity is Roman Catholic in origin. The Catholic Church was the State Church and only Christian Church in England and remained so until the early 1500s when Protestantism was developed from Martin Luther's religious reforms in Germany. In 1536 King Henry VIII ordered many monasteries and churches, including Buckfast Abbey, to be destroyed. He banned Catholicism in England and decreed that people should accept Protestantism, basically because the Pope in Rome forbade his divorce from Catherine of Aragon.

Many churches survived the onslaught and were used for Protestant worship. Local worshippers were fortunate that Holy Trinity Church was spared, but it is clear that the building once suffered extensive damage as it has been restored and extended many times over the centuries. Although now in ruins, it is a Grade I listed building and the Cabell tomb is a Grade II listed building.

It was believed that the spire was an addition which was made towards the end of the sixteenth century. The church register dates from 1602 and the inscription in the interior of the church from 1600. There might well have been a fire in about 1600, which would account for the omission of earlier registers and the later style of architecture in the main body of the church compared to the tower and chancel. In 1793 T. Bilbie of Cullompton, making a peal of seven, recast the five bells in the tower and the bell that was at the Vicarage.

English Heritage recorded that a thorough restoration was made in 1844/45 by John Hayward of Exeter, which included new roofing and the upper part of the spire. John Hayward was the leading Gothic revival church architect in the Exeter diocese in the 1840s and 1850s.

The life of Holy Trinity came to a dramatic conclusion in 1992 when it was burnt down. The fire that razed the 800-year-old church took place on the night of 21 July 1992. Police confirmed that it was arson and there were suggestions that it was the work of Satanists because of previous incidents in the church and the fact that the fire was ignited near the altar, although this idea was never proven. The fire began just after midnight and smouldered for several hours before becoming an inferno.

It was a devastating shock, not only to Revd Paul Wilson, the vicar of Buckfastleigh at that time, John Irwin, the curate, and the parishioners, but also to the whole town. Many local firefighters attending the scene had either been married in the Parish Church, or their children had been christened there, and they were equally devastated.

Paul Wilson told journalists that nothing had been stolen '… and the safe holding valuable chalices and parish documents was still intact when it was salvaged.' Paul Wilson and the PCC were determined to rebuild immediately and plans to build an ecumenical church on the site of Holy Trinity Church with the £1,228,000 received from insurances were discussed by the PCC – it was not to be.

The Church of St Luke's once stood in Plymouth Road in the centre of Buckfastleigh. Even in the 1850s it was recognised that the remote situation of the Parish Church was a drawback. In fact, many of the evening services were held in the National Schoolroom in Chapel Street. In 1858 a decision was taken to build a smaller church in a central position but, being unable to achieve the funding target, the plans had to be dropped and the contributions returned to their subscribers.

Buckfastleigh's new vicar, recognising that the town still needed a centrally-placed church, reopened the building fund on 27 May 1892. The church was built within two years and on 22 October 1894 the Bishop of Exeter dedicated St Luke's.

During the 1960s major changes were made to the back of St Luke's as part of its outreach to the community. It had been agreed that an association be formed to administer money and it was named after Dr Michael Wigram, a well-loved local doctor who had died some years earlier. The project was started in January 1980 by the then churchwarden, John Berry. Within a week he himself had died and his widow, Elizabeth Berry, and the curate, Revd Eric Jones, were asked by the PCC to continue the work.

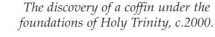

The discovery of a coffin under the foundations of Holy Trinity, c.2000.

The changes included the provision of a kitchen and lavatories which made the church more suitable for public use, such as for coffee mornings where people could meet on a Thursday after shopping in the town. At the time of writing the Wigram Community Association was chaired by John Giles whose father was one of the benefactors.

The second development of St Luke's arose from a proposal made by churchwarden Ivor Thorning to the incumbent vicar, the Rt Revd Steele Perkins, and the PCC for a day-care centre for the elderly and infirm in Buckfastleigh. It was agreed that the rear of the church might be made suitable for this purpose and, in 1989, Ivor Thorning reported the formation of a steering committee to organise the opening of the centre for up to 12 elderly disabled people. A bank account had been opened with £500 from the social services and on Monday 15 January 1990 the centre opened with a further donation of £1,000 from Age Concern. Help was given by willing volunteers who were, in turn, supported by people who could provide professional guidance.

The history and development of St Luke's Church is chronicled by the writer Helen Harris in her book, *The History of St Luke's Church in Buckfastleigh*. What Helen and the parishioners could not foresee was that within a few years of the book being completed St Luke's Church would also be demolished.

There was great concern about the future of the Anglican Church in the town following the destruction of the Parish Church. It was upon the incumbent at the time of writing, Revd John Rowland, that the burden of decision-making fell. John was a Devonian who was born at Elburton, just outside Plymouth, where his father and grandfather had been market gardeners.

John, his wife Penny and their children had been attached to a church with a community centre in an inner-city parish in Liverpool for seven years. It had been a difficult environment in which to live and they finally decided they wanted to come back to their roots. They looked at a church in Cornwall and two in Devon – one of which was in Buckfastleigh. John explained:

We came to Buckfastleigh knowing the situation. We knew that the future had to be sorted out one way or another. So, after six months in the job we started to tackle it. It became very clear that it was not going to be practical to rebuild Holy Trinity. Very few parishioners attended the church and if it had not been burnt down it would have been closed by now – and the Anglican Church could not afford to keep two buildings going.

John Gill, former churchwarden, said:

After the fire in 1992 a survey was carried out at the Parish Church. An ultra scan was used and they discovered the foundations of the original church at the east end of the church – exactly where they wanted to rebuild. To the left of where the altar was before the church burnt down a tomb was found with lead-lined coffins containing three adult bodies and one child. The tomb was right under a loose paving stone. Of course, nothing could be disturbed so we could not rebuild.

I was all for something being built up there even if it was only [that] the east end could be covered in. But I guess the site is too vulnerable up there on the hill and it is too far away from town.

John Rowland continued discussions with the PCC:

There were two options, one was to renovate St Luke's Church in the centre of the town, the other to demolish it. One of the key issues was that we were able to buy the land from David Eales, the undertaker, at the back of the church. The PCC had a meeting and it was agreed that the decision about St Luke's had to be made by the worshipping community and not by the town. After much discussion it was agreed to demolish and rebuild. Then the question of design arose which had to be agreed with the Dartmoor National Park Authority.

We had many meetings together. Finally, at a meeting in Exeter, the chairman said, 'I think we have deliberated about it enough, we need to make a decision' – and they passed it. I remember standing up and saying 'Hallelujah! This deserves a hallelujah!' There was some humour in the situation.

THE CHURCHES: LOOKING OUT TO THE COMMUNITY

Many local people, including some members of St Luke's, were devastated by the decision to demolish the original church, especially since the town had also lost Holy Trinity. By the middle of the twenty-first century there will be few people left who remember either of the churches. A large part of the town's church history will have disappeared.

St Luke's has now been demolished and in its place stands a new church with a very modern hexagonal shape. It is hoped that the new building, also named St Luke's, will be well used by local people in the twenty-first century. It has been designed with the varying needs of the community in mind.

Architect Ronald Weeks, who grew up in Bossell Road, Buckfastleigh, designed the new church. His parents were Fred and May Weeks, who were well known in the town. Encouraged by Revd John Timms, Ron studied architecture at the Bartlett School of Architecture in London for five years in the early 1950s and then, in 1959, he won a scholarship to study at the Ecole Nationale Superieur Des Beaux Arts in the centre of Paris, receiving a grant from the French government. Ron is chairman of a leading London firm, the Percy Thomas Partnership.

When Holy Trinity Church was destroyed by fire Ron wrote to the incumbent at the time, Paul Wilson, offering his services. At their next meeting the PCC discussed the letter Ron had sent them and later Paul telephoned Ron inviting him to meet with the PCC:

They said, 'Come down to see us.' And I did. Of course, Bill Selley was head boy in the choir when I last saw him! I gave them a talk with slides about modern churches around the world and then there was a great meeting of the church. It was packed at that first meeting with people standing up and saying, 'Yes, we need to rebuild.' Then we started talking about whether we should do something at the Holy Trinity site or whether we should do something at St Luke's or a combination of the two.

Finally, the PCC took the momentous decision to knock down St Luke's and I don't think we realised how momentous that decision was. That is how I came to design the new church.

As a result of the desire of worshippers to be able to sit nearer to the altar table the new St Luke's is a hexagonal shape like the Catholic cathedral in Bristol, which Ron designed. The font now stands on an old column from Holy Trinity Church, which is on the same grid line as all the columns in the church, and some of the stained-glass windows from the old St Luke's enhance the prayer chapel.

The Bishop of Exeter, the Rt Revd Michael Langrish, consecrated the new St Luke's on Sunday 13 October 2002. The very wet and dismal day did not dampen the joyous atmosphere of the occasion, nor the thrill for John Rowland that St Luke's was open again.

The Church has always had an important part to play in society and, in smaller communities like Buckfastleigh, it has certainly played a lively role. Even those who are not regular churchgoers recognise the church's function in drawing people together for special occasions, such as weddings and funerals, and for special days such as Remembrance Sunday. All important landmarks in daily life.

Of course, to those who have a strong faith in God, the church is more than that. Revd John Irwin, curate of St Luke's Church, explained that the visible Church consists of a community founded on faith in Jesus Christ, which does what it believes He wants it to do. Public worship is part of that. John explained:

I never see the church just as an asset to the town – that is not its role. The essence of being a Christian is living a Christian life and those who try are drawn together. If you have something very important in your life you want to share it and this is what Christians should be doing: sharing their Good News. To see the Church as a social benefactor is not its primary role, but the care for the community comes as a result of this sharing.

I was born in Oxfordshire but my mother was a Devonian and, after my father's death, [we] wanted to come home. We saw a flat advertised in The Church Times *– it was in Dean Prior Vicarage, so we took it. Sadly, my mother had cancer and only lived for six months after we moved. I gave up the flat but stayed on as a lodger for a while as a member of what was a little religious community. Such happy days!*

I was a churchwarden up at Dean Prior Church for a number of years. On the retirement of the last vicar of Dean, John Timms, the incumbent of Buckfastleigh, became vicar of Buckfastleigh and Dean. Dean is a separate parish but now within the one benefice.

In 1988, while working at Moorhaven Hospital as a psychiatric nurse, I was ordained a non-stipendiary minister in secular employment to serve the two parishes. In his interview the Bishop laid down priorities, 'Your first priority is your family, the second is your job and the third is this ministry.'

I did not have opportunity to do much while still in full-time secular employment, but this increased on retirement in 1992. Now alone, I could do much more were it not for the passing of the years.

Sue Irwin, John's wife, was a very able person and greatly respected in Buckfastleigh. John met her when she travelled to Totnes High School (now KEVICC) by bus when she was 15. After she left school Sue went to Avery Hill College to train as a teacher and it was during this period that their friendship blossomed and they married after Sue finished college in August 1964.

After she married she taught for six years at Ipplepen, leaving when she was expecting her son,

Left: *A Merrie Meeting at the Methodist church, c.1900.*

Right: *A presentation was made to Revd Twiston Williams outside the Methodist manse, Bossell Road, c.1900.*

Left: *Revd Balch preaching at the Methodist church harvest festival, c.1910.*

Right: *Alfred Arscott and Fred Chivell at the Methodist Church harvest festival, 1910.*

THE CHURCHES: LOOKING OUT TO THE COMMUNITY

Jeremy. Then she started working at Buckfastleigh School, firstly as a volunteer mum, then a dinner lady and then a classroom assistant, all the while looking after Jeremy. John remembered:

Finally, Mr Shinner, the head teacher, persuaded her to be a supply teacher. Eventually, he persuaded her to go full time and she worked for four years as a teacher. She retired early on health grounds.

Sue Irwin was active in the Church, especially as a Sunday school teacher. She and four other people were the original founders of Action Research and put a tremendous amount into the organisation. For the last 18 months of her life, Sue was also a member of the Town Council. Sue died suddenly in 1999 leaving not only John, her son Jeremy and Mary, her daughter, bereft, but also local townsfolk as well. The church was overflowing with people at her funeral service, many of them children, all wanting to say goodbye to a lady who always had time to help people and had been 'a force to reckon with' in the community.

Dom Gabriel Arnold is the parish priest for the Roman Catholic Church of St Benedict's in Chapel Street, which was built in 1939, just before the Second World War. Father Gabriel said that he did not know why St Benedict's, built by Hoskins the builders, was built with Buckfast Abbey in such close proximity. However, the Roman Catholic Church was in an expanding mode at the time with the Abbey itself having been completed less than a year before. Father Gabriel had been unable to trace any records, letters or papers relating to the building other than the tenders for constructing the church, none of which were over £2,000. However there is a plaque in St Benedict's with the words:

In Grateful Memory of
EDITH CHARLOTTE HAMILTON
(Née MILDMAY) to whose zeal and generosity was due the undertaking of this House of God in 1939
R.I.P

Buckfast Abbey was re-established in 1882 on the site of an old monastery and the rebuilding of the church by the monks began in 1907.

The Roman Catholic parish of Buckfastleigh includes Bickington, Ashburton, South Brent, Buckfast and Buckfastleigh, all along the A38. There are churches in Ashburton, Buckfast (St Mary's Abbey), Buckfastleigh and South Brent, each with their own priest in charge. 'We are supposed to be one Catholic community,' commented Father Gabriel, 'but all the communities are separate.'

In 1947 Father Gabriel came to Buckfastleigh to join the monastery of the Buckfast Abbey Community. In the late 1980s he was seconded by the Abbot to the Plymouth diocese to be at the disposal of the Bishop of Plymouth. He recalled:

To all intents and purposes I practically ceased to live the monastic life as I was involved in working with the parishes, returning to the Abbey about every six weeks. I went to help the Bishop for about four months but continued working for him for ten years. I was doing short-term work in various parishes throughout the Plymouth diocese, which covers Cornwall, Devon and Dorset. Sometimes I stayed in a parish for a few weeks, sometimes I stayed for a few years.

Some years ago Abbot David turned up on my doorstep in Tavistock where I was parish priest at the time and asked me to come back to Buckfastleigh as parish priest. So I came back to live in the monastery and to be in charge of the parish of Buckfastleigh where I knew some people. I have been a parish priest here for over five years.

Buckfastleigh is quiet by comparison with other places. But I am only part-time parish priest. The rest of the time I do my monk thing.

St Benedict's has about 30 church members and it is not self-sufficient. If it wasn't for the Abbey subsidising St Benedict's we could not maintain it. The Abbey also subsidises the Ashburton and South Brent churches. If there weren't local churches worshippers would have to go to Ivybridge or Totnes – there would be no parish at all without Buckfast Abbey.

The rule is that a good Catholic must go to Mass on Sunday. Both the laity and clergy have been brought up within a very hierarchical, very clergy-dominated Church and it is difficult to change a tradition that has been going on for centuries.

We depend upon those who move into the town to build up our congregation, but it is a very fluid congregation. The Roman Catholic Church is traditional in its worship. We don't have extempore prayer! I wonder if our characters and personalities decide for us which church we shall join? Our prayers are short and sharp. We pray for this one day and for something else the next day and so on. It is like sending a telegram to the Lord.

Spontaneous, or extempore, prayer is, of course, an aspect of worship very familiar to those who belong to the Methodist tradition of worship. The founder of the Methodist Church was John Wesley who, with his brother Charles, started what could be called a 'spiritual revolution'. John and Charles had been meeting for prayer, worship and Christian service with other Protestant Christians at Oxford University where they were studying in 1729. Other students called them 'the Holy Club', or 'Methodists', referring to the methodical way they carried out the rituals and duties that they considered were required of them, and the name stuck.

John and Charles, a hymn writer, were sons of an Anglican rector. Dismayed by the attitude of the day within the Church and the social conditions that prevailed among the working classes, John Wesley travelled around the countryside on horseback, often in the West Country, where he preached to the working classes in particular. He visited Ashburton in August 1776 when he recorded in his diary:

In the evening I preached in the street at Ashburton. Many behaved with decency; but the rest, with such stupid rudeness as I had not seen, for a long time, in any part of England.

One wonders what John Wesley thought of Buckfastleigh for, as Revd Dr David Hardy the Superintendent Minister for the Totnes Methodist Circuit (of which Buckfastleigh is part) says, 'John Wesley must have passed through Buckfastleigh as there was no bypass around the town as there is now.' Even if John Wesley merely passed by his influence was still strong, as two Methodist churches existed before the present one was built in 1835. The first Methodists in the town met in a small building where Orchard Terrace ends and Hamlyn's Way begins – a building that eventually became the mill office before that too was knocked down to make way for the building of Hamlyn's Way.

'The Ham', the land on which the present church was built, was sold by Joseph Hamlyn to William Tucker, the Superintendent Minister at that time, Revd John Worden of Ashburton, and others – most of whom were from Buckfastleigh. Revd Dr David Hardy pointed out in his booklet *A Short History of the Present Church from 1835–1997* that it is interesting to note the occupations of the other Buckfastleigh signatories with William Tucker and Revd John Worden. They include Walter Soper (serge maker), Edward Reed (miller), John Barns (paper maker) John Petherick (paper maker), John Furneaux (yeoman), John Shapter (draper), Joseph Hamlyn the younger (tanner), James Tozer (cordwainer) and Richard Butchers (cordwainer). The price of the land? £45.

Methodist properties are controlled by a trust and at that time all Methodist churches had their trustees appointed. It was their responsibility to ensure the smooth running and the maintenance of the building. Most probably the original trustees were those who were involved with the purchase of the land. Today the responsibility lies with the Church Council.

It is interesting to look back on the development of the Methodist church in Buckfastleigh, which in 1913 had a Sunday school of 200 children. It has a large and spacious interior with a gallery above the main seating area of the church that indicates a congregation which was probably full to overflowing in the very early days. Naturally this has to be put in context of the times when going to church was very important for most people. Local benefactors, including members of the Hamlyn family, were regular churchgoers during a period when it was customary to rent the pew in which you sat each Sunday. This not only brought in regular income but also ensured that no one else sat in 'your' seat!

Joan Gill from Jordan Street, who was brought up as a Methodist, remembered that even during the 1930s where you sat in church reflected which part of town you came from. If you lived in Higher Town – Jordan Street, Market Street and Bridge Street – you sat on the left-hand side of the church, which was nearest to Higher Town, and if you came from Lower Town – Chapel Street or Fore Street – you sat on the right-hand side, which was the Lower Town side!

Methodism is built upon the participation and involvement of qualified lay preachers under the leadership of the minister of a church. Each church belongs to a circuit and in 1803 Buckfastleigh Methodist Church was part of the Ashburton Wesleyan Methodist Circuit that included the oversight and support of Methodist churches in surrounding towns and villages.

Since then there have been many changes. In 1956 two new circuits were set up, one of which was the Buckfastleigh Circuit. Buckfastleigh took over the responsibility for many Methodist churches including Totnes, Harbertonford, Cornworthy, Ashburton, Woolston Green, Broadhempston, South Brent, Poundsgate, Scoriton and Buckfast.

Buckfastleigh Methodist Church has always been lively with keen and committed membership assuming various responsibilities including work with children and young people. Music has always played an important part in its life with special musical concerts being given on Good Fridays, even as far back as the 1930s.

The contribution to the town through its music was at its height when Revd Leslie Hayes was the incumbent minister from 1951–60. Violet Hayes, Leslie's wife, had been a professional pianist before her marriage and under her influence Buckfastleigh's Methodist church choir and that at Ashburton, together with guest soloists and some members of the Congregational church choir, gave mighty renditions of oratorios such as Handel's *Messiah*, *The Creation* or *Elijah* each year on Good Friday.

After the special afternoon Good Friday service there followed a Faith Tea in the schoolroom beneath the church. Then, in the evening, the whole town turned out to hear the choir's performance and the church was always packed.

Laura Harris came to live in Buckfastleigh in 1949 after her marriage to Stanley Harris. Stanley was a staunch Methodist and Laura gave herself wholeheartedly to the church and its activities:

I was in the choir and what an excellent choir it was too. I played the piano for the Sunday school, the Women's Fellowship meetings and the Girls' Brigade, which was formed in Revd Chamberlain's time (1948–51). Unfortunately, the Girls' Brigade ended when the

THE CHURCHES: LOOKING OUT TO THE COMMUNITY

Chamberlains left Buckfastleigh. I enjoyed the harvest festival suppers and, of course, the oratorios the choir gave on Good Friday. The Easter oratorios were quite an event. The service at 4p.m., the tea at 5p.m. and the performance at 7p.m. People like to look back on those days because it has all gone now. I enjoyed it all, even pastoral visiting.

Several social evenings were held in our church. There were enough young people in the church at that time who were the right age group to do these things. You miss those people now and everything was so well organised. We had a youth club, a children's club and a fellowship group in addition to the Sunday school. There was something for everyone to be involved in.

Laura and Stanley's son, David Harris, was also very much involved with the Methodist church. In 2003 David was the main organist and over the years has been called on countless times to play for other Methodist church services around the area and for the Anglicans and Buckfast Abbey.

Laura and David are communion stewards, which involves the preparation of the bread and wine for communion service. 'It is a great honour to be asked to do this job in the church,' said Laura. She continued:

Life has changed so much. I think the television has got a lot to do with the change in family life. Years ago you could feel it was a Sunday. There were fewer cars and life was quieter – there were no shops open on a Sunday. And when you organised events everyone supported you and turned up! All the parents came out for Sunday school anniversaries.

Another aspect I enjoyed was entertaining. I got a thrill entertaining visiting local preachers (lay preachers) and ministers. They would come to lunch after the morning service and you did what you would do for your own family – and after that they would usually just want to sit and be quiet, especially if they had another service in the evening.

In 1990 Idwal Williams, who had just retired and was a circuit steward for the Portadown Circuit, one of the largest circuits in Northern Ireland, applied for a position as lay pastoral assistant for what is now called Buckfastleigh Methodist and URC Church:

My wife became ill and wanted to retire to Devon where she grew up. When the vacancy arose for a lay pastoral assistant I immediately applied for it and was offered the position. So my family and I came to Buckfastleigh in 1990.

Revd Peggy Hiscock, the first lady minister at Buckfastleigh Methodist Church, with Adrian Dawe, c.1980.

As a lay pastor, Idwal was responsible for covering Buckfastleigh, Buckfast, South Brent and Scoriton. Buckfastleigh no longer had its own minister and was not the main church in the circuit. Numbers had declined and one minister, then based in Exeter, was responsible for all the churches in what is now the Totnes Circuit and includes Totnes, Cornworthy, Harbertonford, Buckfastleigh, Buckfast, South Brent, Scoriton and Woolston Green.

Idwal's contract ended in 1993, a year after his wife's death, and he decided he wanted to stay in the town:

I liked Buckfastleigh and the people. I had got to know everybody and they had got to know me. I was called 'vicar' on several occasions – even though I am a lay person. I was still conducting baptisms, weddings and funerals because the minister responsible for the church then lived near Exeter. The only thing a lay person cannot do is celebrate Holy Communion.

At the beginning of the '90s the impression I received of Buckfastleigh was of a run-down place but local people were very helpful and they were looking forward to the time when it might be improved – and, of course, it has now.

The Church here is quite different than in Northern Ireland where it is still the done thing to go to church on a Sunday and there are large congregations. Here the congregation was much smaller when I first came, and an elderly one too, with no children which surprised me. But we accepted it and worked from there.

Twelve years later there has been a tremendous growth – one doesn't expect it quickly and the work put in by previous ministers over the years, and the current minister, Revd Dr David Hardy, has begun to bear fruit. We have had several new members coming into the church, too, who have worked extremely hard and that has resulted in many changes for the better, including a children's club and a Sunday club, which is run by Jill Elliott supported by other members of the church, a music group, which is coordinated by David Harris and Rachel Ellacott, herself an organist, and a regular coffee morning which is very popular with local people. The coffee morning was established initially to raise funds for our church's restructuring of the building but has become an established part of our weekly activities.

I feel that all the churches in the town are looking out towards the community so much more than when I arrived 12 years ago. This is reflected in the rebuilding that the Anglican Church has undertaken and what the Methodist and URC Church has done with its building to make it more inviting and easily accessible to local people.

The roots of the Congregational Church, the oldest Nonconformist sect, were founded in the sixteenth century. Its belief that the Church should be independent of ecclesiastical authority and that the only head of the Church is Jesus Christ brought them into conflict with the newly established Church of England which had become the State Church after Henry VIII broke with the Roman Catholic Church. An Act passed in 1592, 'for the punishment of those obstinately refusing to come to church' (and largely designed for the punishment of this sect), allowed for the hanging of two founder members, Henry Barrow and John Greenwood, at Tyburn.

The conflict between the Protestant Church of England and the 'Independents' as the Congregationalists, Baptists and Presbyterians were called, resulted in believers fleeing to Holland and joining other persecuted Christian sects on the *Mayflower* for the voyage to America in 1620.

In 1682, in the reign of Charles II, an Act of Parliament was passed called the Act of Uniformity, which compelled clergymen to announce that they firmly believed in the contents of *The Book of Common Prayer*. As many as 2,000 clergymen were deprived of their living and reduced to poverty because they would not agree to do this.

One of them was Revd Richard Bickle, the rector of Wembley, who preached at various places in the area. He captured the interest of Samuel Cabell of Brook Manor, brother to the third Richard Cabell (1622–72), who gave him leave to preach in the 'Cheape' House, the market house that once stood in Market Street adjacent to the bridge. Eventually Richard Bickle became the first Congregational minister in Buckfastleigh. It is surprising that he gained the support of Samuel Cabell as the family were staunch Protestants and persecuted Nonconformists.

The unsettled state of the times and the revolt of the Duke of Monmouth that brought so much suffering to the West Country had its effect on Christian worship generally. After the death of Mr Bickle the Independent Congregationalists' numbers were so low that the few remaining members travelled to Ashburton, where there was a small worshipping group that existed under the strong leadership of local merchants.

The baptismal records of the Independent (Congregational) Church in Buckfastleigh start from 1787, and in the 1851 religious census it is recorded that the Independents founded Higher Chapel in 1787. This might refer to premises in Higher Town but, in 1798, a tenement building standing on waste ground was purchased from William Cole, a serge maker, for £90 which, in time, became known as Chapel House. Most probably it was sometime after 1798 that the street in which the chapel was situated became known as Chapel Street.

The trustees appointed were William Fabyan, John Berry, Peter Sharke, Philip Wotton, John Hurst and Roger Maunder of Ashburton, Thomas Cewney, Stephen Searle, William Hall, John Ireland and William Baston.

The Congregational Sunday school was extant in 1830 and, in 1837, a school for girls opened in the schoolroom, 'the young females of the said school to be taught spelling, reading, sewing, knitting and catechism and attendance from four to eight pm.'

The foundation-stone of the present building was laid by Mr Hubbard of Plymouth on Whit Monday 1872 and an agreement was signed between Frederick Weeks, a Buckfastleigh builder, and Andrew Warren (senr), John Warren, Thomas Hunt, Christopher Warren, Andrew Warren (junr) and Robert Chaffe (senr).

In 1972, 100 years later, the Congregational Church in England and Wales and the Presbyterian Church of England decided to unite to form the United Reformed Church (URC) – some individual churches opted out and many Congregationalists joined the Congregational Federation.

The Congregational Church in Buckfastleigh had been active until the 1960s. Finally, however, the numbers dwindled until the remaining members were unable to support their own minister. In 1975 they closed their building and the remaining members opted to join with the Methodists on the other side of the street so that the Methodist Church became the Buckfastleigh Methodist and United Reformed Church.

The late Ann Klemm, the pastor of The Christian Community in Buckfastleigh, spoke not long before her death about how The Christian Community started and how they came to be based in Buckfastleigh. She described how, after the First World War, the young people in Germany felt that there was something missing from their faith and needed to find answers to the questions that other young Germans were asking. The questions may have reflected the unease and uncertainty felt by many during the political and social turmoil following the First World War – there were issues they definitely needed to confront as Christians and they came together to explore their faith.

These young people wanted to bring about something new that would speak to people of today and were helped in this by Rudolph Steiner, who gave them advice through a series of lectures and discussions. Those who heard him were inspired by his thoughts but were hindered from putting his suggestions into practice within their respective churches. So they gathered as many people as they could to start an independent movement. This was quite a task in a time of hyper-inflation and severe economic difficulties in Germany, but finally 'The Christian Community Movement for Religious Renewal' was founded in Dornach in Switzerland in 1922.

The Methodist and Congregational church in Chapel Street, c.1900.

There were a good number of Catholics among those early supporters, but the majority came from the Lutheran Church. The group were surprised when Rudolph Steiner said that true renewal of Christianity would mean a renewal of the sacraments. He also considered it important that both men and women would be accepted equally into the priesthood. So, right from the beginning, both men and women, married or single, could be ordained. The sacraments were retained in their seven-foldness but in a renewed form for the twentieth and twenty-first century.

The Christian Community was founded in England in 1929 by two members from Germany but grew very slowly. There were also branches in Prague, Norway, Sweden, Holland and France. The movement was banned in Germany during the Second World War, but in England The Christian Community was allowed to carry on and spread to other centres in due course.

One congregation was based in Bristol and a house was bequeathed to them by a man from Chawley who was very interested in the movement. The Bristol group sold the house and bought one in Exeter which was run by pastor Elizabeth Roberts for three years, but when a study confirmed that most of those attending Sunday services at Exeter were from the Buckfastleigh area the community decided in 1991 to buy the old YMCA, which was on the market at the time, to use as their base. After some reconstruction the chapel was consecrated in 1992. Ann described the community:

I sometimes feel that this house in Buckfastleigh was waiting for us to come. The building is owned by The Christian Community nationally, we are expected to maintain it. We receive small donations from people and receive a little income from the guest rooms. It works.

Ann was born in America but spent much of her time in Europe after a year in Switzerland when she was four. She spoke German, French and Italian fluently and had a degree in German and History of Art. Having previously spent two years in Germany she returned when she was 22 and worked there for her doctorate in History of Art.

Certainly the rooms in The Christian Community Centre are spacious, light and peaceful. The colours used for the décor reflect a tranquility that pervades the whole building. Ann felt the Sunday service reflected this:

It is a more meditative kind of service. The main thing you would notice on coming here on a Sunday is that there is not a lot of outward activity amongst the congregation. We do sing songs and we stand up for the gospel reading but that is all that is required outwardly. Newcomers find that the service frees them up as they are not obliged to say anything with which they would feel uncomfortable.

The pastor at the time of writing is Jens-Peter Linde who has worked for many years in the Camphill Communities, and more recently has been pastor of a church in Ireland. Jens-Peter says:

A different way of worship, a different perspective on God, Christianity and the sacraments can be experienced in The Christian Community, but it is not exclusive, the article in the title is part of the name and therefore capitalised. Perhaps one can see it as an all-embracing gesture. The sentence in their creed which refers to this says: 'Communities whose members feel the Christ within themselves may feel united in a church to whom all belong who are aware of the health-bringing power of the Christ.'

Leaders and members of the more established churches may well find it difficult to understand and accept the theology of The Christian Community as they did in Germany in 1922, but today individuals feel more free to worship in the way they want and to believe in a creed that is meaningful to them. Thus it may be very fitting that this movement has found its way here to become part of the rainbow of religious endeavours in Buckfastleigh.

What a wealth of history our churches hold and what fascinating stories emerge of the struggle of men and women over the centuries to be free to express their particular beliefs, and to make the Church's message relevant to a new generation.

But whatever one believes, whether one is a churchgoer or not, John Rowland expressed perfectly why the church is important from the community's perspective when he wrote, in his introduction to the Order of Service for the Consecration of St Luke's, on Sunday 13 October 2002, that: 'In the midst of any community the church stands to remind us that God is interested in our lives.'

Above: *The Co-op annual fête, Molesfield, Barn Park/Crest Hill.*

Left: *Fore Street, Buckfastleigh, early 1920s.*

Below: *Chapel Street, Buckfastleigh, c.1930s.*

Sixteen

THE JOHN LOOSEMORE CENTRE: A ROUNDED EXPERIENCE

When the Congregational church became redundant in the early 1970s it stood empty and forlorn for some time. People passing by probably wondered what would happen to the gracious building now that it was no longer a church. The Congregational Union were determined that it would not become a bingo hall or a supermarket so, when the late Gordon Stone heard that John Wellingham, the head of the organ department at Dartington Hall, and Bill Drake, an organ builder, were looking for somewhere to start an organ centre, he approached Dartington Hall, offering the Congregational church as a venue. John Wellingham explained:

I had been at Dartington Hall since 1960, I went to set up the organ department and to teach. Through another colleague I met Bill Drake who passionately wanted to be an organ builder, and he came to learn how to play the instrument from me before going off to work in Germany. I took a group of students on a visit to Göttingen where Bill was working and, through talks and sharing of ideas, we decided that what we wanted was a centre where people could study with the organ builder and the organ teacher together. So that was where the dream started. We came back to England to talk through ideas and I talked to the Dartington Estate manager who was in charge of buildings. It was through the estate manager that we heard about the approach from Gordon Stone concerning the old Congregational Church building. Bill came back from Germany and he and his mother came over to Buckfastleigh to look at it.

It was a spacious building but it needed a lot doing to it. It needed totally rewiring – the plaster was falling off the walls and, in fact, the walls were even beginning to fall down. It was in a real state.

In spite of the state of the building the two men decided it was perfect. Bill Drake continued:

At the beginning Dartington were the leaseholders of the building with Gareth Keene, the bursar, and Jack Dobbs, head of musical studies, as the main trustees. They were the most appropriate people to be trustees and we sublet from Dartington until the John Loosemore Association, which was formed as a registered charity, bought part and we bought the other part. We had a committee, of course, to oversee the project.

The correct title for the centre is the John Loosemore Centre for Organ and Early Music. It is named after a seventeenth-century Devonian who built an organ, the casework of which still stands in Exeter Cathedral. John Wellingham remembered the early days of the centre:

Right from the start the local community was wonderful and there was always a group of people from Buckfastleigh who supported us throughout the years. We wanted a choir for the opening ceremony at the official opening and we got together a community choir thanks to Father Sebastian at the Abbey, who joined forces with us, and the choir from the Anglican Church. My mother and aunt were Methodists and they went to the Methodist and United Reformed Church on the opposite side of the road. The church members had offered to do the catering for us so, after the official opening in the John Loosemore Centre, we went across to the Methodist and URC Church where we were made to feel so welcome, especially by Stanley, Laura and David Harris (who is an organist like his father).

One of the first things we did was to organise classes for village organists from Dean Prior, Rattery and Buckfastleigh who, without much experience, found themselves in the position of having to play for Sunday services. I used to talk about providing simple music for services and the basics of accompanying hymns and we had a lovely time.

One of John's favourite organs is a dance organ which is in a castle in Denmark and dates back to the seventeenth century:

It would have been in the great hall of the castle to accompany a feast or the dancing at the end of the day, so organ music would not only have been played in churches.

At Dartington I taught the harpsichord, the recorder and dance as well. I didn't believe in the organ in isolation. Organisations need to learn about making music, so early music became the focus in our recorder classes for adults and children and in our historic dance classes, choirs and study weekends.

In addition to these many activities the centre also received students from Oxford and Cambridge Universities, and elsewhere, who studied the organ with John and learnt about organ building with Bill. 'Right from the start in 1975 we had a number of full-time students here,' said Bill. 'They came to improve their organ technique. I gave lectures on the history of the organ, organ construction and so on. It was quite a rounded experience.' John continued:

I am still working at Oxford and Cambridge Universities and I am told that those students who have worked with Bill and me for six months before they went to university were much more prepared than the other students who had gone straight to Oxbridge. Several famous professional musicians became our patrons and firmly believed and supported us in what we were doing.

The John Loosemore Centre was the first institution to bring Continental musicians to England. John confirmed this:

Now it is much more commonplace around the country. That wasn't happening in 1975/76. Buckfastleigh is well known for this now.

After about 15 years we began to run out of steam – or rather I ran out of steam. Other academies started to do what we had initiated and then our centre started to become redundant. We realised that we needed a long rethink about what we wanted to do. Finally, I resigned and Bill continued on his own. However, we had been open for 15 years and were the only organ study centre and the first early music centre in Britain.

Bill Drake continued the story:

After John left, a number of activities still carried on here. The chamber choir carried on for a number of years under Graham Treacher, who was the appointed conductor, and we had dance classes but no longer any organ playing. I carried on organ building.

Bill's interest started at an early age, 'I enjoyed everything that went on in front of a church, including organ playing.' Bill was brought up in Baltimore, USA, until he was about 11 years old, by his American-born mother and his Devon-born father:

I came back to England and went to school in Tavistock, where I played the organ, and then went to Dartington for a year where John Wellingham was my tutor. It became quite clear that music was not going to be my profession but, because of my interest in organs and in the mechanics and sound, I thought an apprenticeship in organ building would be a good idea. I went around all the organ builders in England to see about apprenticeships but, as I was over age and most of the firms were union affiliated, they were reluctant to take an apprentice whom they would have to pay according to age rather than experience.

I looked at places in Europe and finally found a firm in Austria which was happy to take me and where I was happy to go. That was in 1963. I spent three and a half years there and then six and a half years with a firm in North Germany. At the end of my apprenticeship I took my exams and then took my Master's Certificate in Organ Building at the Chamber of Trade in Stuttgart at the end of my period as a journeyman.

After the fruitful 15-year partnership between Bill and John had ended, the John Loosemore Association decided that it would be sensible to sell the building, as it was no longer being used. Bill explained:

That's when I decided to buy the centre for organ building. There are a couple of hundred organ-building firms around the country and different firms do different aspects of work. There are some who only do tuning and small repairs, others clean and rebuild them. There is only one other firm in the country which does what we do – exclusively restoration work and the building of new organs in historic styles.

Anyone interested in music, or more specifically in organs, would find a walk around Bill's workshop fascinating. It is especially intriguing to discover how an organ is built and the mechanics of making everything work together to produce the sounds that we are so used to hearing in church.

Bill and his colleagues have built a small new organ, based on Loosemore's pipes, from the organ at Nettlecombe Court. The Nettlecombe organ was dismantled and brought to the workshop for restoration, but lack of adequate funding prevented this project from proceeding:

It really is a most charming instrument. The sound is very much the seventeenth-century level of sound. These days one has become used to louder levels of sound because of amplification and church organs are very much louder. In those days chamber organs were very intimate instruments and designed to be accompanied by other instruments such as viols and small groups of wood instrumental strings.

At the time of writing the workshop also contained an organ from Spitalfields Church in London. The church is awaiting restoration and, as soon as it is ready, Bill and his men will restore the organ so that it can be returned to Spitalfields. Gilded pipes from the organ in Buckingham Palace are also awaiting restoration. Bill explained:

We have been restoring the organ over a number of years. The organ stands in the ballroom where all the investitures and banquets take place. It is a very busy room when the Queen is in residence so we can only work there when she is away doing other things, or at Sandringham, Balmoral or Windsor.

Near the palace organ pipes, at the time of writing, stands an organ that dates back to 1745 from a church in Deptford, in south-east London. There was a fire in the church that caused the surfaces of the case-work to blacken. The surface has to be stripped and repolished so that the mahogany underneath can be seen. The organ itself has suffered over the years and has been altered considerably. The fire gave the church authorities the courage, and the money, to restore it. A new organ is to be built inside the mahogany case in the style of the original instrument of 1745. Bill talked of the organ:

It is just the sort of work we love because it demands a certain amount of research and rethinking about how we do things. It is a good challenge to reproduce something that has been lost and to be able to recreate it. [Bill walked over to the far end of the room.] *This large organ was to be thrown in a skip. It was built in the 1840s by a firm called Bishops and comes from Clapham Grammar School. Someone from Holland happened to hear about the organ, came and rescued it and took it back to Holland where it was stored in a barn for many years. Then the Dutchman heard that I had some space here (I used to have space here!) and brought it over to me because no one in Holland seemed to be interested in it. I am afraid that has been our experience in England too. It is a slightly unusual organ but we haven't lost hope that somewhere in the country we shall find a home for it.*

Bill Drake has a unique business in Buckfastleigh and the town should be proud to host men as skilled as Bill and his team. They are able to restore organs which are as much a part of history as the churches and buildings in which they once stood. We should be delighted that inspired men like John and Bill strove to make their dream a reality – and found a welcoming niche in Buckfastleigh where they have fitted in so well. As Bill said, 'There is only one other firm in the country which does what we do here.'

'Greetings from Buckfastleigh', a postcard from the town.

The Ashburton and Buckfastleigh Cottage Hospital, c.1915.

A view of the Ashburton and Buckfastleigh Cottage Hospital, c.1900.

Seventeen

THE LOCAL HOSPITAL: SMALL AND FRIENDLY

Cottage hospitals began to develop during the nineteenth century. They were usually small buildings with few beds and were positioned in places where facilities were rare, such as rural areas, as most major cities had free hospitals. The term 'Cottage' is not usually used now.

On 28 August 1875 a public meeting was held in Ashburton under the chairmanship of Baldwin John P. Bastard of Buckland Court, Buckland in the Moor. A plaque in the Ashburton and Buckfastleigh Hospital bears witness that:

> ... at a meeting held in Ashburton this day it was unanimously resolved that an effort should be made to establish a cottage hospital for the benefit of the labouring classes of Ashburton, Buckfastleigh and the surrounding district who are now, to a greater extent, precluded by distance from sharing in the advantages of the larger County Establishments at Exeter and Plymouth.
> Signed Baldwin John P. Bastard, Chairman, Buckland Court, August 28th 1875.

By November of that same year £300 had been received through donations and subscriptions and a new house, situated near the railway station, was offered by Mr W. Mann for the hospital's first premises at a yearly rental, including rates and taxes, of £25 per annum.

Of course, although charges were kept to a minimum in order that those who needed the service most would be able to use the hospital, patients paid 1s.6d. (12.5 pence in modern money) a week towards their keep whilst in hospital. Subscribers paid 10s.6d. (52.5 pence) a year and working men 2s.6d. (12.5 pence) per year or 1d. a week.

Eight beds were provided for a total population of 8,000 people. A medical officer had been appointed and this was followed by the appointment of a nurse. Some 38 patients were treated during the first year.

By 1886 the decision was made to build a new hospital and the site in Eastern Road, which was offered by Mr R.G. Abraham, was accepted with grateful thanks. Donations towards the new building flowed in from generous benefactors including Messrs Berry of Buckfastleigh who donated £50. On 14 August 1889 the hospital was officially opened by Lord Clinton, Lord Lieutenant of Devon.

Jean Starkey and Joan Norwell started working for Ashburton and Buckfastleigh Hospital in the 1960s when Frances Fox was matron. Jean recalled:

> In those days you had a matron. A matron was responsible for everything that went on in a hospital – from budgeting to hiring staff.
> There were 14 patients in Matron Fox's time – now there are 16 beds. It is a general practitioner's hospital and they send in patients when a bed is required for them. In the old days people thought they were being sent in to die and some refused to come. Of course, there were many very elderly people coming into the hospital who had been ill for a long time and it was quite obvious why they died – but no one took into account the many people who went home well!

Joan remembered the running of the hospital:

> The Ashburton and Buckfastleigh doctors were on a rota which they worked out between themselves. One night it would be a Buckfastleigh doctor who would deal with the casualties and any other emergencies, and the next night an Ashburton doctor. All the doctors worked as a team and our casualty department was open 24 hours a day, and, in fact, it still is.
> We did night duty mostly, up to the mid-1970s. Night duty has a different feel to it and patients are quite different at night-time. We had to work hard during the night though, mending sheets, pillows and nightwear, sewing on buttons, etc. and doing all the repairs on an old Singer sewing machine that chugged along merrily. We only mended up to midnight though, because of the noise. We were part of a lovely team and we all worked well together.

Jean continued:

Surgery was once a month. Then our local GP, Dr Mills, was the surgeon and he did appendices, hernias, tonsils and complaints like that. We had no infections at all because of thorough cleansing. Everything was used more than once but all the instruments were boiled for three minutes. It was our responsibility to prepare all the cotton swabs, sterilise everything, clean out the steriliser, clean all the instruments that were needed – there was no pre-packed equipment in those days. Everything had to be ready for surgery the next morning. In between rolling the cotton balls we would be seeing to patients as well, then doing the bread and butter and getting the porridge ready for breakfast. In spite of all the different tasks we had to undertake there was no infection.

We had our own gardener and we grew all our own vegetables. At harvest time goods came from churches all around the district and the night staff used to peel and quarter apples galore. It was always done at night and the next morning the cook would prepare them and put them in the freezer for use throughout the year. The vegetables were prepared in the same way. The matron would prepare jars and jars of chutney – it was her speciality. We had a store cupboard that was full all year round.

The hospital also had a mortuary and the nurses were porters too:

We had to take the bodies to the mortuary at night – you couldn't do it when patients were awake because there was no one else to look after the wards – so we had to do it when we could be sure that they were all asleep. We couldn't do it in the morning, anyway, because people going to work wouldn't want to see dead bodies being carried around on mortuary trolleys.

One night we had to take a body from the hospital to the mortuary, which meant you had to go outside and along the front of the hospital, round the corner and up the steep slope where the physiotherapy department is now situated.

When someone dies there is a peculiar sensation – you are on edge. On this particular occasion it was pouring with rain and there was a howling gale. The nurse with me dropped the key to the mortuary. She bent down to pick it up and the dead patient's arm flopped out from under the cover and hit her on the head! She screamed and the trolley started rolling down the slope. I tried to hang on to it but the patient was a heavy man and it was very difficult!

The patients came from a large catchment area but the hospital had a very personal feel to it – it was small and friendly. If patients had to go to Torbay Hospital it would take them all day to get there by public transport – especially if they lived on Dartmoor. If they lived alone on Dartmoor they may have had no visitors in Torbay, but in our hospital there would always be someone there who would know them.

The doctors knew the patients very well – perhaps for most of their lives, and they would know if they were having difficulties at home, or on the farm. It wasn't just their medical condition that they were interested in. Dr Moore and Dr Wigram were always interested in their patients.

There is not such a personal feel to the hospital now although it is still relaxed and informal. The staff have so much recording to do now. We earned very little in our day but we enjoyed it and it was more like a vocation. Nowadays staff get stress counselling – then we just had to get on with it.

Since Jean and Joan's day the hospital has been upgraded and extensions have been added including a quiet room which can be used by staff who need to talk to the relatives of patients, or for interviews between patients and social workers. The newly upgraded hospital was officially opened by the Right Honourable Lord Tebbitt CH PC on 11 December 1992.

Annette Bowen from Buckfastleigh, who joined the hospital as staff nurse in 1999, considered that the hospital still had a relaxed and intimate feel to it:

I am a staff nurse and part of my role is to work closely with social services. It's lovely – the district nurses, the physiotherapists and the occupational therapist – we all work closely together. The size of the hospital has got something to do with it – we are such a small hospital. We have close contact with the domestic staff as well. We have a very good cook and all the domestic staff get on well with the patients. We probably would not have that close contact if we were a bigger hospital.

Visitors are a great asset to us too, as well as to the patients they are visiting. Sometimes we have to ask them to wait if a patient they are visiting is receiving treatment but usually they fit in quite well and many of them do a considerable amount of work to support us.

In the twenty-first century roles are much more clearly defined and, although there is no longer a matron, there is a senior sister and two part-time locality managers. Annette explained:

The senior sister deals with the nursing side and the managers look after the financial side and other problems which might arise. The bosses are really good, they always listen to what we have to say.

We try to look at the patients holistically. We get a lot of patients in the hospital whom we know and knowing something about their background helps them. Our doctors are very supportive too. They are on a call-out rota and if we need a doctor we can phone whoever is on duty, either from Ashburton or Buckfastleigh, and they will come straight away.

If Torbay Hospital is really pushed we take patients from out of the area – there is no boundary as such.

Sometimes we have mostly Ashburton patients, at others mostly Buckfastleigh. It is a doctors' hospital and the doctors decide whether to send their respective patients to the hospital or not. Most patients do very well when they come to Ashburton. They now know that they are halfway home when they come in. We get younger patients coming in now too.

In 2003 Annette, who trained in North Devon, was working day shifts, although the internal rotation system meant that she had to do night duty occasionally. There were only two permanent night staff on duty. Like Jean and Joan, Annette found working at night very different from working during the daytime. 'Patients are a bit more disorientated,' said Annette, 'but they also talk to you more.'

Jan Walker is the senior sister at the hospital, and Annette's boss:

We have been in a transition period as Primary Care Trusts have been created. We were in level three Primary Care Group and have moved into level four and our structure has changed.

Since April 2002 we have been part of Teignbridge Primary Care Trust. Our GP services and all our hospital services will now be managed locally. The trust will be based in Newton Abbot and have Newton Abbot, Teignmouth, Dawlish, Bovey Tracey, Ashburton and Buckfastleigh under its care.

Since 1996 there has been a locality manager who is responsible for the district nursing service, the health visiting service and the hospital service which are all responsible for the healthcare of Ashburton and Buckfastleigh. We are now managed as the 'Moorland Locality' sharing our manager with Bovey Tracey and this is a bonus as we get to share ideas and help each other.

In our hospital I am called the sister in charge or ward manager. My remit is to manage the 16-bedded ward and the minor injury unit – and have some responsibility for the building – because the locality manager is not based on site I am the most senior person here five days a week. I have staff nurses, like Annette, a team of qualified nurses and auxiliary nurses who are untrained staff, who make up the team. We try to simplify the process.

There is a district nurse team leader based here with her team, and the health visitor, and we all work closely together. Because the locality manager isn't a nurse I am responsible professionally as a nurse to the trust lead nurse – but I am responsible to the locality manager on a management level. We have very close links with the social services, too, and those links will become stronger now we are under Teignbridge.

Our minor injury unit – colloquially known as the casualty department – provides a 24-hour service for minor injuries. Major hospitals that provide more services will have an accident and emergency department. We don't have enough cases to have an extra staff member to run the unit, so it is staffed by existing hospital ward staff. We are all trained and have qualifications to run the unit. Anything major will be dealt with by us initially and then we send that patient to one of the bigger hospitals, however, emergency services will take direct to Torbay Hospital.

Only the GPs have the power to admit and discharge patients, nurses don't. We have a good team of doctors from Ashburton and Buckfastleigh and work closely with them. If a district nurse goes into a patient's home and thinks that person would benefit from being in our hospital and we have a bed for them she'll ring the doctor – and the doctor usually agrees with the district nurse. Hospitals are becoming more nurse-led and probably, in the future, nurses will be able to admit and discharge patients.

If someone has had a minor stroke and the doctor and family consider that it would be preferable for them to be in hospital, but it is not necessary for that patient to go to a major hospital, then that patient would be sent to us so that we can keep them comfortable. We give palliative care here too, for people who are at the end of their lives.

The success of our hospital lies in the fact that we are in a rural area – somewhat isolated – so that we don't get the pressure that bigger hospitals get, and yet have all the facilities we need here. In addition to the wards and kitchens there are clinics for visiting consultants, chiropody, and physiotherapy outpatients. There are offices for the health visitors, district nurses, school nurse, occupational therapist and physiotherapist. Additionally, there are consulting rooms for psychologists, psychiatrists, speech therapists, gynaecologists and orthopaedic consultants. Every Wednesday the consultant physician from Torbay Hospital holds a clinic in one of the rooms and visits the wards.

Jan started nursing at 18 in Rochdale and went straight into surgery and then into intensive care:

Nursing was all I ever wanted to do. I decided to come down to Torquay to have a break from working in big city hospitals but after a year working on a busy surgical ward in Torquay as staff nurse, a post came up in Newton Abbot Hospital for a sister. So I applied and got that and loved the job. My first post as sister. Part of the ward was a surgery, and part was like a cottage hospital. You could get to know the people and community better and I realised that I liked that. Whilst the senior sister was ill I managed the whole hospital for a while which I enjoyed.

Then I had a baby and there was time then to reflect on what I wanted to do. Needing a job with more regular hours I was offered a secondment back at Torbay Hospital running the ear, nose and throat department. I stayed five enjoyable years doing that but kept hankering after work in a cottage hospital. I particularly enjoyed working with elderly patients so finally I applied for, and was given, the post of senior sister here which was just what I wanted.

Jan felt that the Ashburton and Buckfastleigh Hospital was fortunate in having a supportive League of Friends:

They have funded the refurbishment of reception and they are very involved with the hospital. They have also provided us with a lovely Trolley Shop. Recently a new system was set up for obtaining funding through the League of Friends. We have a meeting once a month with the team leaders from all the different disciplines at which there is a slot to discuss the funding available through the League of Friends, and we thrash the subject around. We all want money and we have to set priorities and decide what is most appropriate. When we have finally come to a consensus the locality manager puts the formal proposal to the League of Friends.

Buckfast Abbey is very supportive to our hospital. In fact, all the churches are good to us. We have a chaplain appointed to our hospital who comes in for one session a week. His post is paid for by the Primary Care Trust.

It seems that the Ashburton and Buckfastleigh Hospital is a thriving and important facility for communities in the area. It is a hospital started by local people who recognised the need for such a facility in 1875, and a hospital which has continued to serve local people for nearly 130 years. The hospital is supported by committed local doctors and a wide range of paid staff and volunteers, such as the League of Friends. As the hospital is situated in Ashburton it is likely that much of the burden of support has fallen on Ashburton, but Buckfastleigh has played its part well and continues to do so.

'Greetings from Buckfastleigh', a postcard from the town.

Eighteen

THE 1980S: A TOWN IN DECLINE

The Conservatives came into power at the beginning of the 1980s with Margaret Thatcher as prime minister. The plight of the economy and problematic industrial relations dominated the national scene and the steel workers were on strike. By the autumn of 1980 two million people were out of work and the economic and industrial climate was worsening. The miners went on strike in 1984, in protest at the numerous pit closures that brought chaos and misery to many parts of Britain.

Internationally, the situation was still grim as the Russians became entrenched in their war with Afghanistan and 53 American hostages were held by Iranian fundamentalists in Tehran. The Lebanon was torn apart by war and Terry Waite was kidnapped in Beirut in January 1987.

Britain was shocked when, on 2 April 1982, Argentina invaded the Falkland Islands and Britain went to war. Two years later the nation was shocked again when the IRA blew up the Grand Hotel in Brighton during the Conservative Party conference.

With famines and air disasters, the assassination of John Lennon, and the fire that cost the lives of so many football fans at Bradford City ground, it seemed that very little had changed for the better either in Britain or overseas. The one bright moment was the marriage of Prince Charles to Lady Diana Spencer in 1981, which was followed by the birth of Prince William in June 1982.

Although Buckfastleigh had not fully recovered from the closure of the woollen mill in 1975, building work on 42 new flats in Hamlyn's Way, 19 of which were warden-controlled, started in 1983, on the site of the old mill.

As the population increased in Buckfastleigh so there was a need to accommodate the numerous elderly inhabitants. Hamlyn's Way and the warden-controlled bungalows at Barn Park had gone some way to supporting elderly people able to live on their own but, as always, there was a need to provide accommodation for those unable to look after themselves.

In September 1984 it was announced that Rock House was to become a home for the elderly. The Smiths became proprietors in 1987, succeeding the Thomas family. Ruth Smith remembered this period:

There was a recession in the mid-1980s and my husband had a building business in Cheltenham where we lived. Our children had grown up. There was no point looking at the building trade at that time so we decided to follow my career direction. I had been a nurse and later worked as carer in a home, so my husband suggested we bought a residential home of our own. I was horrified at first because I knew how much work was involved but he was convinced it would be okay.

Eventually we found Rock House in Station Road, which originally belonged to the Coulton family and which had since been a school and a restaurant. Initially we registered it as a residential home and took in people who needed care but not intensive care. Later, as many of the patients had mental problems, and psychiatric nursing is my 'field', I registered the home as one for the elderly mentally infirm (EMI). It is more interesting and more of a challenge. Redmount and Abbotswell were then residential homes and we three owner/managers became good friends.

Rock House is the only home in the area serving the EMI and has a catchment area that is much wider than just Buckfastleigh. 'The working day is quite hard,' continued Ruth, 'and for a long time we did night duties and all day – we never slept in the little cottage down the road that we had bought.'

Rock House employs about 12 to 15 care staff, most of whom are full time because of the particular duties they perform. They are recruited mostly from Totnes, Buckfastleigh and Plymouth. Ruth continued:

You need to have the energy to work with people and you need to be compassionate and to be able to build up relationships. We have a lot of fun here with the residents and we love them all, but I know that I could never look after anyone of them on a 'one-to-one' basis.

Redmount, on Old Totnes Road, was opened as a residential home in 1988 by Sheila and Roger Bowley. The house had previously been owned by Dr Ironsides, followed by Revd Eric Jones and, latterly, the West family. Trish Durman, who is the secretary at Redmount, explained:

The Bowleys hadn't run a residential home before but Sheila had been a registration and inspection officer with the local authority and they had been around to visit several homes and then she thought, 'I can do that!' so they bought Redmount in 1988 and opened in a small way with nine residents.

It became dual registered in 1993. We have 35 nursing beds and seven residential. We are the only dual-registered home around here and it is much needed. The good thing about Redmount is that often clients come in requiring residential care only and then need to be nursed and we can keep them here – they don't have to be moved. If you are elderly and have to be moved from one home to another that can be very upsetting. Similarly, we receive clients who come in because they need nursing care and then stay on in the home on a residential basis when they get better.

Sheila and Roger ran Redmount as if the clients were an extended family. Roger used to do all the shopping with his shoes on but without the laces done up! Then he would come back and leave those great big shoes at the front door. If anyone came to the front door they would know that he was in. If the shoes weren't there they would know he wasn't!

The news that Fullaford House, which had been built in 1876 by John Hamlyn, the son of Joseph Hamlyn senr, and which had been recently used by Devon County Social Services as an observation and assessment centre, was to close in 1983 was a blow to the local populace as it meant the future of the house was now uncertain. By 1986 suggestions had been made about redeveloping the house and turning it into an old people's home, flats or other residential development. However, plans were temporarily thwarted when squatters from an arts-and-crafts co-operative in London moved into Fullaford in July 1987.

Local people were not unduly upset as the squatters appeared conscious of the graciousness of the house and its history and whilst they were 'in residence' no moves could be made to destroy it. However, by August the squatters had been successfully evicted and had then moved to live in Market Street, leaving Fullaford House to be sold.

In March 1983 there were boundary changes which moved Tweenaways from South Hams District and Dean Prior to Teignbridge District and Buckfastleigh Parish. Betty Northcote, former Town Clerk, elaborated:

Originally Tweenaways was within the Totnes Rural District Council boundary. We used to pay our rates and rent to Buckfastleigh Urban District Council and they would have to pay the rates back to Totnes. Now we are all under Teignbridge District Council.

We are surrounded by South Hams District, even Dartbridge Inn comes under South Hams. Everything the town side of the old A38 comes under Dartmoor National Park, but the bungalows and housing in Strode Road, for example, do not. The old A38 is the dividing line.

Debbie Griffiths, head of the Dartmoor National Park archaeology department, stated:

National Parks are a hybrid in terms of their function. They are a member of the local government family but they are unlike County and District Councils in many ways. Most people think of us as a planning authority first and foremost. We are the planning authority but we do have other roles as well. Our other principal role is the management responsibility we have to conserve the special qualities of Dartmoor National Park as a whole and to enable the public to understand and enjoy the National Park's special qualities. We try to maintain a balance.

Sporting clubs and groups developed and changed during the 1980s. Two floodlit tennis courts opened at Hamlyn's Playing-Fields in May 1986 and, in 1989, the bowling club opened its new one-level, six-lane green with a pavilion and toilets. Two-thirds of the £30,000 cost was met by Teignbridge District Council and one-third by the club. The pavilion was used by the tennis, bowling and netball players.

The Women's Institute celebrated its 40th anniversary in 1986, the Town Hall its centenary in 1988, and in 1989 the Buckfastleigh Amateur Dramatic Society celebrated its 50th anniversary.

The Buckfastleigh Amateur Dramatic Society was started in 1939, at the beginning of the war, by Frank George who owned Mount Pleasant Garage. The founder members included Edith Blight, Evan Scoble, Fred and Elsie Churchward, Caroline Wilton and Flora (OE) Hoff. Marian Hoff, who, in 2003, was the social secretary for what is now called the Buckfastleigh Drama Group, recalled:

Edith (Babs) Blight was teaching at the primary school and lodging at Mount Pleasant and when asked if she would play the female lead in the society's first production said that she would if Frank found someone nice to play opposite her! Frank invited Evan (Dick) Scoble to play the male lead and it was through the play, Tilly of Bloomsbury, *that Babs and Dick met and later married.*

Those who took part in the first production were: Henry Peters, James Jordan, Mildred Beard, Aline de

Lalier, Edith Blight, Evan Scoble, May Badman, Dennis Luke, Dorothy George, John Bickford, Will Giles, Will Paxman, Thelma Coode and Maud Murch.

The Amateur Dramatic Society's productions were always a special occasion. At the first performance, *Tilly of Bloomsbury*, there was incidental music under the direction of Mr Bray but, for later productions, there was an orchestra led by Edith Warren (later Edith Walters), which added to the atmosphere of anticipation.

Tilly of Bloomsbury was performed again in 1940 in support of the British Red Cross Society and it played to a full house each night. Marian had fond memories of the performances:

The military command accepted an invitation for 25 members of HM Forces stationed in the district to attend each performance. All the productions supported the war effort. The society raised money for the British Red Cross Society and the BRCS Prisoner of War Fund, the Ambulance Fund and the Ashburton and Buckfastleigh Hospital. After the war the society continued giving to charity.

It was a wonderful social life through the society. In the old days you had to be invited to join but today we welcome anyone who is interested in joining us.

The Royal British Legion Women's Section celebrated its 60th anniversary in 1987 with a party at the Town Hall and a thanksgiving service at St Luke's Church. A certificate marking the section's anniversary was presented by Mrs W. Horrell, county vice-chairman, to president Mrs G. Lang.

The women's section of the British Legion, which started in 1927, was particularly active during the Second World War when, together with other local women, they knitted socks, scarves and gloves and other items of clothing for the men in the services.

Phyllis Voisey, president of the BLWS, recalled Netta Tonkin inviting her to join the women's section in 1948. The meetings were held in the back room of the King's Arms Hotel and stalwart members included Olive Cann, Nellie Hayward, Netta Tonkin, Mrs Broomfield, Mrs Goodman, Winnie McCarthy and Dorothy Knowling. They all worked very hard raising money through jumble sales and whist drives and enjoying social evenings. Phyllis remembered:

Once a year we would have a supper in the Town Hall with the men from the British Legion. The men would set up the long tables and forms and we women would bring the tablecloths, flowers and all the other paraphernalia – and, of course, the food: sponges, trifles, tuff cakes, butter, milk, tea, etc. George Lewis would always provide the pickled onions and beetroot and Netta would have negotiated a special price for the ham at Hoffs (usually 8d. a quarter, but less for her). We all loved it, packed tight on the forms. Afterwards there were recitations, piano playing, stories. Then, when all the visitors had gone, we would set to and wash up and set the room to rights.

The women's section has worked hard throughout the years in support of the men in the British Legion. It has organised the annual poppy collections and is consistently ready to raise funds for worthy causes. At the section's 25th anniversary Mrs E. Rashleigh, chairman of the southern area said:

There is more pleasure to be gained in legion work than in any other organisation. Today there are wives and mothers suffering as we did in 1914–18 and in 1939–45, and while such suffering exists, whilst there are wars, our work will go on.

Staff from Redmount Nursing Home at the raft race.

The Royal British Legion Women's Section Christmas party, 1980.

Older and smaller in number at the time of writing, the Buckfastleigh branch remains just as committed.

At the beginning of the 1980s a new organisation was started which was concerned with improving the appearance of the town and providing amenities for the residents to enjoy in order to enhance the quality of life in the area. With Buckfastleigh in decline it was the comparative newcomers to the area who believed that the town was worth looking after and who convinced the established residents that things could be changed for the better. The new organisation was the Buckfastleigh and District Society. An open meeting was called by the Town Mayor in 1979 and Jim Searle and Gordon Stone, both councillors, were asked to form a steering group. By the beginning of the 1980s the society was established with a committee, a membership and regular meetings with speakers. Stalwarts included Rupert Watson, Ann Attkey, Mary Riley, Len Dwight and Jill Stubbs. The Buckfastleigh and District Society, however, is much more than just another social group. Within two years and with Mick Henley as chairman, the Christmas shop-window contest had been introduced along with a 'Buckfastleigh In Bloom' competition for shops and private houses, when window-boxes, tubs and hanging baskets are much in evidence.

The society was responsible for convincing the Teignbridge District Council to convert the orchard between Station Road and Elliott's Plain into a small park to be known as Millman's Orchard. Money was raised through well-supported events and by donations from a number of organisations, with particular support from the Dartmoor National Park Authority which gave money, advice and materials.

The Dartington Bridge Agency, on behalf of the Manpower Services Commission, constructed a footbridge over the stream leading to the orchard and helped in many other ways. The bridge was formally opened by Mr Couch, a former Mayor, and some weeks later, on the first fun day that the society had organised, the Mayor officially opened the orchard. Since then the society has organised an annual fun day, which is always well supported, and the orchard, now officially called the Orchard Millennium Green, is under care of trustees who are responsible for its management.

Mick and Peggy Henley came to live in the town when Mick retired in 1979. Mick recalled:

Our first impression of the place was that people were friendly but it took us a lot of time to get used to the slow pace of life. We were used to shopping in places where you could get in and out in quick time. Here, you start chatting to people and hearing about Mrs Jones' baby! Within a few months we were like everybody else though.

I became involved with the cricket club and started looking after the colts in 1980 and did that for 11 years. I was chairman and then a president too. Peggy and I got to know other people in the town through the various clubs we joined, Peggy became a councillor on the Town Council. Now, of course, you go through the town and it takes half an hour because of the people you stop to talk to.

In 1989 St Luke's Church opened its doors once a week as a day centre for elderly disabled people and substantial donations were made by the social services and Age Concern to support the project. The idea for the scheme came from churchwarden Ivor Thorning who had suggested to Revd Steele Perkins that the rear of the church might be made suitable for the purpose. Mick continued:

Peggy became involved and then I started helping by picking people up in my car. Later I became treasurer and then took over as organiser from John Giles in 1995. Some of the local people who used the centre in the late 1980s were Lilian Warren, Kaz Stryjski, Ernest Coleman, Gertie Manning and Elsie Jeffries.

The project is supported by committed volunteers with representatives from several church groups and women's groups, including the Catholic Women's League, the Mothers' Union and the British Legion Women's Section, who prepare the room, serve coffee and tea and biscuits, chat with the group, lay the tables and serve lunches. The lunches are cooked by Kenwyn Residential Home in Ashburton and are collected by volunteer drivers, who also pick up the members from their homes and take them home again afterwards.

Jacquie Kilty moved to Buckfastleigh with her family in the mid-1980s during a time when there were many new families moving into the town:

I found it quite hard getting to know local people to begin with as they were always friendly but cautious. It took a few years of being in the town to make friends. Now it feels like home.

Both my husband, Gavin, and I started to get involved in the community and have met many local people. Gavin was a founding member of Buckfastleigh Arts Group with a small committed group. I was a founding member with other young mothers, inspired and led by Philippa Wood, of the Buccaneers, a group for promoting activities for children living in the Buckfastleigh area. This started in 1988.

We started by holding a Children's Festival in Victoria Park and also organised many other events within the town through the year including maypole dancing, teddy-bear picnics, puppet shows and separate events through the school holidays.

After three years the Buccaneers was granted charity status which enabled us to apply for funding.

It took a while for the town to recognise our scheme but we were supported by the Town Council, and had support from the then Town Mayor, Doreen Trude.

Fund-raising for the Buccaneers was more difficult and we needed constant backing from local people to keep going. Eventually, after many years' hard work, the original group moved on as their children grew up and other young mothers took over to bring in fresh ideas and more energy – which is as it should be.

Although there were many positive developments in the town during the 1980s there were two decisions which infuriated local people. One was the closure of the Co-operative stores with the exception of the food store in 1987. A public meeting was held in protest at the closure but the Co-operative Wholesale Society went ahead; they stated that the stores were 'not economically viable and [that they] could not maintain the losses of recent years'. It was a blow to those who relied upon the Co-op for their daily shopping, and a blow historically – the stores had been there for 118 years.

In November 1987 the Buckfast Caravan Park was closed after 33 years. In 1982 the caravan park had been bought from Teignbridge District Council by Buckfast Abbey and now its closure, to make way for expansion by the Buckfast Spinning Company, meant great losses for the traders of Buckfastleigh. Harry Kayley, with his wife Doris, ran the greengrocery on the corner of Fore Street and Station Road:

When we first came to Buckfastleigh in 1986 to run The Fruit Basket there were more businesses down this end of the town. There was the off-licence, Stark's the jewellers, Johnson's hardware, the 16th-Century Eating House (now the Tourist Information Office) and an antique shop in Station Road.

It was a very active little shop when we first came and we built up the business and it really thrived but we lost a lot of business like several other traders in the town when the Buckfast Caravan Park closed down. Holiday-makers used to arrive on Friday evening or Saturday morning and on Saturday afternoon they used to come into the town to buy food and drink.

We found people in the town very friendly when we first came to Buckfastleigh. It gave us a lovely, warm feeling to be invited to lunch on Christmas day and to be made so welcome by local people. We did not find the town too quiet at all.

Larry Areco worked as a waiter in Italy when he was young and most of his customers were British. He wanted to travel and work on a cruise ship but he needed to be able to speak English fluently. He found a job in Scotland initially and used to come down twice a year to London which he loved. 'I had come to England to learn English,' said Larry, 'and never did properly.' He worked in various places in England before returning to Italy for a brief period of employment on an Italian cruise ship but he missed England, came back and eventually opened his own restaurant in Chippenham, where he met and married Diana.

When their first child, Nathan, was three months old they came down to Brixham on holiday. Diana liked Devon so much that she decided she did not want to stay in Chippenham any more.

'I would never have left Chippenham,' said Larry, 'but Diana wanted to come to Devon, so we came to look for a property. When we came to view the Baker's Oven we liked the look of Buckfastleigh.'

'We looked around the town,' said Diana, 'especially at the school as Nathan was five and Matthew was three. We liked what we saw, so we bought the Baker's Oven!'

After they had been running the Baker's Oven for a short while Larry had grave doubts about staying in the town:

'Let's leave,' I said to Diana. 'I shall never make a living here!' However, Diana was adamant that she wasn't going to leave. So we stayed on. The children loved the school and everyone was so friendly and took to us. Now we have been here nearly 20 years!

The shops have changed so much since we came and I think we are among the traders who have been here the longest, but when we first came in the '80s it was a strain to work for yourself. Custom was sporadic.

You have to stick to one thing, pizzas are my thing! My own food is fresh – pizzas cooked fresh. I do my best to give good service. I had my life when I was young and then when I married I wanted to make a good family.

'People have been very nice and we love it here,' said Diana. 'You feel that people stick together and help each other as best they can.'

During the 1980s traders came and went. Many wanted to stay but there was competition from the larger supermarkets in the area which offered free transport for local shoppers. Doris Kayley explained:

The social situation had changed and many people did not want to cook, which affected what they bought. Supermarkets were responding by providing a wider variety of frozen food and fast food for people on the move. Many customers coming into The Fruit Basket did not know how to cook things like cabbage or spinach – or what kind of flour to use to bake a cake. One young person did not know the difference between cabbage and cauliflower. Eating habits have changed.

In the end we started writing out recipes and putting them on the counter to explain to customers buying our fruit and vegetable how to cook them. Even I did not know how to cook a squash when they first came in.

Society was changing and the tempo of life was much faster. People moved around the country more and were more prepared to move in order to look for work – especially if they were buying their own home. The extended family, living together in one town or village, was no longer the norm and, with a higher rate of divorce, the number of one-parent families increased accordingly.

The national changes had a knock-on effect on life in Buckfastleigh where, in comparison to previous generations, there was a higher number of single-parent families, increasing unemployment and a much looser support network.

Traffic in Buckfastleigh, particularly in Fore Street, was becoming a nuisance. By 1985 further problems had become obvious; huge lorries were causing damage to buildings and other vehicles in Fore Street. Initially it was considered that the solution would be to have traffic lights or to employ a warden. However, the problem was caused by heavy lorries using Fore Street to gain access to the Mardle Way industrial site, and first mention was made of a link road via Higher Mill Lane and Deepway. By 1988 a relief road was seen as the only solution to the problem.

At the end of the decade a situation arose which proved to the people of Buckfastleigh that they could work together for change. Texaco Ltd put in an application to Teignbridge District Council to build a motorway service area on the A38 between Buckfastleigh and Ashburton which would include a hotel with 40 bedrooms, a restaurant, a shop, a petrol station and a lorry park.

The objections to the development by Teignbridge Council were based on the 'seriously prejudicial impact' it would have on the landscape in the Ashburn valley and that it would 'encroach into the flood plains of the River Ashburn'. Local objectors focused on the urban sprawl which would develop between Ashburton and Buckfastleigh, the catastrophic effect on the 'pleasant green valley on the edge of the National Park' and the adverse effect it would have on traders in both towns where petrol stations, shops, hotels, etc. already existed.

The planning application was turned down by Teignbridge District Council and when Texaco decided to appeal against the decision, local people, in both Ashburton and Buckfastleigh, joined forces with Wilf Joint, Mayor of the Buckfastleigh Council, and the Dartmoor Tourist Association, the Dartmoor Preservation Society, the Buckfastleigh and District Society and other agencies in order to protest against the application appeal.

The appeal was held on Wednesday 29 March and Thursday 30 March 1989 at Forde House in Newton Abbot. Texaco lost the appeal and there was jubilation and relief that those conducting it had listened to local people. It was an example of how collaboration and co-operation could work successfully – a lesson which would prove equally effective in the next decade.

Nineteen

Sport: Playing for the Town

Sport has always been enjoyed in Buckfastleigh with football, cricket and rugby being particularly popular amongst the town's young men. The football team, which is known as the Buckfastleigh Rangers, is over 100 years old and Cyril Heath declared that 'the cricket club celebrated its centenary in 1962 making it now nearly 150 years old.'

The Youth Club Football Team, 1939. Left to right, back row: Mr Stuart, Jim Stuart, Gerald French, Leonard Bragg, Pat Stuart, Lloyd Routley, Graham Lock, Henry Brown; front: John Stuart, Roy Bonathon, Jim McCarthy, Tommy Stuart, Arthur Burge.

Maurice Lane was born in 1916 and during the 1930s played for the Youth Club Football Team, which was started by John Stuart's father. Maurice recalled:

The Youth Club Football Team used to play against the Buckfastleigh Rangers and after the Second World War I played for the Rangers. In 1948 we won the Torbay Herald Cup which was the year my daughter, Janice, was born. We have never won that cup again because it is so hard to win. The cup final matches are played on Good Friday and up to 500 teams play for the cup.

That was the football team's heyday and the team included Kenny Bowden, John Stuart, Bill and Arthur Honeywell, Bruno Zacher and Alfred Howe, who was one of the best footballers in the town at that time.

Cyril Heath played for the Rangers before the war and remembered the training the team undertook:

For exercises we used to run up Church Steps, 197 steps, twice a week. We would run up and walk back and Herman Myhill and I would run or jog twice a week up to Wallaford Down Gate.

Cyril Heath and Maurice Lane also played cricket. Cyril was the captain of the First XI for 25 years and cricket club chairman for over ten years. After the war the team included, Cyril, Maurice, Bill Dawe, Evan (Dick) Scoble, Ted Coode and Cyril Doidge who, Maurice said, 'was much younger than we were' and who played cricket for the second team.

'They were such happy times,' recalled Maurice. 'We used to play up at the Recreation Ground – the cricket and football teams sharing the ground between them.'

Both Cyril Heath and Cyril Doidge, who was 16 when he started to play cricket, endorsed this comment. Cyril Doidge explained:

I was then called up by the Army, in the late 1950s, as compulsory military conscription to the Forces was still in place. Whilst I was in the Forces I played cricket five times a week. I had a great time!

Cricket has played an important part in Cyril Doidge's life and it also provided him with the opportunity to meet his late wife, Barbara, when the cricket team went to Yelverton to play a friendly match against the local team:

When we started to play matches on Sunday, we had to get permission from the church first as the land belonged to the Church Commissioners. We were granted six matches a year and they had to finish by six in the evening before the evening service began.

During the early 1960s the cricket club bought the

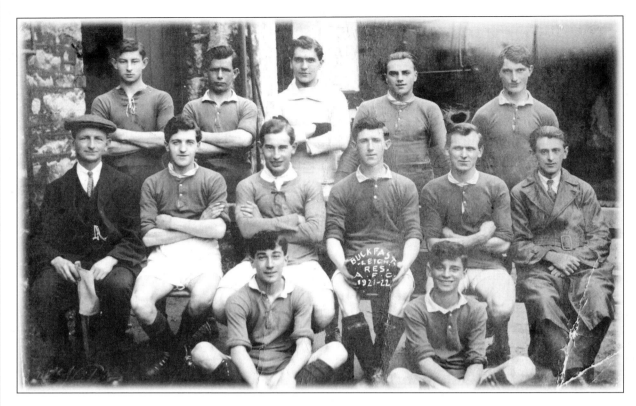

The local football team, 1921/22. Left to right, back row: Bob Barden, John Ford, Bill Legg, Harold Austen, Charlie Willcocks; middle: George Foster, Fred Roberts, Jim Harvey, Jack Willcocks, ?, Claude Richard; front: Fred Lane, Bill Stuart.

The Second XI cricket team, 1954. Left to right, back row: Marge Hayman, Martin Hayman, Cyril Doidge, Maurice Lane, Derek Voaden, Fred Lane, ? Rogers, Ken Bowden; front: Michael Parsons, Evan (Dick) Scoble, Charlie Hayman, Eric Evemy, Trevor Turner, Bill Dawe.

SPORT: PLAYING FOR THE TOWN

Right: *Buckfastleigh Cricket Club vs Showbiz XI. Left to right, back row: W. Dawe, John Reed, C. Hayman, C. Heath, Evan Scoble, ? (carnival princess), D. Peters, ? (carnival queen), J. Harvey, Wendy King (princess), E. Coode, C. Doidge, M. Kelly (Torquay Cricket Club), Michael Abbot; middle: ?, ?, Ernie Wise, Eric Morecombe, Joe Church, C. Voisey (kneeling). The names of the people in the front row are not known.*

Recreation Ground, which was 11 acres, from the Church Commissioners for £2,000, thanks to Richard Willcocks who was a long-standing member, a president of the club and a Church Commissioner. The Rangers continued to share the ground, paying rent to the cricket club, but eventually it was considered appropriate for the football club to find their own playing-field and they were given a field at Duckspond (previously the town's rubbish tip) by BUDC when Dick Scoble was both chairman of the council and president of the cricket club. The club was still based there at the time of writing.

Initially there were drainage problems with the Duckspond site. After the drains were put in and the pitch levelled off, the pitch again collapsed because the drainage was inadequate. The problem was resolved and, on the same land, there is a clubhouse, which is used for various functions.

In 1962 Buckfastleigh Cricket Club celebrated its centenary with a dinner and dance at the Trecarne Hotel in Torquay on Friday 27 April 1962. The president of the cricket club was R.W. Coles, the managing director of Bulley Cleaves Quarry, who had been president for many years.

Both Cyril Heath and Cyril Doidge felt that the end of an era had come when overseas players were sponsored to play for cricket teams around the country. During one season Buckfastleigh received a young Australian for whom accommodation and temporary work was found in return for the young man's cricketing services. It was a scheme designed to give young players experience, but this 'perceived' payment in return for cricketing services seemed to change the nature of the matches, which hitherto had all been friendlies. Cyril explained:

Since the cricket club first began all the matches were friendlies. Then the Devon Cricket League was formed, everything changed and it became much more serious. When we played friendly matches our conduct was good and we dressed properly on the field. When the league was introduced it was as if conduct suddenly went out of the window!

As the game became more competitive so the players' behaviour worsened. There was no dress code and the players seemed more aggressive, shouting and swearing at each other. Emphasis was on the results, not on the sport. Cyril Doidge recalled:

Competition was fiercer so the chances for youngsters became limited. In a friendly you tried to give as many players as you could the chance to play. There is no doubt that in a friendly match you played to win, but if you were winning easily you would ease off the pressure and you would give someone else the chance to learn how to bowl, for example. I accepted league rules for the First XI team but not for the second team which was there to encourage youngsters.

The same problem existed within the Buckfastleigh Rangers, as Donald Joint explained:

I played football and cricket in the 1950s. I started playing football when I was 15 and I played cricket with Dick Willcocks and Jago Searle. I was on the football committee for many years and I used to help with the over-16s. When they started paying footballers things changed. I remember saying to Peter Warden there will come a day when there are no Buckfastleigh boys playing for the Rangers. Of course, that day came. Eventually we were relegated from the Devon League and now they are in the premier division of the South Devon League. But the day of Buckfastleigh paying for footballers has gone and, gradually, there are more boys coming back into the team, although there are still local lads playing for other teams.

Michael Roberts was a Buckfastleigh footballer who played in goal for Torquay United and Alfie Howe was one of the finest footballers to come out of Buckfastleigh. He had a chance to play football professionally but he was unable to get out of the apprenticeship he was in.

However, the Buckfastleigh Rangers had a notable success when local football player Colin Lee was recruited as a professional. Colin was born in Buckfastleigh and attended St Mary's Catholic School in Buckfast and then St Cuthbert Mayne School in Torquay. He started playing football for Buckfastleigh when he was a young teenager, but he

The CWS football team, c.1960. Left to right, back row: Maurice Soper, ?, Reg Laity, Ted Coode, Alan Chaffe, ?, ?, Neil Peardon; front: Lloyd Routley, ?, ?, ?, Eric Livermore, Cyril Doidge, ?.

also used to play for the Tortrojans on Sundays which is where he was spotted by a scout for Bristol City football team.

'When he left school he went as an apprentice to Bristol City,' said his mother, Mary Lee, 'where he played for the youth team. After playing for Bristol City he went to play for Torquay United.'

'He played for Torquay United for quite a while,' said Donald Joint, 'and then he was spotted by a scout for Tottenham Hotspurs. They knew Colin was doing well and they signed him on. He scored four goals in his first game.' Mary continued:

Colin has finished playing now. After playing for Spurs he went to Chelsea. He has been manager of Watford, Wolves and is manager of Walsall.

Colin's brother, Francis, played for Buckfastleigh. He had trials with Torquay United and played for the reserves for a short time. My other son, Michael, played football too, for Rangers and Liverton and my father and husband played rugby for Buckfastleigh Ramblers.

Donald said:

Colin is the only boy from Buckfastleigh who went away and made a name for himself in sport for a very long time. Timmy Crimp, who lived up at West End, used to be a scout. He would spot these young boys playing football and if they were good we would take four or five boys up to football trials.

Timmy was scouting for Watford and said to me one day, 'Would you do me a favour, Donald? How would you fancy taking some boys from Devon and Cornwall up to Watford for football trials? We'll pay for everything.' I did that whilst Colin Lee was at Watford. On this particular occasion there was a match whilst we were there and Colin Lee said to me 'I would like a word with you after the game, Donald, I can't talk now as I have to see the players before the game starts.' He was the manager, of course.

So, I watched the game and I waited in the tunnel after the match. On this particular day Watford had a very unexpected win and when Colin came down all the reporters wanted to get at him. He stopped them as they started to ask questions and said, 'I don't want to talk to any of you before I have a talk with Donald.' I was absolutely chuffed. After all, football was his life but he remembered that he had promised to talk to me. He wanted to thank me for bringing the boys up to Watford.

The rugby club's team, the Buckfastleigh Ramblers, was founded during the early 1920s. When the war broke out the rugby stopped, as with many other sports, only to resume again in 1947. Sadly, two of the Ramblers' members had been killed in the war.

Nicknamed the 'Glory Boys', the team went from strength to strength during 1938 and 1939, drawing in the Devon Junior Cup and winning the annual challenge match for the Barry Cup, playing against Salcombe. On their return to Buckfastleigh the town band led them through the main streets with the whole town coming out to cheer them.

The headquarters for the team was the White Hart pub as the landlord, Bert Cambridge, was the team's full back. Their home pitch was the Recreation Ground and, before the games, the town crier, George White, would go around the streets advertising the fixtures with his booming voice!

Horace Smart played for the Buckfastleigh Ramblers during the 1940s and '50s:

I used to play and then took over as secretary after the war. Bill Hayman was treasurer, and Bill Roberts from Glovers Park (now Bossell Road) used to walk up to the Recreation Ground, whatever the weather, to mark up the pitch. Bill Hayman and I used to spend night after night doing the posters to post up all through the town.

It is a tidy walk up to the Recreation Ground and not many people had cars in those days. Many of our supporters would be older men and now that I am that age I realise what it is like to walk up there in all weathers. Sometimes we would meet the referees off the 3p.m. bus from Plymouth and race them up to the Recreation Ground to start the match at 3.15.

We used to have an old tin bath in the hut up there and whilst the game was being played Bill Hayman used to stoke up the boiler in the shed. After the match all the players, that was 30 of us, used to bath in the same water! The visiting team would be offered the bath first, so we got all the dirty water! Then I used to come home and have another bath!

My bath at home would be in a tin bath in front of the fire but we had to hurry as Ann and I had to be up at the Town Hall for six o'clock because there was a dance nearly every Saturday evening, except when we were playing away.

Ann Smart recalled how the rugby club always organised the dances. 'We had Terry Lamble's Band

and Herbert Owen who played the saxophone,' she said. 'If they weren't available then we would have a ladies' accordion band up from Plymouth.' Horace remembered those days fondly:

We used to have some fun and the young players were so keen. On a Monday evening we would have a meeting to select the team for the following Saturday and when I got home the lads would be queuing up outside my home to find out whether they had been selected.

It was a special era for all the sporting clubs. They played for the town and the town supported the teams. Sadly, although the Ramblers continued successfully up until the 1960s, the club folded in 1967 due to a lack of interest.

Martin Baker, from Buckfast, has the unique record of having played for the Ramblers in every decade since the 1950s:

I played my first game for the Ramblers in 1959, so I played for them in the '50s, and then the '60s, '70s (a one-off friendly match in 1979, despite the club not functioning), '80s, '90s and I even played for them in 2001 when I was 57 – just to make up the numbers!

In 1980, thanks to Martin Baker, the team started up again, only to close down after three years because they were unable to find a home pitch. It was a hard blow. 'The interest was there,' said Martin, 'but we couldn't move forward because we had no home ground.' Betty Major explained:

You can't run a club if you haven't got a ground to play on. However, in 1992, ten years ago, suddenly everyone was keen on rugby again after there had been a successful World Cup. Keith Miller called a meeting and I was asked to attend as I had been treasurer in the old days and I still had the cheque book!

We formed a committee and then reformed the team playing friendlies, and the football club let us play our first few matches on the pitch at Oaklands. We had a meeting with the cricket club and they agreed that we could use their facilities. In 1998 Martin Baker came back as manager.

It is a very friendly club. We play our matches and we feed our players afterwards and we cook whatever we can – usually chips!

Ten years on the Ramblers were still doing well. 'We have a great reputation in the South Devon League for providing a good meal after the match,' smiled Martin, 'thanks to a good team of women.'

The Buckfastleigh Ramblers share the clubhouse facilities with the cricket club who still own the ground. The clubhouse is called the Buckfastleigh Sports Club and it is run by a consortium of cricket and rugby players. Betty talked of the club:

I am the treasurer of the sports club too. We manage the clubhouse and, of course, it has to pay its way. Both the cricket club and the rugby club contribute rent and the sports club keeps all the bar takings. Of course there are bills to be met such as telephone, electricity, rates and a hefty building insurance.

Like the old days there is a real community spirit in the club, most of our players come from Buckfastleigh and we are not in the business of paying players. One of our players from outside the town is deaf. His name is Tony Alderman and he went to New Zealand in the summer to play for Wales in the Deaf World Rugby Cup, and Wales won! So we have a player who has played in an international match.

We have found that other rugby clubs are very helpful – it is much more of a social thing. Last year [2001], because we are within the Dartmoor National Park Authority boundaries, we were not allowed to play at home because of the foot-and-mouth disease outbreak. Other clubs out of the area allowed us to use their grounds for our matches.

The Exeter Chiefs have been down to play at Buckfastleigh and they came again this year. It is because we are a grass-roots rugby club and they are not. Their supporters particularly enjoyed coming because they found everyone here so friendly.

Martin continued:

The Exeter Chiefs are professional players but they came down and treated us as if we were professionals. They treated the match as if it was a full-scale practice game. 'We are not going to treat you as a junior club,' they said, and we didn't want them to. They beat us 80 points to 9 but we respected the fact that they didn't patronise us.

At the time of writing committee members included Betty, her daughter Susan Farley (chair and secretary), Martin Baker, Vaughan Smith, Cid Tozer, Mike Maslin (coach), Andy Rowe, Andy Wells, Angus Cann and Geoff Partridge (captain).

Betty emphasised the high number of dedicated people working for the rugby club and pointed out that the traders in the town, including all of the pubs, provide the club with a lot of support, the main sponsor being Celtic who supplied all of the shirts.

Buckfastleigh Ramblers celebrated the tenth anniversary of the reopening of the rugby club with a champagne party and many of the players from more than 50 years ago were invited. 'I was surprised when I discovered that 12 of my old team mates were still alive,' smiled Horace Smart. 'Of the 1950s team only three had died. Some of them came to the reunion although they don't live in Buckfastleigh any more.' Ann Smart said:

When we were at the party there was the same feeling there that existed in the old days. A lot of the younger

Left: *The Buckfastleigh Ramblers, 1953/4.* Left to right, back row: *W. Roberts, J. Stevens, G. Hayman, G. Battye, J. Ford, D. Evans;* middle: *W. Lee, F. Goodman, D. Hayman, H. Smart, R. Stevens, J. Porter, F. Robinson, T. Hayman;* front: *W. Legg, I. Chiplin, I. Voisey, H.J. Smart, J. Harvey, E. May, W. Hayman, J. Miller, R. Pulford.*

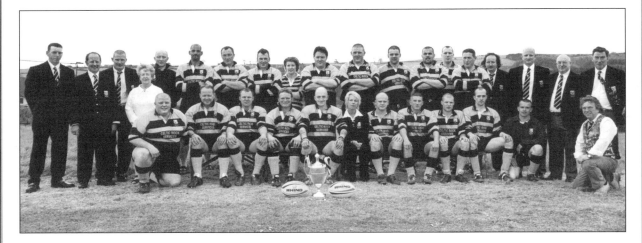

The Buckfastleigh Ramblers, 2002. The photograph shows the team with Cid Tozer (president), Susan Farley (chair) and Steve Chapple (captain).

Right: *The Dart Vale Wheelers, 1936/7. Included in the group are: Bill Roberts, Bill Hayman, Sid Ford, Edgar Reed, Clarence Lock, Bill Lane, Annie Lewis, John Furneaux, Bill Smerdon.*

lads we didn't know but they were very friendly and made us feel so welcome. It was a lovely evening and the present Rugby Club Committee work so hard.

Football, rugby and cricket were not the only sports played in the town, of course. The Hamlyn Playing-Fields in Bossell Lane, donated by the Hamlyn family in 1921, is the home of the bowling and tennis clubs. It was also used by the netball club until the group closed through lack of interest. John Hoff, a former chairman of the bowling club recalled:

In the old days the bowling club had six rinks on three terraces and the tennis club had three courts on three levels. During the Second World War two rinks of the bowling-green and two grass tennis courts were dug as part of the 'dig for victory' campaign. This left four bowling rinks on two levels and one grass court. The remaining land became allotments until the late 1980s.

Brian Norman and his wife, Betty, joined the bowling club in 1970. Brian, the president of the club and president of the Hamlyn Playing-Fields Association, explained that the association is made up of trustees from the participating clubs who administrated the association.

The trusteeship of the land was taken over by the former Urban District Council to whom the bowling club paid only a nominal rent to cover the cost of maintaining the peripheral grassed areas. All the maintenance of the bowling-green itself was undertaken at the expense of the bowling club.

Upon the reorganisation of the local authorities in 1974, when Buckfastleigh Urban District Council was disbanded the trusteeship of the playing-field was automatically assumed by the Teignbridge District Council. However, at the time of writing, ownership of the land was still uncertain. John Hoff explained:

When Teignbridge District Council took over from BUDC in 1974 they took over responsibility for the Hamlyn Playing-Fields, although the bowling club still retained ownership of the clubhouse (pavilion). A new pavilion was built in 1988/89 with 20 per cent of the costs being met by the new Hamlyn Playing-Fields Association.

The new association was formed at that time in order to raise the necessary funds, and to ensure that the new facility would be shared by all clubs using the playing-fields area. The association raises funds to cover ongoing expenses for the pavilion only.

The pavilion is run by the Hamlyn Playing-Fields Association on which members from both the bowling club and the tennis club are represented. The trust ensures that the pavilion is run properly and subscriptions are collected from the members of both clubs towards the cost of running the pavilion.

In 1989/90 Teignbridge District Council initiated a scheme to reconstruct a new six-rink (flat) bowling-green on the old terraced areas. Again a substantial contribution was made by the bowling club and Teignbridge insisted that all peripheral works were to be undertaken by the club itself.

Grants were obtained from the Sports Council, Devon Playing-Fields Association, the Town Council, club members and local traders. A substantial interest-free loan was obtained from the Devon County Bowling Association and a number of small loans were obtained from the club members themselves. Eventually, Teignbridge District Council was able to construct a six-rink bowling-green whilst the members installed an automatic watering system when the new green was built. Brian Norman stated that club members, but primarily Vic Manfield, the groundsman, constructed retaining walls, gates, fences, paving, site scoreboards, signs, and undertook landscaping. John Hoff approved:

The playing facilities were a great improvement. When the bowling club started there weren't any female members. Bessie Lang became one of the first lady members and eventually the ladies formed their own section. The ladies' section is separate and they make their own decisions, but otherwise they join together with the men for decisions affecting the whole club.

Bowling is very popular now. Of course, the facilities are much better and once the financial situation improved the club started to flourish. The beauty of bowling is that anyone can be a reasonable bowler in half a day. But to be really good you have to practise very hard!

The ladies' section began in 1958. Jeanne Pinney and Pauline Manfield started bowling almost 20 years ago. Jeanne had fond memories of the club:

I often used to go up and look over the hedge and watch the bowling. Then my aunt mentioned it to Bessie Lang and she invited me to go up and have a go. Les Lane showed me what to do. Then I persuaded Vic Manfield, who looks after the green, to bring Pauline along which he did. Pauline and I with Diane Raggett, Ann Smart and others, were the youngest there then, and we started the trend for younger people to go bowling. We struggled for a while as we were there with all the older ones, Amy Peachey, Carrie Wilton, Edith Walters and Bessie Lang and Mary Chapple.

I am chairman of the ladies' section and Pauline is captain of the ladies' team. Four of us are represented on the main committee. To start with we only had about ten ladies. In the past we played two games a week if we were lucky, now we play about four or five times a week. I like bowls because of the challenge. When I used to watch it over the fence I thought it looked easier than tennis. When I started playing I realised that there was more to it than I thought.

Buckfastleigh Bowling Club ladies' team, 2002. Left to right: Betty Norman, Diane Raggett, Pauline Manfield, Jeanne Pinney.

The rules have been relaxed quite considerably. We don't have to wear hats now but we do try to look smart. Some people have passed comment about how smart we dress. We do turn out looking the part. Our uniform is white and red. Trousers came in for women for the first time this year, some women look grand in them, some don't.

Pauline talked of the merits of the bowling club:

Bowls is more relaxed. Everywhere you go you meet a lovely lot of people and we get on so well together. Members were more cliquey in the past but we try not to be.

For a small club we have done very well. The women have done so well and I think we are more competitive and certainly more aggressive when we play than the men are.

Brian Norman continued:

The women have done exceptionally well but the men are equally as good and in 2001 we were in the premier league of the Mid-Devon League. In fact we had two teams, A and B, participating for the first time.

David Werry came to live in the town in 1983 and, as a tennis enthusiast, he joined the tennis club at the Hamlyn Playing-Fields and is now secretary:

We are just a small club, we've always been a small club really, but our membership has declined over the years because there do not seem to be the young people coming through to replace the older ones as they drop out. I'm one of the oldest players. There just doesn't seem to be the same interest as there used to be. Twenty years ago the membership was about 40; we only had one court and a tumble-down shed and toilet. Now we have around 20 adult members who enjoy the use of two courts and a modern pavilion, built in the late '80s and shared with the bowls club.

We don't have many teenagers, but then school sports facilities seem to be so much better nowadays. Teignbridge District Council are keen to encourage as many people as possible to play sport so they have recently scrapped the rent we pay in Buckfastleigh.

We are not a competitive club although we still belong to the South Devon Tennis League. Those of us who come just enjoy playing our tennis. Our club nights are Tuesdays and Thursdays. Years ago there were people who played in the winter as well as the summer, but we play mostly in the summer. Teignbridge give us free reign because they want to encourage the club to continue, but to get a club to continue you have to encourage people to come and play.

David and his wife, Ann, enjoy living in Buckfastleigh. David worked for Lloyds Bank when he first came and, in 2003, worked in Buckfastleigh Post Office:

We came from Kingsbridge and people said, 'Well, if you are going to Buckfastleigh you will need to take your boots and shovel because you are going out on the moor, it can be pretty miserable up there weather-wise.' That's not really fair. It's no wetter here than anywhere else, certainly little snow. Buckfastleigh is quieter than Kingsbridge, but it has a character all of its own because it is an industrial town, whereas we have been used to Cornwall and the South Hams which are mostly holiday areas. We have enjoyed it here but it works both ways: if you put something into a place you get something out of it.

Buckfastleigh Amateur Athletics Club started in around 1924 with events, open to towns and villages in the area, taking place in Victoria Park. Later the venue was moved to the Recreation Ground.

Buckfastleigh Club hosted two Devon County Championships, the 100 yards and the 440 yards, and provided two champions, Ralph Dunning in the 100 yards (c.1920), and Leslie Lane in the 440 yards (1927). J. Ford was the 1-mile champion in the 1930s. The coach was George Skewes and there were 50 members in the club which ran successfully until the start of the Second World War when it folded.

The YMCA building on the corner of Chapel Street and New Road is now the home of The Christian Community. Formerly, however, it was a flourishing club for young men with facilities for snooker, billiards and table tennis. Cyril Doidge's father was the YMCA secretary for over 20 years:

When I was 11 years old I would go to the YMCA on a Saturday morning with Dad when he went to do some paperwork. I used to play on the tables. He cut off a cue to make a smaller one for me to use and I used to stand on a box to reach the table. There were two snooker tables – one was a really good one for the experienced players and one was for the less experienced players to use. I mucked around a lot but was good enough by the time I was old enough to join the YMCA properly at 15 years old (previously 17) and to play on the top table. John Pearse and I were the only players who won all three cups at the same time (snooker, billiards and table tennis).

The YMCA was very popular when I started in the early 1950s. It was open Monday to Saturday each week and, in addition to snooker, billiards and table tennis, there were cards, board games such as chess, and there was frequently a whist drive. My parents ran that for years. Ern Pope was the caretaker then and he and Mrs Pope, along with my mum, used to help with the cleaning and serving refreshments. We had a drama group, too, and used to put shows on. There were probably over 100 members, although there wouldn't be as many as that coming in each evening. No youngsters were allowed in and no alcohol was allowed. There wasn't even a coffee bar.

The Young Men's Christian Association (YMCA) was formed in Buckfastleigh in 1889 after a group of local businessmen decided that it was important to provide recreational facilities for the young men of the town. It was agreed that they would construct new premises and the YMCA building, which cost £1,370 to build, was officially opened on Tuesday 15 February 1898 by Dr C.A. Hingston of Plymouth, the president of the South West District of YMCAs.

Dr Hingston described the building as:

... prettily constructed of local limestone with white brick facing with its title in full 'Young Men's Christian Association', on the façade, [and] is a distinct acquisition to the town.

He announced that the vice-president and treasurer was Mr C. King-Smith and the hon. secretary Mr W. Chaffe. The committee members were Messrs A.G. Abbot, W. Bradford, J. Weekes, G.H.A. Northcote, M. Hoare, J. Taverner, W. Shute, A. Butcher, P.H. Wills and F. Pinkhern.

After the opening the men attended a public luncheon in the Town Hall at 2p.m., over which James Hamlyn JP presided.

Local business and professional men had done a superb job in providing such excellent facilities and by 1907 the membership was 34 with 76 associate members, although there was a weekly attendance of only 20 young men.

The YMCA was in existence for exactly 100 years. On Thursday 15 January 1989 the board of management decided at a committee meeting that, in view of their desperate financial situation, the YMCA branch should close on 30 September 1989.

In giving the reason for the closure of the YMCA in 1989 the chairman said that:

... in view of the complete change over the last decade in the social and recreational activities of our local population we feel that there is little desire on the part of the local people to join the branch in its traditional form. Consequently, our income has declined and there is, in our opinion, no longer the prospect of an active branch which will withstand time, and progress in the way that all local branches should progress.

As well as sport teams and the YMCA Buckfastleigh has always abounded with leisure clubs and societies. For the past 100 years the swimming-pool, in particular, has been a favourite place during the summer for children and teenagers to socialise and enjoy a swim. It is still the principal facility in the town for young people and one can only applaud the forethought of the Hamlyn family for providing one for the use of the town. Although Teignbridge District Council have now taken responsibility for its maintenance, the swimming-pool actually belongs to Buckfastleigh.

The Buckfastleigh Swimming Club began in April 1990 and a month later, at a cost of £8,000, the newly heated swimming-pool opened for the summer. Jacqui Butler, a member of the swimming club committee, explained:

Over 80 children have enrolled in the swimming club and we have two galas which we organise. We are concerned about the short time the swimming-pool is open during the year. It opens late in the year and closes before the children go back to school. Often we have had lovely weather during the late summer months and we feel that it could be open longer. Adults want it open earlier too. Usually it has closed before they get back from work in the evenings.

Most of the children spend a good deal of time in the swimming-pool, as do our children. We have excellent swimming instructors on site and I know that the children are in safe and competent hands.

Have Buckfastleigh's sports clubs – football, cricket and rugby, in particular – withstood the test of time? Are they progressing as all clubs should progress? Certainly, the bowling club appears to be attracting relatively younger members, with women members as keen as the men. And there are now aerobics classes, and a women's running group in the town that has about 30 members in total.

'Women want to improve their fitness,' said Jaine Swift, who is the women's running group leader, 'but also they enjoy the social side and are concerned about safety and running on their own.'

Women are more interested in participating in team activities in the twenty-first century than standing on the sidelines and, gradually, more young men are opting to play for their local football, cricket and rugby teams again, but will the clubs continue to attract younger members in the future?

Above: *The Town Council led by Town Mayor Doreen Trude, 1993/4. Left to right, back row: Jim Mabin, Ivor Ford, Graham Dandridge, John Bovey, Peter Thornhill, John Bolton (councillors); front: Anne Ryan, Joan Lock, Peggy Henley (councillors), Jim Elliott (deputy mayor), Doreen Trude, Yvonne Bevan (Town Clerk), Janice Palmer (councillor).*

Left: *Mayor Jim Mabin with former Town Mayor, Doreen Trude, 1996.*

The opening of the new relief road from Buckfastleigh to Buckfast, 1997.

Twenty

THE 1990S: WORKING FOR THE TOWN

The last decade of the twentieth century was chaotic on a national and international scale, and the impact of the Gulf War, and the war in former Yugoslavia, was considerable. It was, however, countered by some good news, such as Nelson Mandela's inauguration as the first black president of South Africa.

In Britain the repercussions following the introduction of the poll tax by Margaret Thatcher, with demonstrations regionally as well as nationally, were enormous and even in Buckfastleigh anti-poll-tax protesters confronted the MP Patrick Nicholls at Furzeleigh Mill near Dartbridge. The fierce controversy surrounding BSE and CJD, which led to the banning of British beef, was especially felt in farming areas like Devon. There was a national sense of uncertainty about the future as the divorce of the Prince and Princess of Wales in 1996 was followed by Diana's tragic and untimely death in 1997.

At the beginning of the decade inflation was at its highest for ten years and unemployment figures were rising for the first time in four years, whilst crime had increased considerably, often due to the influence of drugs.

A report by the Buckfastleigh Health Centre indicated that the population of Buckfastleigh suffered from rural isolation, high unemployment and low income and these factors affected particularly the high numbers of lone parents and their families who lived in the town. Housing was another concern, some privately rented housing was sub-standard and the percentage of rented accommodation was higher in Buckfastleigh than anywhere else in England, with relatively fewer people owning their own homes than in any other place.

Crime statistics for Buckfastleigh were low at the beginning of the '90s compared to the average for Devon as a whole. However, the town had almost three times the incidence of drug offences than had occurred in the whole of Devon.

Throughout the decade vandalism and petty crime increased the same as elsewhere in the country. However, townsfolk were unprepared for the major crimes that were committed over a four-year period, in a town that still had a population of under 4,000 and no resident police officer.

Holy Trinity Church after the fire.

Serious crimes included a night attack by an intruder on a couple in their home at Bossell Park in March 1993 – it was later revealed that the attack was drug-related. In 1996 a local man was convicted of the murder of a stable-girl who worked in the vicinity.

A sensation was caused in 1992 when a man who had previously lived in Buckfastleigh for a short time was arrested and convicted for several bizarre murders of homosexual men in London. The media had a field-day and, if they did not realise it then, by the end of the decade local people were forced to recognise that Buckfastleigh was neither a backwater nor a rural idyll any longer. The town reflected the vulnerability and increase in violence that affected towns and cities across Britain.

One crime that hit hard was the arson attack on Buckfastleigh's 800-year-old Parish Church, Holy Trinity, on the night of Tuesday 21 July 1992. So fierce was the blaze that by the time the alarm was raised it was too late to save the building. The clergy, church members and local people were devastated but there was a determination to rebuild and funds started to pour in for the new project.

However, the decision by the Parish Church Council not to rebuild on the site of Holy Trinity, but to knock down St Luke's Church in Plymouth Road and build a brand new one on the same site, was met with disbelief by many people who did not want to lose another church. However, Revd John Rowland

and the PCC were convinced that the town should look to the future and build a church in the centre of Buckfastleigh that would meet the needs of people in the twenty-first century. The decision to build was made and it took six long years from start to finish. It was an act of faith by a membership that recognised that the Church needed to adapt and change if it was to survive and be relevant to the lives of the community it served.

In March 1993 the new health practice building was completed. Dr James Hedger explained:

It is a timber-framed building which is triple-glazed and very efficient energy-wise. We won the SW Electricity Board Small Business Award for the Environment and went down to the Plymouth Pavilions, where we had a nice dinner and received the award.

We moved out of the health centre next door, which has now been converted into three houses, and built this practice on what used to be the ends of the gardens of two houses in Crest Hill, and a spare bit of field which used to be owned by the health authority. However, five years after the new building was completed it became apparent that it wasn't big enough and now we have completed our extension.

Dr Derek Moore, the well-known and respected family doctor who had been practising in the town for over 30 years, retired on 2 October 1993, a few months after the new health clinic was completed. He would be greatly missed. The remaining partners, Dr Edwards, Dr Tessa Barton and Dr James Hedger, chose Dr Jonathan Towers to join them in general practice from 3 October 1993. This strong partnership, supported by other medical centre staff, would be responsible for the town's health for the rest of the decade and into the new millennium.

In the mid-1990s there was a growing awareness of local people that the town needed to change and that if they did not instigate the changes no one would. Doreen Trude was elected Mayor in 1994:

I was quoted in one of the local newspapers as saying Buckfastleigh was dying on its feet. Of course, I didn't realise then that there was a reporter within hearing [range]. I did not want it to get into the press but it did. But, after it was printed, several people came up to me and said, 'You were right, we are dying on our feet.'

Buckfastleigh is always left out on a limb. With the reorganisation of local government in 1974 we had a chance of going with Teignbridge District Council or with South Hams. I remember discussing it with Clarence Northcote who said it doesn't matter who we join up with, we shall still be left out on a limb.

Julia Cross from Buckfast agreed:

1974 was when everything stopped happening. In 1991 the precept was £15,000, which would go nowhere, it wasn't going to attract captains of industry. The local council had no power to do anything and there was a great loss of interest. There was no money to spend.

Doreen Trude considered that Buckfastleigh had become a commuter town:

People live here and eat here but go out of town to work and do their shopping. I stood in Fore Street one night before the one-way system was introduced, watching all the cars coming up Fore Street, and there was one continual stream of traffic. I wondered where all the traffic had come from and then I realised that they were all coming back from work.

It was not only Doreen who had noticed the flow of traffic – Fore Street became a considerable problem for local people who found that if you were elderly, walking with children or pushing a pram, you were taking your life in your hands. Julia Cross, who had moved with her family to Buckfast in 1983, could not understand how people could live with the nightmare of heavy lorries passing through.

James Price and Julia and Ann Howkins, who lived at the off-licence, got eight people together to see if they could solve the problem. Ann's business had suffered. She had been writing constantly to her local MP but the MP could only send one letter to the County Council and it was clear that a single person was not going to achieve much. Julia explained:

We could achieve much more by working as a group. Some of the members were Conservatives but then we invited others in and became a non-political group all working for the town.

It was precisely this determination from several different groups of people in Buckfastleigh that encouraged a new awareness among local people. It did not matter that people did not always agree with the proposals, it was important that local people were involved in the decision-making at all stages.

It was agreed that a relief road was needed to take all the heavy traffic in and out of the town. During the next five years the Traffic Action Group worked extremely hard, studying the highways and transportation programme for the county. They lobbied every quarterly meeting with photographs and circulated information to the members of Devon County Council about the progress of the Traffic Action Group, even placing slogans in front of them such as, 'If Fore Street was your street you'd do something about it.' Julia explained the campaign:

We needed to get the support of the Dartmoor National Park Authority who were sympathetic. Finally, our submission worked its way through the system, although in the interim period the system and the funding rules changed.

THE 1990S: WORKING FOR THE TOWN

There was not a lot of money for all the major schemes that were needed in Devon but they were impressed with the Buckfastleigh scheme and one of the key things was that we took a ten-minute video of Fore Street. It was a horrendous afternoon, and very wet, and in ten minutes we had enough material to make an impression when we gave our presentation to the council. One of the councillors said, 'It is unreal.' I replied, 'It's not unreal it's happening, it is there on your video tape and something has to be done about it.'

There was opposition to the route that the Traffic Action Group recommended. A group under the acronym CARES (Campaigning for Alternative Routes that are Environmentally Sensitive) opposed the scheme due to its environmental impact and road safety. They proposed a shorter level route through Millman's Orchard and Lower Town. Stuart Barker noted that CARES was effective in that the objections caused a public enquiry. Finally, however, the County Council decided that the route the Traffic Action Group recommended was the feasible one. The contracts were awarded and the work started in 1996, spanning two financial years.

In 1997, when the road was finally completed, there was an enormous sense of satisfaction amongst campaigners. Julia recalled:

Later at the official opening of the relief road we were told that we had conducted a civilised campaign which was well thought-out with proper arguments. We kept the campaign to the real issues and we played the cards of the blight on the town, the damage to the buildings, the fact that no one wanted to invest here and so on. As a group we considered that we had achieved more than we could have achieved by being on the Town Council. But we did need the council's support and the former Mayor, Jim Mabin, gave us his backing.

Stuart Barker continued:

After the road was started we wanted to know what the community thought of their town and what they wanted to see happen, so we sent out a questionnaire to all the residents in the town. We were staggered when 1,200 forms came back – about 38 per cent of the population. It was a huge representative sample. People wrote very gloomy things about the future of the town and its problems but many also told us their aspirations, the things they wanted to see happen. Things that they thought would make a difference to the town. There were so many suggestions.

What matters is that you care about Buckfastleigh. You are a Buckfastleigh person if you live here now and care about the people and the town. It's not about where or when you were born – it's about whether you care.

Some 150 people cared enough to attend a meeting of Buckfastleigh 2000 which was set up in 1995 to look at the needs of the town and its community. Initially, it was chaired by Stuart Barker and then by Julia Cross, who recalled:

We went out of our way to consult local people. Buckfastleigh 2000 was quite small at the end but we achieved quite a lot. The best part was the support that we received from all the agencies – Dartmoor National Park Authority, Devon County Council, the Community Council, Teignbridge District Council and other bodies that are interested in what we are doing. They all came to the meetings.

Stuart Barker commented:

We had to address the concerns of local people and removing large lorries from Fore Street was people's number one concern. By that time the town had been killed, of course. People were quite right about that. No one was coming to the town to shop and no one was taking up the options to buy empty premises in the town. The community realised that.

Having sorted out the relief road and removed the lorries local people then wanted wider pavements. The pavements were too steep in places and not wide enough for a young mum with a pram and kiddy in tow, or for a wheelchair, and people were falling over on the narrow slippery surfaces. Vehicles were always mounting the pavements, forcing pedestrians into doorways to get out of the way. The damage to Fore Street was very evident. 68 per cent of those who answered the questionnaire wanted traffic sorted out and wider pavements.

It was agreed that after the opening of the relief road they would wait six months before doing an evaluation of the town centre to see whether a traffic scheme was needed. Was it the lorries that were causing the problem or the volume of the traffic? Six months later another evaluation of Fore Street was undertaken and found to be just as bad. There were fewer lorries using it but it was choc-a-bloc with cars. Stuart explained:

Most of the chaos in Fore Street would be people coming home from work in their cars, not bothering to use the relief road, blocking Fore Street in each direction and getting angry – and people wanted something done about it.

Plans were drawn up for a traffic centre management scheme for a one-way system. The scheme plans all included wider pavements and loading bays to give pedestrians better access to all the shops. On the working party were members of the Traffic Action Group, retailers, people from the community, members of the District Society, Chamber of Trade, and representatives from the industrial estate. They worked closely with the Town Council.

Left: *In the past pear pies were baked and a general fête held in the town on a day known as Pear Pie Day. The tradition was resurrected and this photograph shows the Pear Pie Day celebrations in 1999.*

'We met with several head engineers from the County Environment Department and had to convince them that the scheme would work,' explained Stuart. 'Not everyone on the council agreed with the decision but it was the majority decision.'

During 1995 and 1996 there were not only changes to the town itself but also tensions within Buckfastleigh Town Council, about its organisation, support and independence. The end of 1996 saw the resignation of both the Deputy Mayor and the Town Clerk.

Stuart Barker was elected as Deputy Mayor in 1997 and later Town Mayor when Jim Mabin stood down. Stuart recalled:

I was determined to get things right and the interim Town Clerk addressed many of the problems of the council and put us right. The role of the Town Clerk is very important and it is a difficult role. It is a job where you have to be everything. You have to be a solicitor, an accountant, a caretaker, a hall-booking clerk, clerk, computer operator, telephonist, mentor and take on board everyone's concerns and problems. The Town Clerk would have been the chief executive in the era of the Urban District Council. It is a very important job. Now they do not have such a high status.

After a period of instability Sarah Woodman was employed as Town Clerk:

I got the job of Town Clerk after seeing an advert in the paper. I had worked in local government for a long time, mostly in housing. When my children were small I worked with my husband doing computerised accounts and that was the kind of experience that was required in Buckfastleigh. Accountancy requirements have become more important.

My latest contribution has been to introduce coffee into council meetings! Before I came, members of the council used to spend long hours deliberating with only water to drink. My only worry about introducing coffee was that the councillors would then prolong the meetings!

Being Town Clerk is a really enjoyable job – and it is what you make of it. I have got quite involved in promoting tourism, partly because when I started there wasn't anyone doing that. We produce a town diary now and we have a town guide so our role has expanded quite considerably. [Sarah is responsible for serving the council and looking after the Town Hall.] *The Town Hall Trust used to be called the Town Hall Trust and Institute, now the word 'Institute' has been removed from the title. I used to be secretary to the Town Hall Trust and the Buckfastleigh Trust. The Town Hall Trust is made up of town councillors so when the councillors change so do the trustees of the Town Hall.*

Stuart Barker continued:

The Buckfastleigh Trust is an umbrella group which facilitates local projects. There is a need for a registered charity to access funds. Through the Buckfastleigh Trust we have been given a considerable amount of grant-aid for the benefit of the town – somewhere in the region of half-a-million pounds. We persuaded English Heritage to put money into the town to enhance the infrastructure because comments in the questionnaire we sent out were concerned with the dilapidation of properties. We have actually spent over £3 million. Local people have been shocked by this amount. Not pleased, but shocked, because they think the money should have been spent on something else. But if we hadn't spent the money on the town it might well have been given to Scarborough, for instance. All grant-aid is designated for a specific purpose – it can't be spent on just anything we want to spend it on.

The Town Enhancement Scheme was funded partly by English Heritage, the European Regional Development Fund, Teignbridge District Council, the Town Council and Devon County Council. It was a true partnership scheme.

The work started in March 1999 and finished in August 1999. 'It caused a lot of disruption,' said Stuart, 'and it was when the work started that we received criticism – probably because local people suddenly realised the enormity of it all.'

Buckfastleigh was presented with the South West Award for the best town enhancement scheme in the

South West after the completion. Stuart commented:

Buckfastleigh is now on the map. A few years ago no one had heard of Buckfastleigh. When I was Mayor I went to many committee meetings all over the place and those in authority now know that Buckfastleigh stands for the community and for the community wanting to improve the town. That is something we should be quite proud of. Whatever people think the money has been wisely spent and traders are doing more business.

Over the years the Town Hall premises have been vandalised by children and young people who enter the building unsupervised. Sarah recalled problems:

One of my first jobs here was boxing in all the electrics, because children used to come in and turn off the electricity when performances and other events were in progress. It was dangerous, as you had to get down to the entrance hall to get to the box. Now we have CCTV cameras which have proved very effective and we don't get so much trouble.

I didn't know Buckfastleigh at all well before I came. I live at High Beara and my children went to Dartington Primary School, so I always used to go in that direction. I used to come to Buckfastleigh occasionally when the children were younger, and in pushchairs, and I must admit I found Fore Street very difficult to negotiate. As I didn't enjoy it I used to go elsewhere. Of course, everything is different in Fore Street now.

I used to feel sorry for Buckfastleigh as it always looked rather a depressed sort of place which didn't seem to be going anywhere at all. That was my first impression of the town. It was just like a black hole in an area that seemed so thriving, on the surface anyway. I know that most rural areas aren't affluent at all and hide quite a high level of deprivation.

However, when I started working here I was struck by the very good sense of community that exists which I found quite exciting, I admit. As Town Clerk you realise how many people there are who give of their time. They don't expect anything back – they are just remarkably generous people, I find that rewarding.

Dr James Hedger, a partner at the Buckfastleigh Health Clinic, agreed with Sarah Woodman:

In the early '90s we doctors sensed that there was a lot of despair in the community, mainly through unemployment, drug abuse and a few cases of Aids. It seemed that Buckfastleigh was going nowhere but by producing our report on the Town's Health we got a community worker, Carol Cowell, and the despair that we felt then seems to have dissipated. Things have moved on now. A more positive atmosphere has come about since the community worker has been here, among all sections of the town.

Sarah continued:

We have laid the bare bones of improvements for the town and now we need the traders to help and the tourist organisations to encourage people into the town. It is going to be fascinating to see how Buckfastleigh develops over the next few years.

Although there were those who disagreed with the changes to Buckfastleigh's town centre, as the 1990s and the twentieth century drew to a close, apathy and depression gave way to a more positive outlook. There was a greater determination by many people to make Buckfastleigh a more vibrant town in which to live, and when better to put these dreams into action than at the beginning of a new century?

Cottages in Station Road. (Photograph taken by Patricia Cairn-Duff)

Buckfastleigh farm-hands, c.1930s.

Henry and Mary Hoare at the stables, 1912.

Twenty-One

FARMERS AND FARMING: A WAY OF LIFE

The relationship between rural people and the land has always been a compelling one. Much of Devon's land is lush and fertile and, in South Devon in particular, it is redder and richer, with orchards and water-meadows enticing the wealthy landowner and farmer alike.

There have been, and still are, many farms surrounding Buckfastleigh. Some, centuries old, still exist – farms like Bilberry, Bowden, Wallaford, Button, Rhyll, Beara, Dean Court, Caddaford and Bigadon.

Local people have worked in agriculture as well as in industry and it is inevitable that women, like men, have been tied to the land over the centuries, as farmers' daughters or wives, or labourers.

In 1843 the Poor Law Commission stated that farm work was a most laborious task for women, literally a back-breaking job. A farm journal from 1800 revealed that women's work included weeding and gardening, spreading dung, haymaking, hoeing turnips and digging potatoes. The men's jobs, in comparison, were shepherding and ploughing with oxen or horses.

The contribution of women to agriculture was quite considerable in Devon until the middle of the nineteenth century, when agricultural machinery was introduced into farming. With men monopolising the machinery women were left to do the more manual, less interesting jobs, until female labourers started to abandon agriculture for other work.

The Boveys were important landowners and possessed much of the ground surrounding Buckfastleigh. They intermarried with the Furneauxs and were an important family in the town in the 1880s, their family tree dating back to William the Conqueror's time and before. John Bovey's grandfather, who was farming in 1855, was always known as Squire Bovey and was treated with great respect by local people. He seemed to have been a fair man who would give a couple of days work to anyone without a job.

Feeding the hens at a farm near Buckfastleigh, c.1930.

Betty Martin and her parents came to live at Hillside, Old Totnes Road, in 1947/48. Betty grew up with animals around her, but it was not until she married John Bovey in 1949 and moved to Merrifield, just past Barn Park on the Hapstead Road, that she lived on a farm:

There was no electricity so we used candles to go to bed and also prepared oil-lamps during the day. My mother-in-law Ethel, who everyone knew as Paddy, would put the candles in their holders for each bedroom on the kitchen table with a box of matches, ready for the evenings, so when we wanted to go to bed we just picked up the candles and lit them.

On smaller farms it was the farmer's wife herself who did most of the dairy work. Betty continued:

The men used to get up first to do the milking and then we got up. I used to bottle the milk every day by hand. After the cows were milked the milk came in and it went through the strainer and cooler. The big pan of milk was given a good stir to mix the cream back in or otherwise one bottle would have all cream and the other ones wouldn't.

I would get the pint dipper (a pint measure with a handle), line up the bottles and fill them with milk. Then I got the bottle tops – the cardboard ones with the hole in the middle – and I went along all the bottles putting the tops on.

We did quart (two pints) bottles and one-pint bottles.

It took most of the mornings to do the dairy work and for John to do the milk round. The dairy was cleaned and scrubbed out before John got back from his round. We never had lunch until all the bottles had been washed in hot water with washing soda.

We always had South Devon cows because of the quality of the milk. A bit later, when we started sending milk direct to the milk factory instead of bottling it ourselves, we bought some Friesians that gave quantity instead of quality. Different cows produce different kinds of milk. It all got tested when it got to Daws Creamery in Totnes, near the Railway Station. Putting milk into churns saved us a tremendous amount of work.

Paddy was such an interesting person. She was responsible for all the chickens, ducks and geese – feeding, looking after them, plucking and cooking them. We used to have goose for Michaelmas, which was a farming tradition. Paddy was a marvellous cook and you should have seen what she would turn out on the big, black range that she had to cook on. Breakfast was a proper cooked breakfast with fatty bacon and double-yolked eggs, if we had some, and hogs pudding. Paddy did all the cooking, I helped with the vegetables and we'd do the washing together.

We owned 28 acres and we could only take nine or ten cows. It wasn't a lot to work on but we made a living. Hay was needed to feed the cattle, which meant that certain fields had to lie fallow for a short time. We also grew beets and swedes to feed the animals. In the winter we brought in the beets and we put them through a beet and chaff cutter – that was one of my jobs in the afternoon. All that had to be prepared before the cows came in. We would mix the chopped beets with the chaff whilst the cows were being milked. I loved the way of life and preferred what I did to housework.

In the winter we used to go up to Deepe, where we had a field, with a horse and cart to cut hay out of a hayrick. We used a big, long hay knife, with a double handle on the top, and would cut out the rick, put it onto the cart, and bring it back to the farm and store it in the hayloft.

After my children were born I would take them up to the field in summer and plonk them on a blanket under a tree, give them some sweeties and toys, and I would turn the hay by hand, working up there all day by myself, except for the children. In the evenings local people would help to gather it all in and we always provided a load of sandwiches, tea and buns for them.

We all worked from dawn to dusk. Most of my farming memories are of Paddy because we worked together in the house but I went out with John, as well, to do the hedging and other jobs. That is, he would do the hedging and I would sweep up the road after him! We grew potatoes that we could sell to make extra money.

It was a hard way of life, and in many cases farmers were only tenants of the land they lived on. Sometimes farmers could not afford to pay labourers, which is why the womenfolk were an important part of farming life. Yet, for both male and female farmers, it was a life they understood and loved, however hard. They had a rapport with the land and the animals, which developed in most cases when they were children growing up on a farm.

Betty Tucker grew up at Bilberry Farm. Her parents, the Rowlands, were tenant farmers and her paternal grandparents lived at New Park, further along the valley:

Mr and Mrs J. Hoare and family at Caddaford Farm, 1914.

I used to help on the farm when I was on school holidays. Horses were very special to me and I used to ride everywhere. My grandfather had 21 shire-horses that were very lovely gentle giants, really. He was very strict about the care of the horses and stipulated that if any of the men ill-treated one of them they would be sacked immediately. He would not tolerate his horses being cruelly treated. If at any time I didn't have a horse to ride he would send one down to me.

My parents were dairy farmers in the 1930s and '40s. We had Guernsey cows so the milk was thick and creamy. We used to start milking at five in the morning and by seven the milk lorry was in the yard ready to take the milk in bulk to Totnes Creamery, now Unigate.

I always did the night call when the cows were calving, to help my Dad. We had dogs, horses, pigs, an otter as well as cows, and some of the cows were tame.

On Sunday I was allowed to bring the milk in to Buckfastleigh by pony and trap. Mr Parsons, who was at the Co-op dairy in Chapel Street, used to help lift the milk out of the cart. One Sunday there was another man there called Charlie Lewis, and he said, 'Let's have a race.' We agreed that we should race up to the chapel and then turn the horses around. It was six on a Sunday morning and all the mill workers would be having a lie-in and wanting to rest. Anyway, someone told my Dad and I got into trouble.

My grandfather used to have grazing rights from Wallaford Down to the Avon Dam. We did a round-up in September, driving the cattle and Dartmoor ponies over to Cornwood for branding. I used to go with my *father and the other men and my father would say, 'You realise that you have to ride all day? We can't come home with you when you are tired.' By the end of the day I was practically asleep in the saddle but I never gave in.*

Bilberry had seven acres of orchards. In the autumn local people would come along and pick up the apples and would get sixpence a sack. All the apples went for cider making to cider makers called Manning from Tuckenhay. Sadly, the orchards are gone now.

It was a way of life but it wasn't always easy, but if you are brought up on a farm you are part of the land.

We didn't live far from John and Betty Bovey and Betty Wilton lived at Wootten Farm. If anyone called out 'Betty!' we would all answer! Oh, it was such a happy life and we had a lot more than many other people. My Mum was very good and she always had other children to stay in the holidays. There was so much laughter in our home.

When my father died we moved to my maternal grandparents' home at Dean Prior. They were called Mitchell, and grandfather Mitchell was a miller. He allowed me to keep pigs. I was given a pig when I was small and they just grew on me! Anyway, we lived at the Mill and the Coultons lived at Dean Court adjoining the Mill.

Bilberry Farm now belongs to the Coultons. Jack and Joy Coulton bought Bilberry Farm when my father died and Mary Truman, their daughter, inherited it.

Garth Grose's mother, Mary, grew up at Caddaford Farm, near High Beara. She was born in 1894 and went to Buckfastleigh School around 1899/1900. 'She used to walk from Caddaford to school and back and she had a pet lamb which used to come with her!' laughed Garth.

Although Garth lived in Ashburton with his mother as he was growing up, he spent most of his time at Caddaford Farm, by that time rented from the Church Commissioners by his aunt:

I loved growing up on the farm and I was out there most weekends and holidays. My aunt had six children and I was the extra one when I was out there but I used to work to make up for it. I used to collect the logs in, milk cows by hand or make ricks. That was where I learnt how to farm and from where my interest in farming came.

They used to throw me up on the cart-horses and I used to ride one occasionally into Mr Carne, the blacksmith, at Dean. He would shoe the horse and then chuck me back up again! They were huge horses and the one I rode mostly was called Jubilee. Probably after King George V.

One day I was riding Jubilee past the old paper-mill up the Totnes Road. I didn't see the train that was coasting quietly down the line. Just as we got to the top of the hill it suddenly let out a blast of steam and didn't Jubilee rear! A man in his garden called out, 'Hang on to him, boy, hang on to him, you'll be all right.' It frightened me and the horse.

Up at Caddaford there are some cottages called Well Cottages and there was a place there for keeping cattle in and a chap used to look after the cattle. I was sent there one day to give him a message and I had just gone up Caddaford Hill and was walking along the road when I saw something in the distance. 'What the devil is this,' I thought. It was rats, dozens and dozens of rats! I shot up on the gatepost as all these rats went by. Big ones, little ones squeaking in the hedges, some dragging their tails and some clearly old ones. I watched them all go by and then went up on the road and met a man called Mr Wallace.

'Mr Wallace,' I said, 'I've just seen hundreds of rats!'
'Hundreds, boy?' he asked.
'Yes,' I replied
'Ah, that's good,' he said.
'What do you mean?' I asked.
'They're changing house,' he replied. 'They've been and eaten all they could find down here and they've moved on up to the next farm.'

All the walls around were stone walls and the rats used to burrow underneath and live on the corn from the cattle feeds. Once they brought concrete in that was the ends of the rats. We used to catch them by putting cakes in a barrel and trapping the rats in the barrel! That was before poisons came in.

I used to drive tractors in all kinds of weather. Even if the weather is bad you can still enjoy it because you can watch the birds. When I have been ploughing new ground I've seen seagulls fly over and almost get buried with the ploughing they have been that eager to get the worms. On occasions you might get between 400 and 1,000 birds flying behind you all through the day and gradually they would fly off to the coast. Then as the afternoon goes by you would end up with one last one who would be desperate to fly off but couldn't resist going after one more worm.

Henry Hoare, farmer.

Garth has a keen eye for nature and he recorded his

observations in the poems that he wrote. His love of farming and the countryside, especially Dartmoor, is heart-warming:

One summer night we were coming back from Caddaford after cutting the corn with scythes and stacking it up when I heard a weird noise in the field. So I went back and peered through the gate to the field and there, down beside the corn, having just come out to have a look around, were two corncrakes with their chicks. Since that day I haven't seen any more corncrakes. We used to hear them in the corn and the grass in those days, but they have all gone now because of the different methods in farming. In those days the corn wouldn't be cut until the end of July. The birds were quite common then but through cutting the corn earlier the corncrakes have gone. I think you can still see those funny-looking birds in Ireland and on the coast of Scotland.

The first signs of changes in the environment – unnoticed by most people, and, perhaps, as far as corncrakes were concerned, of little consequence, started to appear with changes in farming practices, especially when mechanisation arrived. Garth, who spent most of his adult working-life at Bowdley Farm, continued:

Later we had a self-binder which cut the corn and tied the corn up into sheaves. All we had to do then was stand the sheaves up. The self-binder was a vast improvement on cutting the corn with scythes.

Cutting corn was hard work but you were able to lift what you could. If it was too heavy you just shook some off. Now with the great big bales you either lift them or leave them there. They are too heavy. It's man against the machines.

At Caddaford, before the war, local men, and sometimes whole families, used to come out to help with the harvesting. Some men would come just for the free cider. Auntie would come out with the rhubarb jam sandwiches and jugs of tea and a can of milk. I used to catch harvest mice and shove them inside my shirt or pockets but they all escaped. Sometimes they would run up the corn, bite off the head and run back down the stalk and eat the corn.

John Bickford who, with his father, was a tenant of Dean Combe Farm, part of Lord Churston's estate, also described the work that had to be done to get the corn in before the war:

We cut the corn with three horses and a binder. We then stood the corn in stiches of six sheaves for two weeks and then it would be put into a rick. The corn would be threshed in the barn with a stationary engine. Later the travelling thresher came to the farms until the advent of the combine harvester. Local people would come and help us when we were cutting the corn. We would have great fun in the fields and there would be hogsheads of cider for everyone to drink.

After the war everything was different, combine harvesters came in and a different type of tractor. We had a bar thresher and a stationary engine. The sheaves would be put into the thresher and they would be threshed. You can imagine the dust this caused. It was terrible. It was the dust that caused my chest problems.

John Bickford was fortunate that his wife, Joan, had grown up on a farm, worked as a Land Army girl during the war and enjoyed farming. 'Joan could milk cows and drive a tractor,' said John, smiling. 'That's why he married me,' laughed Joan.

It was certainly an advantage to have a wife who was skilled, or willing to learn, and worked hard. John and Joan's daughter, Margaret, also worked on the farm for several years and was an invaluable support to her parents. John continued:

Farming was a hard life. Joan used to do bed-and-breakfast to help us to make ends meet. But it was a bind that whatever you did during the day you still had to milk the cows at night. It was hard, especially when you were harvesting.

In 1970 I gave up milking and went on to beef farming because I had grazing rights on Dartmoor and I could get a hill cow subsidy. That meant you were paid for every cow you had. The grazing rights went with the farm which I bought in 1961 after Lord Churston decided to sell up.

John and Joan have retired – John believes that there is far too much red tape and bookwork. 'Every cow has to have a passport now!' exclaimed John. 'Looking back they say that there were the good years and the bad years – but you got over the bad years.'

Most farmers consider that the Second World War marked the changes in farming practices. Bob Beard, whose farm is on the edge of Buckfast in Buckfastleigh West, also inherited his farm from his father:

In the 1930s it was mixed farming. There were five people employed here then. We had the big barn roof to thatch, hayricks to thatch, hedges to pare and repair, stables and cow sheds to clean out, cows to milk morning and evening and horses to groom. There were no tractors then. When the war came most of the fields were ploughed up. Eventually, my father sowed the fields back to grass with his own grass seed. The cornricks and the hayrick were threshed. All the grass in the fields was grown from our own seed. The war didn't help but it was after the war that things changed.

I had trained as an engineer and then got a job with the Milk Marketing Board. There wasn't enough money in the farm to pay me and the labourer who was employed by my father. Then, when my father died in

Hoare ploughing match, 1911. Henry Hoare is sitting on the ground (second from left), *John Hoare is in the second row* (seated, far left) *and Ralph Hoare is standing in the third row* (centre right) *wearing a pale suit and a flat cap.*

1973, I took over the farm, but the death duties made life difficult. They were a millstone in those days.

However, I worked for 30 years selling and servicing garden machinery and chainsaws. This was a business that I ran alongside the farm and because I had the business I could afford to have someone come in and do some of the odd jobs that needed doing.

The land belongs to the family. We raise the grass to make hay. We make hay in the summer and in the autumn the cows come in and eat the rest of the grass. In the winter and spring we do repairs, grass combing and rolling the fields for the next crop of grass. A local farmer pays for the use of the fields for grazing for his animals. The same family have used it for over 40 years.

Adrian Dawe's father was farming in Cornwall until 1964. Adrian joined him as a teenager in 1962 and, being the only son, his father took him into partnership with him. It worked well and they bought Tordean Farm in March 1964:

Tordean was a mixed farm then, which included sheep, fattening cattle and rearing calves, a few pigs, poultry, corn, making our own hay and silage. Before we came it had been a dairy farm but neither of us were keen on dairy farming. Even in 1960 it had been clear that you had to have a good number of cows to make it viable. We did have cows and suckling calves and grew corn for the first few years and put in 70 acres of barley. By 1967/68 the farm was in great order and we did well from then on.

Adrian's father then started to diversify into the meat trade. Although the farm was beginning to respond, they did not feel that they were getting a good return on their capital and considered they should be looking for something more profitable. At the end of the 1960s, disillusioned with traditional farming, and with contacts in the meat trade and an increase in the sale of freezers, the Dawes converted the dairy into a butchery:

My father was a buyer for a couple of abattoirs at the time and also supplying carcasses to Smithfield, via Newton Abbot, and consequently people would say, 'Can you do me half a lamb for the freezer?' or 'I'd like half a pig put away,' and that's how it started and it just grew and grew from there.

I devoted most of my time to butchering and went on a crash course to learn the rudiments of butchering. Then the work got to be more than I could cope with so I employed a butcher, and then another, and by 1974 the business was doing really well.

There were fewer supermarkets then and butchers weren't too keen on bulk orders initially, that was to our benefit. We invested in equipment, improved the premises and got a licence from the local authority to make sausages. We were still running the farm but by then, with the high rainfall in the area, we found it more economical and it suited our schedule to grow grass. Eventually we started selling grass to local farmers for grazing.

Adrian missed traditional farming:

I used to enjoy ploughing on a nice, sunny morning and I used to enjoy sheep shearing. I don't miss the dusty jobs like cereal harvesting, and haymaking, because I suffer from hay fever, but I miss handling the animals and the tractor work and so on, although I am still living on the farm.

Farming is harder now than it has ever been, including farming in the 1930s depression. The difference today is that farmers borrow money and have credit problems, whereas in my grandparents' day people didn't borrow that much money. They would sit back on their haunches, tighten their belts and stick it out.

The National Farmers' Union is active and has become more active since the farmers' crisis. In the old days people didn't have much time for the NFU but now the NFU is filling a much-needed role.

At the time of writing John Thorn farmed out at Beara. His parents came to live on Beara Farm in 1939 at the start of the war. The house dates back to the 1300s when it was a one-up one-down cottage:

Before the war our farm was 78 acres and used to carry one full-time labourer, whereas now we have 110 acres and a campsite, and I do it on my own.

My father carried on until 1976 and after I left school and started working I kept a few sheep and cattle, and rented a bit of ground here and there. Some of the land was at Brook Manor and some up at the church, which I have still got. I remember when I used to come up through Buckfastleigh about six on a Sunday morning with the sheep in the late 1960s. We would go up Market Street, then Silver Street, that way. I used to walk in front of the sheep, the dog behind and my father in the car behind the dog, so he could bring me home later. Imagine doing that now.

Back in the late 1700s there was the Fleming estate, the Churston estate and opposite my farm all the land belonging to the Church Commissioners – all big farms and big estates. Some were gradually sold off due to inheritance tax and death duties, probably. Gradually, farms became smaller, and now the small farms have gone back into bigger ones. There are only a few farms around here now probably farming about 1,000 acres apiece. At one time you could make a living out of 100 acres, but now that's impossible, which is why farmers are doing different things. For example, I am running a campsite and many others have part-time jobs.

I keep sheep and beef and I have had my campsite since 1959 with a licence for 25 caravans and tents, which means I have to work very hard. Every day I have to clean out the toilets and showers, sort out the rubbish, collect the fees, deal with phone messages, make bookings and do the bookwork. I do the bookwork at night. Every animal [on the farm] has to have a passport, which is an identification document detailing when the animal was born, for example. Because of the outbreak of foot-and-mouth disease in 2001 I only have a few cattle left.

There were no markets throughout that year but there were auctions, and farmers had to bid for the animals. I just sat tight for a while, but I am going to start buying again soon. I sell the cattle to West Country Beef since the foot-and-mouth outbreak and I take them into Tom Langs in Ashburton to be slaughtered.

I remember when they used to kill cattle in the slaughterhouse in the bottom of the town next to the Valiant Soldier. John Hoff, the butcher, used to slaughter his own meat too. Now they have done away with small slaughterhouses.

The foot-and-mouth disease that erupted in February 2001 affected most of the rural parts of Britain. Even in the Buckfastleigh area, which was mercifully spared, farms were under quarantine. One of the reasons for the disease spreading throughout the country, instead of being contained in one area, is that now farmers and their livestock have to travel considerable distances to bigger abattoirs.

In 2002 the Women's Institute conducted an investigation into abattoirs and prepared a comprehensive report. Councillor Lucille Whitehead, who is a member of the Buckfastleigh WI, said that the investigation found that 'supermarkets now sell 75 per cent of retail meat and require increasingly uniform and high standards, and want to deal with as few abattoirs as possible.' Local smaller abattoirs have declined considerably. In 1938 there were 13,000 abattoirs in Great Britain; immediately prior to the foot-and-mouth outbreak there were only 387. In this part of Devon the only abattoirs now existing are in Ashburton and Kingsbridge.

Although local farmers are fortunate that Ashburton is on their doorstep there is a high demand for slaughtering services. A vet has to be in attendance and it is his responsibility to examine the cattle as they are unloaded to ensure that the animals are healthy enough to be slaughtered for human consumption. The whole procedure can be a costly one for farmers. John Thorn commented:

I remember when they had cattle sales in Ashburton in the late 1940s. All the cattle used to be trucked up country afterwards by the steam train and I used to lie in bed at night and hear the train going down the line about nine at night from a November sale. It would be dark and you could hear all these animals bellowing and it was quite eerie. The train would take the animals to

Totnes and then put them on a mainline train to wherever they were going. It was really sad.

The emphasis in farming today is on protecting the environment. The Countryside Stewardship Scheme has begun whereby farmers are paid to allow their property to grow wild in order to protect wildlife like bats and butterflies. The farmers are, therefore, paid for not maintaining the land. Farmers, however, are used to routine and order with a schedule of tasks to be undertaken at certain times throughout the year – tasks such as mending fences, trimming and cutting hedges, maintaining the standard of the soil, haymaking. John continued:

In Buckfastleigh there is one of the largest colonies of Greater Horseshoe bats, with another colony at Bulkamore Mine, and my farm is in the bats' flight path. So if I don't cut my hedges and just let them grow up and grow wild for four or five years the Department for Environment, Food and Rural Affairs (DEFRA) will then pay me to layer them afterwards, so much a metre to put the earth back up and so much a metre to fence them both sides. So they will be paying me to put the hedge right – but if you trim them each year you don't get paid at all!

Garth Grose commented:

Farming has been subject to constant change. Between the 1950s and the 1970s farmers were encouraged to destroy hedges in order to create larger fields for corn growing. The removal of the hedges destroyed wildlife and plant growth. Now we want the hedges back!

John added his views:

At one time I cut down acres of orchards but now I am paid to maintain and keep my orchards because the public can see them from the roadside and they look nice. I only have two-and-a half acres of orchards now and they are all around the farmhouse and buildings. My neighbour, Luscombes, has a cider factory and he buys the apples from me (I am organic in the orchard, but only in the orchard), crushes them and makes them into apple juice that is served on Concorde! They want Devon apples grown in Devon!

'Most root crops such as mangels, turnips, swedes, marrow and stemmed kale have gone,' said Garth Grose. 'They have been replaced by large fields of rye grass for silage and large bales of hayledge. Many farm workers have left the land,' he continued, 'as their work has been taken over by contractors who now do the ploughing, hedge trimming and do the harvesting with combine harvesters.'

Farmers have faced, and are still facing, an uncertain future because of changes in the economy and a decrease in income. There are demands for agricultural reforms and changes in the food market. On the other hand, policies are being implemented to conserve our environment, there are moves to ensure that people are aware of the importance of buying local produce – often regarded as better quality – and there is constant promotion of the area to encourage tourism.

Although Buckfastleigh sits in the hinterland we are part of Dartmoor National Park. John Weir, head of communications for Dartmoor National Park Authority, made the following comments:

Farming has shaped most of the Dartmoor landscape and has contributed greatly to the area's wildlife and cultural value. It also contributes significantly to the local and regional economy. It has a long history, spanning at least 4,000 years.

Change has occured down through the millennia, but continuity also survives in the people of Dartmoor. The daily and year-round tasks of sowing, harvesting, lambing and other animal husbandry practices continue as they have done for the last 50 years and centuries before.

Traditions of land management, including common land management with its ancient origins, boundary creation and repair, and pony drifts, survive.

Hill farmers continue to be a vital part of the local community and their actvities maintain landscape beauty and interest and help to encourage the presence of diverse wildlife. The work of the Dartmoor farmer also constantly adds to the quality of our lives – through quality of experience as we wander through the landscape, and through quality of produce. The future of Dartmoor as a National Park will always be heavily dependent upon a viable and bouyant hill-farming community.

There are traditions in the Dartmoor area and we want to see them last. Farming adds to the quality of people's lives not only through landscape but through farmers' markets.

Whether farmers' markets prove to be economically viable remains to be seen, but it is true that we do want our farming traditions to continue, to conserve the flora and fauna of our environment and to eat the produce grown by local farmers because, although it is the farmers who undertake all the hard work, we are part of the land too.

Above: *The Valiant Soldier Heritage Centre, 2002.* (Photograph taken by Patricia Cairn-Duff)

Right: *The interior of the Valiant Soldier. This room was previously a public bar.*

Below: *Fore Street, 2002.* (Photograph taken by Patricia Cairn-Duff)

Twenty-Two

THE NEW MILLENNIUM: LOOKING TO THE FUTURE

The Globe Inn, Weech Corner, Fore Street, 2002.
(Photograph taken by Patricia Cairn-Duff)

New Year's Day, 1 January 2000, dawned fine and clear. It was cold but the sky was blue and the sun shone palely on a Buckfastleigh that was resting after the millennium festivities of the night before. All around the world cities, towns and villages were celebrating the end of the twentieth century and the beginning of a new century, in their own particular way. One thing most of the world's citizens hoped for was world peace and a better time for mankind.

It was not to be. In 2002, existing wars and the threat of new wars continued and terrorism had the whole world in its grip following the devastating attack by Al-Qaida terrorists on New York and Washington on 11 September 2001 and in Bali in 2002.

Britain was dealt a severe blow in 2001 when foot-and-mouth disease erupted in many areas of the country resulting in the mass culling of animals, quarantine, and the ruination of farmers financially and emotionally. Devon farmers and animals suffered during the outbreak and, although the disease did not reach Buckfastleigh, local farmers felt the effects of the quarantine whilst waiting anxiously for signs that the disease was abating. Devon ceased to be an infected area on 1 August 2001.

Due to the enhancement of the town centre Buckfastleigh looks brighter. Fore Street is no longer congested thanks to the relief road running through the Mardle Way industrial estate to Buckfast, which takes much of the heavy traffic. The one-way system in operation in Fore Street also relieves congestion although, according to many, it runs the wrong way and the street still appears empty of people. However, the town is getting there and especially on a sunny morning it is a pleasure to walk through Buckfastleigh.

The initiative that has really placed Buckfastleigh on the map is the Valiant Soldier Heritage Centre. Situated at the lower end of Fore Street, the Valiant Soldier had been a public house for over 120 years until it closed in 1965. Bruce McLellan explained:

The Valiant Soldier had been tied to a brewery. Fortunately it avoided what normally happens to a pub when it closes. Pubs are either modernised or there is a change of use. However, when the Valiant Soldier closed in 1965, it was agreed that the landlords could buy it and continue to live there, on the understanding that it never became a pub again.

Over 30 years later, when the owner's widow moved out shortly before her death, the Buckfastleigh Trust persuaded Teignbridge Council to buy the property on behalf of the local community. The trust recognised the interest that could be generated from a pub that had remained untouched since the 1960s. Nothing had been altered since the day it closed and most of the original fittings such as the optics, glasses and coins in the till still remained in the bar. Numerous other items of historical interest were found in what had been the landlord's private quarters upstairs. Bruce McLellan continued:

I became involved in getting the project under way, but it was Stuart Barker, chair of the Buckfastleigh Trust, Julia Cross and others, who worked hard to obtain the funding and get the project off the ground. We had to raise the money to repay Teignbridge Council and were fortunate in raising it through the European Regeneration Fund and a number of charitable trusts.

My job was more in the background, getting the

building ready to open and working with the volunteers. I then became the project manager and we opened the building as a visitors' centre, with a small museum, in 2000.

Part of the ground floor of the building adjacent to the Valiant Soldier itself is used as a Tourist Information Office. The whole project is run by a team of committed volunteers who have been extremely successful in attracting thousands of visitors to Buckfastleigh over the past couple of years.

The other attraction that brings tourists into the town during the summer months is the open-top vintage bus which came from an idea that developed when Bruce was a member of the Town Council:

Some of us recognised that there were a good number of tourists coming into the area but not into the town. Half the tourists visiting the area arrive by coach, so it is not easy to attract them away from the Abbey, but others arrive by car and want to see all the attractions in the area.

Starting from the South Devon Railway, the vintage bus – which is free of charge – takes tourists to Buckfast Abbey and then on to Buckfastleigh where it leaves the passengers to browse around the town before picking them up again later and taking them back to the railway station. Bruce explained:

It's fun and it's free and certainly eating places, like the Singing Kettle, derive business from it.

The principal funders were the Countryside Agency, Teignbridge District Council, Dartmoor National Park Authority, the Buckfastleigh Town Council and the Buckfastleigh Chamber of Trade. There were, of course, other sponsors, including all of the proprietors of the attractions en route.

Bruce and his wife, Janet, came to live in the town on Bruce's retirement from the Navy (after living in Ashburton for a while). He considered Buckfastleigh to be forward looking. 'Many older people have only experienced decline,' he said, 'the 'up' in the town is relatively recent.'

Buckfastleigh Broadband Ltd is an exciting project which was set up with £500,000 in funding from the Department of Trade and Industry and the South-West of England Regional Development Agency. Part of the funding went towards the creation of a public access internet centre, Wave, based in the former Dartmoor Craft and Coffee Shop in Fore Street. Wave allows local residents, visitors and businesses to access high-speed computers, to experience broadband and the internet in general, to ask questions and learn more.

The founder of Buckfastleigh Broadband is Gordon Adgey who has 17 years' experience in the telecommunications industry. More recently he set up and advised a number of companies in the telecommunications, internet and media industries.

The managing director of Buckfastleigh Broadband is Kathryn Hughes who became a resident of Buckfastleigh in 1988 after moving from San Francisco two years earlier. She has spent the last five years in business consultancy and has an extensive background in design, visual communications and media production, both in the US and the UK:

At the beginning of 2001 we began to explore if and how it would be possible to have broadband in the town. At this time it was only available in urban areas. We recognised that broadband could have a very positive impact on the town through building new skills, creating new opportunities and jobs, as well as helping existing businesses remain competitive.

The eight-strong team of Buckfastleigh Broadband designed and built a broadband network that has provided connections to the library, the primary school, Searle's Business Centre, the Waterman's Arms and GS Multi-media, the company that ran the town's community and Town Council websites.

'Broadband means fun, fast and efficient, saving time, energy and money!' said Kathryn.

Wanting a change in lifestyle Richard Rogers and his wife sold their home and business in London in 1994 and came to live in Buckfastleigh during the late 1990s:

It was through the Rudolf Steiner School, in Dartington, that I came into contact with organic farmers and producers. I was asked in 1995 to help a bio-dynamic farmer with his marketing and he told me that he had heard about farmers' markets in America. At that time they had not made an impact in Britain. I approached Totnes Council seeking permission to set up a farmers' market in their town. They said no, because of the damage it would do to local businesses!

I have always been interested in organic food and wholefoods. Obviously, the object of healthy living is to eat healthily and I am concerned about the quality of food. Most non-organic foods have traces of pesticides, hormones, antibiotics and the chemical fertilisers used in their production. In 1998 I saw the plans for the regeneration of Buckfastleigh and decided I would try to set up a farmers' market in the town, as something needs to draw people in on a regular basis. I contacted Teignbridge District Council and other agencies but did not get any funding. I decided to invest my own money and took the view that as long as I could be repaid the capital outlay over three years I could do it.

Then Richard approached the Chamber of Trade because without the support of the business community the market would not get very far:

At first they were quite anxious about it, fearing

a damaging effect on their businesses, but within a couple of weeks of the market opening they were congratulating me. It was bringing people into the town. Now it is an important part of the town's life every Thursday morning and makes a lot of difference to trade. So, the first Buckfastleigh Farmers' and Local Produce Market was held on 6 May 1999 and has been running weekly since then.

Richard believes that the farmers' market has to operate on a weekly basis in order to pay its way. To keep money in the local economy the frames for the stalls were made at Dean and the covers were made by a canvas-maker at Rill Farm:

The produce has to be local so that growers are not travelling vast distances. Also, so that you can question them and be assured of the food quality and, importantly, help the economy.

There is a concerted effort in the West Country to encourage people, including hoteliers and restaurateurs, to buy locally produced food and drink. Alan Butler from the Singing Kettle said:

We always try to buy as much as we can locally, and from local suppliers, for our restaurant, but it is not always possible. If we can't buy from local suppliers we look for suppliers in Devon and after that we try to stay British. My mineral water comes from Dartmoor, I use the local vegetarian supplier for vegetarian dishes we cook, we buy our meat from local farms and tea and coffee come from local suppliers. It doesn't necessarily mean that their produce is procured locally but it keeps the money in the area.

Tradespeople are optimistic. Jacqui Butler continued:

When Alan and I and the girls first arrived in the town to take over the Singing Kettle I was rather worried about the lack of shops. The Singing Kettle, however, was everything I wanted in a tearoom. As soon as I saw it I knew it was for us.

Things started off slowly but we had lots of ideas and thought that things can only get better and, of course, they did. We have regular customers from the town and customers come from outside the town to see us. We obtained a restaurant licence and developed the garden into a tea garden which opened in 2001 and was such an enormous success that we had to get in extra staff. Some days it was very, very busy.

Peter Collings of Huccaby's agreed that things have improved:

Most businesses in the town have reported that 2002 has been one of the best. Much of this is due to the Valiant Soldier Heritage Centre that has brought upwards of 10,000 people into the town. The vintage

Johnson's Hardware, 2002. (Photograph taken by Patricia Cairn-Duff)

bus is a free service supported by the Chamber of Trade and Bruce McLellan has done a lot towards this. The whole thing is coming together.

Lamb Pie Day, in July, is also becoming a day that local people can look forward to. As the chairman of the Chamber of Trade I organise it with the help and support of other local people and we have had very successful days with several stalls in the street, people sitting outside having a meal and a drink, and the kids coming down and having a go on the fairground attractions. We have even had donkey rides – it is just a fun day. The highlight, of course, is the competition for the baking of the best lamb pie, which has been won for the past two years by Jacqui and Alan from the Singing Kettle. Fortunately we have had the weather on our side for the last two years. Now people are aware it is happening each year and the support is growing.

As you get involved in town life you get greeted by other people. Everyone has time for one another and you become part of the community. Sometimes it can take 30 minutes to walk a short distance through the town because everyone wants to talk. It's a great feeling!

Alan Butler commented:

The Chamber of Trade was set up five or six years ago after a long gap. It is a fairly powerful body. The Chamber of Trade may be informed and consulted by the County Council. We may advise on things like car parking, street layout, parking charges, fees, etc. – because these things impinge on the local business community.

Jacqui elaborated:

The Chamber of Trade, of which Alan and I are a part, has tried to build up the image of the town by putting up hanging baskets and bunting that is put up for the Lamb Pie Day. People have commented very, very positively on the hanging baskets and have said how wonderful they look. It made me very proud. Others have said how nice it is to be able to walk to the Post Office without having to worry about the traffic.

However, some of the elderly people remember how it used to be 50 years ago and have not accepted the changes.

Pat Hedges, Buckfastleigh Town Mayor, commented:

Many people have talked about their memories of Buckfastleigh and say that the town is not the same anymore. Of course it isn't. How can it be? The days when Buckfastleigh was in full swing with industries all around have gone, never to return. Today we have to go forward with the resources we have, and these all lie with tourism – the railway, the Abbey, the Valiant Soldier and the Buckfastleigh Caves.

We are midway between two cities, Plymouth and Exeter, and about 15 miles from the coast, and we sit at the foot of beautiful Dartmoor. We have so much going for us.

Alan Butler felt that if there were no shops in Buckfastleigh then people would leave the town:

So we are doing our best to put a bit of life back into the town. The town is doing well, businesses are doing well and people are using the shops. I think the town is great. Americans who come here think that it is wonderful to be able to walk down through the High Street.

I was brought up in a small village where I knew only a few people and then moved into a much larger town where I didn't know many people and then moved to Buckfastleigh where I seemed to know everybody! It was strange at first to walk through the town and be greeted by lots of people.

Society is changing very quickly, more quickly than we realise. A mark of modern life is the ability to change and how you cope with change – especially the traders. The businesses that are doing well are the ones which are changing to meet the needs of the people.

The chemists in Fore Street has provided local people with an invaluable service for a very long time. Initially owned by Brays, the business was then bought by Bill and Ann Rucker during the early 1950s, who then purchased a pharmacy on the Embankment Road in Plymouth.

In 1972 Roger Simmons and his family moved from Lincolnshire to manage the Plymouth shop. Roger then moved to Buckfastleigh in 1974 to run the chemists and eventually went into partnership with Bill and Ann. Later a pharmacy in Totnes was purchased by the partnership and the Plymouth shop was eventually sold in the 1980s. Roger went on to acquire the Buckfastleigh business in 1991 and Bill acquired the Totnes branch which he sold when he retired in the mid-1990s.

Val Hoare is the resident pharmacist for the shop in Fore Street. She started as a locum for Roger Simmons 12 years ago, covering holidays and one or two days a week until Roger asked her to take over as full-time dispensary manager in around 1999. Moss Pharmacies bought the business in April 2000 and asked Val and the staff to stay on. Val recalled:

I had worked for Moss before as I had worked in 13 of their branches as a locum over the years. The staff found it much more difficult at first going from a one-man business to being part of a business chain.

I am very happy working here. Our shop is a nice building to work in. More importantly the customers are great and the staff are absolutely wonderful to work with. We are a team and work well together. We work very hard, are very professional about what we do and care about what we do. That was one of the reasons why I accepted the position here.

One of the successes of Moss Pharmacies is that instead of developing big High Street shops they have focused on small community pharmacies. This shop is relatively big compared to some of their shops, which are quite small. They focus on service to their customers whereas other companies are renowned for national advertising and particular products.

In a community where many of our customers are retired or are mothers with young children, and don't have access to their own cars [but just] *infrequent public transport, a pharmacy and the Post Office are as essential as any supermarket. Some of the elderly folk like somebody to chat to about their families – not just their health. My staff are in an ideal position because they live in the town and they have known our customers for many years. They know about their background lives and can ask questions that are important to our customers. It is not just their medical*

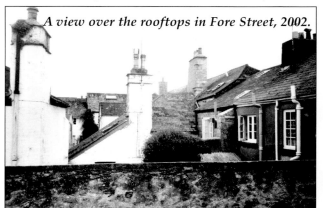
A view over the rooftops in Fore Street, 2002.

Another view over the rooftops, 2002.

THE NEW MILLENNIUM: LOOKING TO THE FUTURE

Fore Street, 2002. Decorated in honour of Queen Elizabeth II's golden jubilee. (Photograph taken by Patricia Cairn-Duff)

problems we are treating but we are able to support and help the whole person.

Dr James Hedger, from the Buckfastleigh Health Centre, agreed that there has been a big change:

We have a problem now in that the country is running short of doctors, and the government is concerned about how we are going to cope with having fewer people around who are trained in medicine and nursing.

The health service has moved from treating illness to preventing illness and this creates extra work. James Hedger considered it much better for the medical profession to act as a knowledge resource and knowledge navigator and thus enable people to understand and deal with a situation themselves. Preventative medicine is improving all the time.

The Labour government introduced a new tier of management, Primary Care Trusts, which replaced health authorities. Every practice belongs to a Primary Care Trust of about 100,000 patients – Buckfastleigh belongs to the Teignbridge Primary Care Trust which has about 110,000 patients within 12 general practices. Patients should have a strong voice on the Primary Care Trust and an increasing say in what the practices provide.

Politically, elderly people are very relevant and as people become older they expect more from life and become a vociferous majority. Elderly people experience increasing health-care costs as they begin to suffer from degenerative diseases like arthritis and cancer, for which new medicines are discovered.

Who will care for the elderly people as they get older is of increasing concern. Abbotswell, one of the three homes for the elderly, closed down in the autumn of 2001. It was partly due to the New Care Standard legislation brought in by the government, which took effect in 2002. The legislation required a higher level of specification for residential buildings like Abbotswell with which, unfortunately, the owners were unable to comply. Additionally the policy concerning the care of elderly people has changed with more elderly people being encouraged to stay in their own homes for as long as possible, with appropriate care being offered on a daily basis. Maureen Maclean, the former proprietor, stated:

It means that when elderly people do come into residential homes they are older, and much frailer, and using Zimmer frames and wheelchairs. Abbotswell is not able to cater for their needs because of the design of the building. We had no option but to close down.

It was a blow to the older populace as it was the residential home most of them wanted to go to when they could no longer look after themselves.

Abbotswell, which is over 300 years old, was first opened as a residential home in the early 1970s by Mr and Mrs Giles, they were followed by the Bolongaros, and then the Kennets who named the house Abbotswell, previously known as 10 Crest Hill. The house was well known by local people because of the tall tree that once grew in the garden and became a landmark.

Maureen, who originally came from Devon, and her husband, Andrew Maclean, had been running Abbotswell Residential Home since 1996:

I had worked in care for several years and Andrew was

a businessman. As we had always wanted to run our own business we decided to use my care skills and his business skills to run a residential home. We looked at 30 places before we came to Buckfastleigh. When we came to Abbotswell the residents were so full of life – funny and ready for a laugh – it was like one big happy family and that's what we wanted – a family home. Abbotswell was so lovely that we decided to buy it.

The maximum number of residents that could be accommodated was 14, and residents in the home, when Maureen and Andrew took over in 1996, included Katie Bragg, Elsie Jeffries, Annie Edgecombe and Ann (Louie) Hill. Michelle Lee, who had been the assistant manager, explained:

We never put an emphasis on routine before their lives. They could do what they liked when they liked. Of course we had to have set times for meals and there were set routines to enable them to be clean and safe. However, their rooms were their private abode and the staff ensured that they had their privacy. The rest of the house was open house with staff and visitors coming in, and if any of the residents wanted to go out and catch a bus to Newton Abbot they could.

'We never wanted to run an institution,' said Maureen. 'In fact, if we were redecorating then we would consult the residents and let them choose their own wallpaper,' she added smiling.

On one important occasion the residents did a display about old Buckfastleigh and Abbotswell became the focus for it. Maureen recalled the project:

The residents even went into the primary school and talked to the children about their lives. It helped that the residents were well known in the town. Not for the first time the chemist's shop would ring us up and say, 'We have so-and-so here, can you come and fetch her?'

The residents always enjoyed a singsong and we had someone to come in and play the piano. The residents' knees were always going! And there would be a service for the residents once a month. They loved to sing and loved music.

Pauline Manfield worked at Abbotswell for over 25 years, starting first as a cleaner and then becoming the cook and a carer, which she thoroughly enjoyed:

I started with Mr and Mrs Giles and they were kindness itself and very, very compassionate. All the owners have been good in their different ways.

I loved all the residents. Of course most of the staff had grown up with the residents as very few had come from outside the town. Katie Bragg was one of the residents and she used to be a real character. She had a lovely disposition and would tell us stories about the past when she was a girl and where she worked.

Katie used to look a picture of health. With regular meals and regular medication and being looked after, and looking after each other, the residents thrived – so much that they could go home. But then, if they went home they would be on their own again and might start neglecting themselves.

That is a real concern with which Redmount Residential and Nursing Home also contends. Redmount is much larger with 42 beds and, of course, with many more staff. 'But we do try to run it as a family home,' said Trish Durman, 'and to make it as homely as possible. There have been changes, but at the end of the day we still give excellent care.'

Roger and Sheila Bowley, who had been running the home from 1988, sold the business in 2000 to an organisation called Your Health. The owner does not live on the premises so the day to day running of the home comes under the overall charge of a matron and deputy manager. Trish explained that visitors are always welcome:

There are more carers from overseas now and we currently have six Philippine carers who were recruited through an agency. The residents love them because they are so caring and so nice.

Representatives of the churches come in to see the residents, Father Gabriel, Revd David Hardy and Idwal Williams. Julie, a young woman from Camphill Community at Hapstead, used to come and play the organ. The residents love visitors coming in. We also had a lady with two pack dogs who came in – specifically to go around the rooms so that the patients could pat them. Now we have a couple living here who brought their dog with them and he wanders around and the housekeeper brings her dog in. It is lovely to see the smiles on their faces.

Camphill Community, with adults in need of special care, continues to thrive and, like other kinds of residential homes, funding, monitoring and accountability is a much higher priority than it was in the past. The organisation is a charity and a non-profit-making company that is self-governing. Although most of the residents are funded through the government Camphill has to find the funding for major renovations and new development work itself. Helen Bennet, who is housemother to five residents at Merrifield Farm in Camphill, explained:

The aim of the community is to provide a secure and stimulating environment. The villagers live in self-contained extended-family households where residents, workers and their families live together, ours is one of the smaller houses.

The residents' day is structured and, as Camphill has 90 acres of land to be looked after, the residents find their days fully occupied working on the farm and taking part in various workshops on offer, such as

THE NEW MILLENNIUM: LOOKING TO THE FUTURE

The Orchard Millennium Green, Station Road, 2002.
(Photograph taken by Patricia Cairn-Duff)

pottery, metallurgy and weaving. Leisure time is important and in the evenings there are films and discotheques and, at weekends, trips out.

The villagers are often seen on a Friday walking as a group around Buckfastleigh when they do their personal shopping and visit the Singing Kettle for a drink. On Sundays some of the villagers attend local churches. They are participating more and more in local events, and there is every encouragement from Camphill for local people to visit Hapstead and to join with the villagers on their special open days.

Some 30 years has proved it to be a successful venture; Buckfastleigh and Camphill have adapted well to living 'side by side'. It is hoped that funding concerns and new legislation will not inhibit a way of life, and a force for good, in the community.

The community in Buckfastleigh is still very strong. With a population that is now over 3,700, there is still a basic kindliness about Buckfastleigh and a willingness to be open and friendly on the part of most people. Whereas in the old days one could walk down through the town and know and greet everyone, now there are numerous faces that one does not recognise. It is still, however, easier to get to know people in Buckfastleigh than in larger towns and there are numerous organisations to join and events in which to take part as the *Buckfastleigh Newsletter*, which is produced once a month and sponsored by the Wigram Society, reveals.

Some organisations are fairly new, some have been going for many years, and all welcome new members. The Buckfastleigh Amateur Dramatic Society started in in 1939 and has been going for 63 years.

'We had a superb party to celebrate our 60th anniversary,' said John Hoff, 'and many past members came and we had photographs up around the room.' The society is looking forward to many more happy years of rehearsing and performing plays in Buckfastleigh.

The 60s Club is over 50 years old and the Women's Institute is now 56 years old. Both clubs still meet regularly, but sadly the Royal British Legion closed in 2002. Terry Hallett said:

It is very sad but there were only four of us remaining. All of us are getting older, annual membership fees are higher, and there have been no younger men coming to join the British Legion.

The Royal British Legion is open to anyone who wears the Queen's Uniform for a minimum of seven days, and includes the fire service, the ambulance service, the police and, during the war, air-raid wardens. It is, of course, open to war veterans of any war, including the Falklands and the Gulf War.

Buckfastleigh is going to miss the British Legion, which has taken part in annual Remembrance Day parades and church services for the past 56 years, has organised the annual poppy collection and fundraised for charities including their own Benevolent Fund. That will now come to an end, except for the British Legions Women's Section which continues.

Colin Harmes, who has completed 25 years as a part-time fireman in Buckfastleigh, is now the organiser for the annual poppy collection. Previously it was Doreen Trude, secretary for the women's section. Colin commented on the task:

It has been an interesting experience and there is more involved than I realised. Nowadays most of the collections are done through retail outlets, pubs and restaurants, rather than house-to-house collections.

As long as wars exist there will always be a need for a poppy collection and remembrance service.

Colin also belongs to the Military Vehicle Trust (Devon Area Group) which has been responsible for a display of military vehicles for the past 14 years, usually on the premises of the South Devon Railway:

It is living history. We are trying to preserve old, wartime vehicles and the uniforms which were worn during the Second World War. Through the organisation we also raise money for war veterans and the British Legion.

As well as the elderly, the town is concerned about its children and young people. Some of the town's young people clearly feel sidelined and their behaviour suggests they are on the margins of the town's community life instead of being an integral part of it – and the town's future.

There are organisations working with children and young people, such as the Buccaneers, which organises events for children. Jacquie Kilty explained:

I was chair of Buccaneers from 1998–2000. It was in this time that we finalised my personal initiative that had started with my sons in 1991. This was to build a skate park in Victoria Park. With the help of our first community delevopment worker, we were able to open the facility for skateboarders, rollerbladers and BMXers in 1999. It has been popular with young people to this day and competitions are held there annually.

Play Zone was set up, run under the wing of Buccaneers, at this time, a very successful after-school club and holiday club. Buccaneers has been renowned for the work it has done for young people in the town.

The Methodist Church runs a children's club, the youth club, run by Adrian and Pauline Distin, is still very popular with a high number of young people using the facility, and the Guides and Brownies are still active.

Originally the Guides started in 1927, meeting in the National Schoolroom, and continued until the early 1940s. It was re-formed in the 1960s by a lady called Rosemary Howell, who was Deputy Lord Lieutenant of Devon, and a Guide commissioner, who lived at Spitchwick Manor. Having persuaded a teacher from South Dartmoor College (then Ashburton School) to start a company (now called a unit) in Ashburton, she then started one in Buckfastleigh which is still active.

Ann Werry, who came to live in Buckfastleigh with her family in 1983, offered to help the Guide company in 1984 when her daughter, Clare, was old enough to join. The Guide captain at that time was Ruth Westall from Ashburton, followed by Sandra King. When Sandra King left Buckfastleigh Ann became Guide captain (Guider):

I have had a lot of help. Some of those who have assisted were uniformed, and some unit helpers. At that time we met in the school but when the school was being extended we moved to the Methodist church schoolroom and got so settled we never moved back.

We miss the school grounds but there are plenty of places in the town that we can go to for outdoor activities and pursuits. The Guides is an organisation that is based on a set of ideals which link with the Guide Promise and we have that to aim for all the time. So it is rather more than a youth club because of all its different facets. The training for new helpers and assistants now is rather considerable, as one is being trained to think of the child as an individual and thinking of all the different aspects of child development. It seems like part way to becoming a teacher!

The Guides plan many of their weekly activities themselves and have a lot of fun. They also join with other Guides at larger events and competitions, and have at least one summer camp. However, nowadays, girls seem to be ready to move on to other things sooner and very few stay on to become young leaders. Peer pressure plays a big part in this trend.

The Brownie unit in Buckfastleigh has remained very successful for a great many years, and always has a waiting list.

Years ago there were very strong Scout and Cub units, but the Scout unit closed about a year ago. The Beavers still run but the Cubs have had to close for lack of leadership.

Maywyn Wilkinson helps to run the AK Club for people with learning disabilities that meets in the National Schoolroom. The club is a great help to parents and thoroughly enjoyed by club members:

They play games like jigsaws and snooker, they have discos and nearly deafen us! In the summer we have barbecues down at the orchard. We provide all the activities that they enjoy and we don't try to organise them and, on the whole, they mix with each other.

There are quite a few young people from Buckfastleigh but we draw them in from Ashburton and other places around. There have to be two leaders on duty each evening, one of whom has to be a community learning disabilities nurse. I am one of the few volunteers left. The club used to meet weekly but now we meet once a fortnight because we can't get the volunteers.

It is a dilemma when good organisations have to close, or limit their activities, for want of leadership, and it is a dilemma that Buckfastleigh faces again and again.

The former Victoria Park caretaker's bungalow is gradually being transformed into a centre for young people called, appropriately, the Bungalow Project. Young people have worked closely with the town community worker and the organisation Sure Start to provide a drop-in centre, a counselling service and a café.

Sarah Small, who is 17, came to live in Buckfastleigh in the 1990s together with her parents, Anita and Philip Small. Anita grew up in Buckfastleigh. 'I didn't want to come here as I had left all my friends behind,' said Sarah, 'but I was surprised at how quickly I felt at home in the town.'

Sarah is a student involved in several community projects, and works at the White Hart part-time as a waitress and chef:

I feel so independent here. Talking to all the people who come into the White Hart has given me a broader perspective on life and it has opened my eyes to what is going on in the world.

She is one of a group of young people, between 14 and 18 years old, and adults who was on the youth sub-group of the Bungalow Project. The youth sub-group has been disbanded now and Sarah is the youth representative on the Buckfastleigh Community Project Committee which has the overall management responsibility. A total of £26,000 has been raised through different funding agencies and Sarah herself raised £2,000 towards the project.

The chair of the project committee is Kathryn Hughes, and other members of the committee include: Kath Kelly, the senior youth officer for the South Dartmoor area; Zoe Lambeth, the community officer responsible for running the Bungalow Project; Bruce McLellan; Malcolm Cowper; Suzanne Potter, a youth worker at South Dartmoor College; and Richard Brooks, a Dartmoor National Park Ranger. Sarah commented:

I was surprised that so many young people are interested in Dartmoor. Two teams from South Dartmoor College took part in the Ten Tors expedition this year, and the Duke of Edinburgh's Award Scheme encourages young people from Buckfastleigh to become involved in activities like walking and community activities. The main problem for young people in the town is the lack of transport.

Pat Hedges, the Mayor, says:

We have to encourage our young people, like Sarah, to work together with the older members of the community, with energy and co-operation, to turn things around, so that young people can feel part of Buckfastleigh. One day they will be able to talk about their own memories of the town with pride.

The Teignbridge Theatre Company was formed in 1981 for the Buckfastleigh and Ashburton area by five couples who had previously belonged to the Newton Abbot Musical Comedy Society. They have had great success over the past 20 years with shows like *South Pacific, Oklahoma!* and *The Sound of Music*, and have had a strong local following. Gerald and Jen Billing and their four children became involved in 1986 and it was when their daughter, Hannah, asked if she could stage a show, that a junior group evolved which has been equally successful. Gerald Billing commented:

The junior group is responsible to the adult group but we allow the young people to run the group themselves with some help and guidance from the adults, but we do not interfere. It depends on the kind of support the young people receive from their parents that decides if the show is going to be successful or not. We gave Hannah and our other children all the support we could.

In 2002, a short time after the new St Luke's Church in Plymouth Road was completed, the newly formed St Luke's Event Group, which comprised members of the Teignbridge Theatre Company and those of St Luke's Church, performed *Joseph and the Amazing Technicolor Dreamcoat*. It was a great achievement by the cast, producers and musicians, and pleasing to see so many children and young men involved.

Led by the Bishop of Exeter, the Rt Revd Michael Langrish, the consecration of St Luke's was held on 13 October 2002. It was a proud moment for the church members and the town, and it is to be hoped that the church will be able to offer the spiritual guidance and support that people need, and are searching for, in the twenty-first century.

In Buckfastleigh the 'ancient and modern' co-exist. As the work of the new church begins to unfold so the remains of an early-Saxon church have been discovered beneath the ruins of Holy Trinity Parish Church. Research into the history of Buckfastleigh, and the preservation of its heritage, continues with genuine enthusiasm. This is balanced by the determination of those who are striving to make Buckfastleigh a thriving and vibrant town once again.

Peter Thornhill is a local businessman who is experienced in IT and internet services. He is shown here in contact, via telecommunication, with the space-shuttle Columbia *during its inaugral flight, early 1980s.*

Buckfastleigh town band with Revd Mylchreest, 1940s.

Buckfastleigh carnival in celebration of Queen Elizabeth II's coronation, 1953. The attendant on the left is Ann Smart, the queen is May Francis (née Wicks) and the attendant on the right is Honor Morton (née Voisey).

Buckfastleigh Town Council

Thanks Sandra Coleman for presenting her fascinating history of Buckfastleigh

Buckfastleigh Town Council holds monthly meetings and considers all aspects of Buckfastleigh – Planning and Highway issues, tourism and economic promotion, the provision of services to parishioners and the hiring of rooms in the Town Hall.

To find out what is going on in Buckfastleigh

- Pick up our Town Guide
- Look at our quarterly Buckfastleigh Bulletin
- Consult our monthly Town Diary – displayed on the Town Noticeboards
- Search our Website – www.buckfastleigh.gov.uk

For more information, phone the Town Clerk on
01364 642576 or
Email: clerk@buckfastleigh.gov.uk

BLIGHT & SCOBLE LIMITED

BUILDING CONTRACTORS & DEVELOPERS

MARDLE WAY • BUCKFASTLEIGH
SOUTH DEVON • TQ11 0JS

Telephone: Buckfastleigh **01364 642253**
Fax No: Buckfastleigh **01364 642074**
Email: enquiries@blight&scoble.co.uk

Building in Devon for over 100 years

Dragonfly Foods
Home of the Beany

Fresh Organic Award Winning Foods

organic Beany® • organic soysage®
organic tofupot® • ok fibre™ organic
organic Tatty® • organic Insider®

Organic Health centre and Food Factory

Dragonfly Foods
Mardle Way,
Buckfastleigh
Devon TQ11 0NR
Tel/Fax: 01364 642700
info@beany.co.uk
www.beany.co.uk

SUBSCRIBERS

Michael Abbott, Glebelands, Buckfastleigh
Simon J. Allan, Darmstadt, Germany
Michael John Stanley Allen, Bossell Road
Mr and Mrs M.W. Ansell, Buckfastleigh, Devon
Martin, Donna and Tammy Baker, Buckfast
Victor Baker and Family
The Family of Len and Anita Barden
Eileen Bartlett, Beer, Devon
Shirley and Peter Berlin, Buckfastleigh, Devon
Jackie Berry, Buckfastleigh
M.B. Berry (family name French), Buckfastleigh
Suzanne Berry, Buckfastleigh, Devon
Master Bradley Bignell, Buckfastleigh, Devon
Gerald A. Billing, Buckfastleigh
Hilary and Derek Bird, Kingsteignton
Tony Bird, South Brent, Devon
Joyce K. Blank, Buckfastleigh, Devon
Patricia Boisey, Buckfast, Devon
John W. Bolton, Buckfastleigh, Devon
Betty Bovey, Buckfastleigh, Devon
Buckfastleigh Primary School
Doreen and Keith Bryant, Goodstone, Bickington, South Devon
Margaret Budd (née Jones), Buckfastleigh
Mrs Pauline Burge (née Boyer)
K.J. Burrow, Bucks Cross, Devon
Alan and Jacqui Butler, Buckfastleigh
Hubert J. Chaffe, Buckfast, Devon
Stella M. Clark, Coombe, Buckfastleigh, Devon
Peter and Barbara Clarke, Buckfastleigh
Anne Coleman, London
E.W. Coode (Ted), born Buckfastleigh 1929 – Nursing Home 2002
D.M. Coombes, Wimbledon, London
Annie Coram and Abbey Tomkinson, Buckfastleigh, Devon
Audrey Coulton, Buckfastleigh
Fernley and Dorothy Cox, Buckfastleigh, Devon
Andy and Dot Cribbett, Buckfastleigh, Devon
Adrian Dawe, Tordean Farm, Buckfastleigh
Helen Dettori (née Midgley), Rome, Italy

Judith Dewdney (née Midgley), Macclesfield
Bob Dixon, born Buckfastleigh 1931
C.R. Doidge, Buckfastleigh
Noel L. Downie
William Drake, Buckfastleigh, Devon
Sue Duquemin, Buckfastleigh, Devon
Kate J. Eagelton, Ewell, Surrey
Ann Eales
Nigel Edworthy and Family, Buckfastleigh, Devon
Jill and Richard Elliott and Family, Buckfastleigh
David Roy Evans, formerly of Hapstead, Buckfastleigh, Devon
Violet A. Farquhar, Buckfastleigh, Devon
Jean Fice, West Huntspill, Somerset
The Family of Leslie Foot, Buckfastleigh, Devon
Pamela Forbes, Buckfastleigh
Nicola Jane Ford, Buckfastleigh, Devon
Kay Fouracre, Buckfastleigh, Devon
John Giles, Buckfastleigh, Devon
G.J. Gill, Buckfastleigh
Melvyn Gill, Buckfastleigh
Ken and Joyce Glanville, Totnes, Devon
Sheila A. Glass, Taunton
Brian and Frances Goss, Buckfastleigh, Devon
Garth Grose
Mr and Mrs P. Grute
Mrs Sheila Grute, Buckfastleigh, Devon
R.G.T. and J.V. Hallett, Buckfastleigh
Rita Hallett (née Wicks), Ashburton, Devon
Hilary Hammond, Southampton
Laura and David Harris, Buckfastleigh
Doreen M. Havill (née Wicks), Buckfastleigh, Devon
Giles, Hannah and Bethany Hawkins, April Cottage, Buckfastleigh
Bet and the late Ken Hayman, Buckfastleigh, Devon
Mr Colin C. Hayman, Buckfastleigh, Devon
David and Joan Hayman, Buckfastleigh, Devon
Mr Martin C. Hayman, Melbourne, Australia
Cyril James Heath, Buckfastleigh
Derek and Pat Hedges and Family, Buckfast

SUBSCRIBERS

Tom Heesom, with fondest memories of The Grange, Buckfast
John Henle, Buckfastleigh, Devon
Mildred Edith Hext (née Penny), Buckfastleigh (1900–1977)
Denise Hinkley, Buckfastleigh, Devon
Dennis Hoare, Buckfastleigh, Devon
J.F. and M.E. Hoff, Buckastleigh, Devon
Christopher Holliday
A. Robin Hood, Barton, Torquay. Memory of Les Neale DSS
K. Hughes, Buckfastleigh Broadband, Buckfastleigh, Devon
Margo E. Hughes, Buckfastleigh, Devon
Annabelle, Jonathan, Alice and Elizabeth Hunt, Buckfastleigh
Martin Hunt and Family, Reading
Nora Jackson, Buckfastleigh, Devon
Dr R. Jackson, Leatherhead, Surrey
Stephanie Jacobs (née Heesom), with fondest memories of The Grange, Buckfast
T. and C. Jeffery, Buckfastleigh
Elaine Jenkins, Buckfastleigh
Donald M. Joint, Buckfastleigh, Devon
Lewis, Lesley and Samantha Jones, Buckfastleigh
Dee and Mike Knight, Buckfastleigh
Elizabeth Knowling, Buckfastleigh
Maurice William Lane, Buckfastleigh
I.S.G. Lang, Bishops Steignton
Mr Andrew Langmead, Buckfastleigh
Mrs Mary Lee, Buckfastleigh, Devon
Rhoda Look, Buckfastleigh
Cynthia M. Maddern, Penzance, Cornwall
Mrs Pauline Manfield, Buckfastleigh, Devon
Francis and Eileen Manley
John and Margaret Mann, Kingskerswell
C. James Midgley, Peterborough
Peter Miller, South Brent, Devon
Carole J. Millman, Buckfastleigh, Devon
William F. Milton, Buckfastleigh, Devon
Stewart and Elizabeth Mitchell, Buckfastleigh, Devon
Honor E. Morton (née Voisey)
Desmond John Mutton, Buckfastleigh, Devon
Derek Myhill, Buckfastleigh, Devon
Janet R. Myhill, Buckfastleigh, Devon
Peter Norton, London
Roger O'Brien, Thirsk, North Yorkshire
Janet Parrott, Newton Abbot
David Penny, Buckfastleigh
Christopher B.T. Perry, Buckfastleigh, Devon
Adelaide May Pinney, Buckfastleigh, Devon
Dorothy and Dennis Pope, Buckfastleigh, Devon
Neil Prentice, Buckfastleigh
Mr and Mrs D.W. Puttick, Eastbourne, Sussex
Tony and Angie Ravenscroft, Buckfastleigh, Devon
Mrs Pamela Redclift (née Bird), Dartmouth
Claire Rhodes (née Thompson), Plymouth, Devon
Mr A.J. and Mrs P.A. Rickard, Buckfastleigh Post Office
Mr T.S. Rowe, Buckfastleigh, Devon
John Rowland, Buckfastleigh, Devon
Michael D. Ryder, Buckfastleigh, Devon
Carol Saker, Oxford
William H. Selley
Jack Setters, Buckfastleigh, Devon
June Setters, Buckfastleigh, Devon
Ruth Shail (née Midgley), Dartington, Devon
Anne Smart, Buckfastleigh, Devon
Dorothy Joan Smith, Buckfastleigh, Devon
Julie Soul, Sherborne, Dorset
Catharine and Victor Sparkes, Buckfastleigh, Devon
John A. Spiller, Palo Alto, California, USA
Graham J. Squires, Buckfastleigh, Devon
Jacqueline M. Stephens, Buckfastleigh, Devon
Marjory Stryjski, Buckfast, South Devon
Mr Anthony Thomas Stuart, Buckfastleigh
Kathryn and Rod Summerfield, Shyrehill, Buckfast
Pamela L. Thompson, Buckfastleigh, Devon
Kenneth and Barbara Thorp, Buckfastleigh, Devon
Sqn Ldr D.P. Tidy, Buckfastleigh, Devon
Mike Tolchard, Buckfastleigh, Devon
Debra Tomkinson, Buckfast, Devon
Mary Trist, Little Neston, Wirral
Doreen M. Trude, Buckfastleigh, Devon
Dennis and Frances Turner, Ashburton
William J. Turner and Family, Buckfastleigh, Devon
Mr and Mrs R.A. Vane, Lincoln
Wyn Varney, Brooklin, Maine, USA
P.T. Voaden, Kaski, Poland
Jean L. Voisey (née Hext), Buckfastleigh, Devon
Keith, Hilary, Nicky and Chris Voisey, Whitley Bay, Tyne and Wear
Mick and Doreen Voisey, Buckfastleigh, Devon
Mr Paul M. Voisey, Saltash, Cornwall
Phyllis M. Voisey
Mr William John Voisey, Buckfastleigh
Alan G. and Sheila V. Wakley, Buckfastleigh, Devon
John F.W. Walling, Newton Abbot, Devon
Peter and Penny Weekes, Buckfastleigh
A. and M. Welfare, Buckfastleigh
Dorothy and Dennis West, Paignton, Devon
Andy and Jill Westlake, Buckfastleigh, Devon
Mrs M. Wigram, Buckfastleigh
Paul and Maywyn Wilkinson, Buckfastleigh
Idwal P. Williams, Buckfastleigh
Mrs Marion S. Zacher

Community Histories

The Book of Addiscombe • Canning and Clyde Road Residents Association and Friends
The Book of Addiscombe, Vol. II • Canning and Clyde Road Residents Association and Friends
The Book of Axminster with Kilmington • L. Berry and G. Gosling
The Book of Bampton • Caroline Seward
The Book of Barnstaple • Avril Stone
The Book of Barnstaple, Vol. II • Avril Stone
The Book of The Bedwyns • Bedwyn History Society
The Book of Bickington • Stuart Hands
Blandford Forum: A Millennium Portrait • Blandford Forum Town Council
The Book of Bramford • Bramford Local History Group
The Book of Breage & Germoe • Stephen Polglase
The Book of Bridestowe • D. Richard Cann
The Book of Bridport • Rodney Legg
The Book of Brixham • Frank Pearce
The Book of Buckfastleigh • Sandra Coleman
The Book of Buckland Monachorum & Yelverton • Pauline Hamilton-Leggett
The Book of Carharrack • Carharrack Old Cornwall Society
The Book of Carshalton • Stella Wilks and Gordon Rookledge
The Parish Book of Cerne Abbas • Vivian and Patricia Vale
The Book of Chagford • Iain Rice
The Book of Chapel-en-le-Frith • Mike Smith
The Book of Chittlehamholt with Warkleigh & Satterleigh • Richard Lethbridge
The Book of Chittlehampton • Various
The Book of Colney Heath • Bryan Lilley
The Book of Constantine • Moore and Trethowan
The Book of Cornwood & Lutton • Compiled by the People of the Parish
The Book of Creech St Michael • June Small
The Book of Cullompton • Compiled by the People of the Parish
The Book of Dawlish • Frank Pearce
The Book of Dulverton, Brushford, Bury & Exebridge • Dulverton and District Civic Society
The Book of Dunster • Hilary Binding
The Book of Edale • Gordon Miller
The Ellacombe Book • Sydney R. Langmead
The Book of Exmouth • W.H. Pascoe
The Book of Grampound with Creed • Bane and Oliver
The Book of Hayling Island & Langstone • Peter Rogers
The Book of Helston • Jenkin with Carter
The Book of Hemyock • Clist and Dracott
The Book of Herne Hill • Patricia Jenkyns
The Book of Hethersett • Hethersett Society Research Group
The Book of High Bickington • Avril Stone
The Book of Ilsington • Dick Wills
The Book of Kingskerswell • Carsewella Local History Group
The Book of Lamerton • Ann Cole and Friends
Lanner, A Cornish Mining Parish • Sharron Schwartz and Roger Parker
The Book of Leigh & Bransford • Malcolm Scott
The Book of Litcham with Lexham & Mileham • Litcham Historical and Amenity Society
The Book of Loddiswell • Loddiswell Parish History Group
The New Book of Lostwithiel • Barbara Fraser
The Book of Lulworth • Rodney Legg
The Book of Lustleigh • Joe Crowdy
The Book of Lyme Regis • Rodney Legg
The Book of Manaton • Compiled by the People of the Parish
The Book of Markyate • Markyate Local History Society
The Book of Mawnan • Mawnan Local History Group
The Book of Meavy • Pauline Hemery
The Book of Minehead with Alcombe • Binding and Stevens
The Book of Morchard Bishop • Jeff Kingaby
The Book of Newdigate • John Callcut
The Book of Nidderdale • Nidderdale Museum Society
The Book of Northlew with Ashbury • Northlew History Group
The Book of North Newton • J.C. and K.C. Robins
The Book of North Tawton • Baker, Hoare and Shields
The Book of Nynehead • Nynehead & District History Society
The Book of Okehampton • R. and U. Radford
The Book of Paignton • Frank Pearce
The Book of Penge, Anerley & Crystal Palace • Peter Abbott
The Book of Peter Tavy with Cudlipptown • Peter Tavy Heritage Group
The Book of Pimperne • Jean Coull
The Book of Plymtree • Tony Eames
The Book of Porlock • Dennis Corner
Postbridge – The Heart of Dartmoor • Reg Bellamy
The Book of Priddy • Albert Thompson
The Book of Princetown • Dr Gardner-Thorpe
The Book of Rattery • By the People of the Parish
The Book of St Day • Joseph Mills and Paul Annear
The Book of Sampford Courtenay with Honeychurch • Stephanie Pouya
The Book of Sculthorpe • Gary Windeler
The Book of Seaton • Ted Gosling
The Book of Sidmouth • Ted Gosling and Sheila Luxton
The Book of Silverton • Silverton Local History Society
The Book of South Molton • Jonathan Edmunds
The Book of South Stoke with Midford • Edited by Robert Parfitt
South Tawton & South Zeal with Sticklepath • R. and U. Radford
The Book of Sparkwell with Hemerdon & Lee Mill • Pam James
The Book of Staverton • Pete Lavis
The Book of Stithians • Stithians Parish History Group
The Book of Stogumber, Monksilver, Nettlecombe & Elworthy • Maurice and Joyce Chidgey
The Book of Studland • Rodney Legg
The Book of Swanage • Rodney Legg
The Book of Tavistock • Gerry Woodcock
The Book of Thorley • Sylvia McDonald and Bill Hardy
The Book of Torbay • Frank Pearce
The Book of Watchet • Compiled by David Banks
The Book of West Huntspill • By the People of the Parish
Widecombe-in-the-Moor • Stephen Woods
Widecombe – Uncle Tom Cobley & All • Stephen Woods
The Book of Williton • Michael Williams
The Book of Witheridge • Peter and Freda Tout and John Usmar
The Book of Withycombe • Chris Boyles
Woodbury: The Twentieth Century Revisited • Roger Stokes
The Book of Woolmer Green • Compiled by the People of the Parish

For details of any of the above titles or if you are interested in writing your own history, please contact: Commissioning Editor Community Histories, Halsgrove House, Lower Moor Way, Tiverton Business Park, Tiverton, Devon EX16 6SS, England; email: naomic@halsgrove.com

In order to include as many historical photographs as possible in this volume, a printed index is not included. However, the Devon titles in the Community History Series are indexed by Genuki. For further information and indexes to various volumes in the series, please visit: http://www.cs.ncl.ac.uk/genuki/DEV/indexingproject.html